EAS

BUDDHIST TEACHINGS ON LETTING GO OF ANXIETY AND ATTACHMENT

BY

JAMES LOW

Published by Simply Being www.simplybeing.co.uk

British Library Cataloguing in Publication Data. A catalogue record for this book is available from the British Library.

ISBN: 978-1-7394572-0-4

All talks/ teachings have been edited by Barbara Terris and some of them have been further extended and revised by James Low.

Cover photograph is courtesy of Robbie Terris.

Content

4

Buddhism and personal identity

AM I KNOWABLE?

This evening we will look at our experience of being in the world, a world that seems to be full of 'things' amongst which we ourselves appear to be 'someone', some particular kind of living thing. Buddhism offers us many different ways of inquiring into the nature and status of everything that we perceive, including ourselves.

Clearly we all have a sense that we exist. Earlier in the day you were somewhere else, doing other things and now you have brought yourself here. That gives us a sense that somehow 'I am in charge of this body'. And yet, in the course of the day, encountering different situations and meeting different people, our mood has fluctuated, bringing changes to our posture, gestures, breathing and so on. In some situations we feel more relaxed and expansive while in other situations we feel more anxious or irritated and we retract into ourselves.

I seem to be myself and yet I am aware that how I am is strongly influenced by what happens around me. My self seems to have an internal definition in the sense that it feels like me. We say: "*I am.*" "*I am hungry. I am tired. I am sleepy.*" We seem to be making these statements about someone who is knowable and who exists before they are known. That is to say, I can know things *about* myself which appear to be true and valid. And yet, if I feel tired, my tiredness has arrived in me, as me, without me deciding to be tired. Being tired, being hungry – these are states of myself which are revealed to me. I become aware that I am tired or hungry. In becoming aware of it I say, "*I am hungry*", as if this were a deep truth about me.

This would indicate that my relationship to what I call 'myself' is a double move. I am both the content of my experience ('*I'm feeling lonely*'), as this feeling arises and expresses me as I am now, and also the aspect of myself which is revealing, showing, or containing this content. This interplay would indicate that we are not one thing.

In terms of the content of my 'self', is there anything reliable and enduring that I can identify? Our thoughts, feelings and sensations change. Even if I make a statement about myself which refers to some quality which continues through time I am in fact referring to an abstract truth which has very little actual impact on my actual lived existence. For example, if I say, "*I am British*" this establishes that I am entitled to a passport and to live in the UK. However, when I am having a shower I don't feel especially British. If I am cleaning my teeth, this is not an expression of intrinsic British-ness. So although British-ness seems to continue through time it is actually not constitutional of the immediacy of my self-experience.

Similarly I know that I am male yet most of the time I don't have a particular sense of maleness. In the airport coming here I saw lots of people wandering around, some male, some female, and they also saw me walking around. My maleness was only a minor aspect of navigating my way to the flight gate. However when I needed to go to the toilet I went into the male toilet, not the female toilet. Is being male something which is definitively formative of experience? Or is it more of a commentary, a set of identifications which I and others apply to 'myself' under certain circumstances? It may always be true yet only occasionally and situationally valid.

One of the functions of meditation is to provide a space in which we can be more aware of the nature of our self-experience. If you see a friend in the distance walking towards you, you recognise them by their posture and their gait, their way of walking. There is a particular recognisable patterning in the way they move, in the way they hold their shoulders and so on. On the basis of our felt sense of familiarity with that pattern, we impute an essence: *"Oh, this is John!"* What is the John-ness of John constituted out of? Tone of voice, habitual gestures, the kind of clothes John wears? What we are seeing is a pattern which would not always have been applicable to John, yet knowing John under certain circumstances, this is the range or repertoire of patterns which we have come to associate with 'this person' we call John. In the moment of encounter there seems to be a facticity to the John-ness of John. And yet, in the course of the day that person will have had many different kinds of experiences of themselves and their environment evoking hopes, fears, expansion, contraction and so on. So what we refer to as 'John' is both ever-changing and somehow reliably identifiable.

How limitations arise

We will now examine the buddhist view of how limited identities and their limitations arise. The basis for our experience in a world where we take ourselves to be a separate individual is the movement of two factors: ignorance and attachment. Ignorance means ignoring how life actually is. Attachment means being attached to and dependent on our ideas about how life is. Even within the framework of duality we can experience the simplicity and immediacy of the unfolding of the world revealed through our senses. The fresh quality of such experience refreshes us and allows us a chance to see ourselves in a new light.

For example, in the summertime you may be walking along a beach somewhere. The light is shining on the water, you feel the sand moving under your feet. It's a very open situation with nothing that would provoke your habitual preoccupations. If you open to that and are not spinning in your head, you can feel quite open. In that situation we feel part of the world, at home in the world and at ease. Everything is here complete as it is and with no demand that we do something with it. This is a delightful holiday experience but when we are back home there are letters to open, phone messages to be answered and so on because for me to be 'me', I have to perform all the tasks that keep the identity of 'me' alive. If I don't work at maintaining 'me' then I will lose my familiar sense of self.

The very fact of my being committed to my individual identity binds me into the world through a whole network of transactions. Indeed, I build the particularity of my own world through my own choices and activity. This is why renunciation is such a major part of the general buddhist teachings and practices. To become a monk or a nun, to shave one's head and beg for food, is to step outside the social roles that bind one into worldly responsibilities. Even if we do not choose that path a regular review of our attachments is helpful for seeing how our sense of self, which claims autonomy, is actually dependent on the availability of many factors which we have to keep in play.

So, are the things I do necessary? If they feel necessary, then for what are they necessary? We could stop doing many of the things we do. We could decide we are going to simplify our lives. And yet we don't. Why not? Because these complex activities create and constitute our dynamic sense of self. In that sense, 'being me' is not really a state of 'being' at all. It's a state of becoming, of doing, of creating and conditioning, of patterned engagement in the experiential field.

In life we are conscious of many phenomena arising and even if we are not fully caught up in them, we are conscious that we are conscious of these arisings. However, given our habit of over-investment in certain phenomena and under-investment in others, it is easy for some appearances and events to seem to have greater importance. Ideas arising from these appearances and events have greater power to pull us into fusion so that we have no consciousness of being locked onto the object of our focussed attention.

For example, if you get caught up in obsessional thoughts and feel that you must do something, the intensity of your commitment to what you are doing blinds you to other possibilities and also to the impact your behaviour has on others. The impulse becomes uninterruptable. For example, you lock your door and go out and then you wonder: *"Did I actually lock the door?"* so you go back and check if you have locked the door. You *have* to go back. In that moment you are caught up in a thought *("I haven't locked the door!")*; that thought catches you, fills you and you can't reframe it. You can't contextualise it and it takes you back to the lock. If we review the aspects of our life that seem vital we may be surprised to see how much of our life is in fact obsessional.

OUR COMPETENCE CAN MAKE US STUPID

Small children often have a resistance to doing repeated activities such as washing their hands or cleaning their teeth. After some years the child performs the activity without prompting; it has become automatic and habitual. This makes life easier, but the fusion with the flow of the task also lets us think about something else. We are both performatively focussed and distracted from our embodied presence.

Through the practice of mindfulness we can become mindful that we are cleaning our teeth, mindful of the reflection in the mirror in front of us, mindful of the pressure in our hand holding the toothbrush, we are mindful of the fact that 'I am cleaning my teeth'. This allows us to engage in activity while having a degree of clarity of over-view at the same time. So there is the subject as an engaged participative agent – the one who is cleaning the teeth – but there is also a mindful observer, a mode of our subjectivity, which is more neutral.

When we are brushing our teeth in a habitual way and our thoughts wander off thinking about something else, there is a lack of reflective consciousness present in the situation. Our very competence is an aspect of ignoring what is happening.

Our competence can make us stupid. Our mobilisation, our gaze, our hearing, our patterns of interpretation become so aligned to pathways which though efficient in their familiarity and seeming clarity, nevertheless obscure what is around by their absorbing self-focus. All other options are functionally unavailable.

We can experience something of this in meditation. We decide we are going to sit and observe our breath or visualise a mandala yet we find that our attention has wandered off and become wrapped up in other mental phenomena. We have become accustomed to being distracted in daily life and so it is not surprising that it manifests in meditation. You are sitting in meditation with an intention about what you are going to do but then, without intending it, you are caught up in another thought which distracts you from your original explicit intention. In that distraction, because you are following familiar kinds of thoughts, there is the clarity of knowing 'what you are on about' since you are thinking about something familiar. This distraction is often difficult to recognise quickly because its focus is on familiar contents of the mind, contents which carry the clarity of immediate comprehensibility. Following the breath is an unusual activity and in itself does not encourage reflective or discursive thought. That is to say, it is not interesting for our ego-self. The distracting thought, however, takes us to familiar territory where we can enjoy our mind at work.

Millions of people watch soap operas on television every day. The stories in soap operas are always full of crises, but they are predictable crises since we know what the characters are like. That is the strangely exciting edge of the familiar. We know that it's not great drama, that the stories are a bit stupid, but if you get hooked in, somehow you want to watch it again and again.

The same involvement occurs with meditation. The function of the familiar patterning of events lies not in its display of intrinsically meaningful content. It is not the semantic content that is important but the dualistic movement of me giving my attention to something that is within the range of my competence. Involvement with my familiar thoughts and feelings brings me to a terrain where I seem to know what's going on and by this I am confirmed as somebody who exists, who is intelligent and who makes sense of the world.

Many Tibetan texts say that if you really want to practise dharma, you should leave your village, leave your land and go to a place where no one knows even your name. What is being renounced by this is not so much the outer objects but the invitation to fall asleep in your life. There is a givenness to our daily routine. We know what to do and so we just get on with it. Sometimes we may be a bit bored but anyway, there is a continuing affirmation: *"I am who I am and I know what I am doing."*

This is what attachment means in buddhism. It doesn't especially mean being attached to a possession like a watch. That is only a small part of it. Attachment is more like a kind of merging with the objects of our daily life so that we take it for granted that things are what we believe them to be. This fusion with familiar objects and events is a way of avoiding the loneliness of the ego. The ego seeks autonomy and independence yet when this is tasted it is a bit bitter since the ego needs the other in order to be itself. Isolation is lonely and depleting to the ego so it jumps to the other polarity and seeks confluence with the object of its attention. In this way it does not find the midpoint of open contact with the openness of the situation.

Contact with the other is, in its openness, non-dual. We are not one and we are not two. We are together with each other in and as the co-emergence of this moment. This is the basis for tantric initiations by means of which the isolation of the student is dissolved in the infinite welcome of the dharmakaya presence of the teacher. Through this unimpeded contact the student becomes able to receive the third initiation which reveals their mind to be non-entitative and non-dual with all that occurs. With this the student's sense of isolation dissolves and they experience non-dual compassion as all-inclusive kindness.

We are locked in the habit of ignoring what is actually here and imagining what we take to be here. When we look at what is 'here', can we actually see what is here? Can we see what is here as it is without telling what is here what it is?

In front of me just now there are three sunflowers. 'Sunflower' is a name. We know this is just a name and not the 'true name' because it has different names in German and in English. When you speak your own language it is as if the familiar name is absolutely connected with what you see. When we learn other languages we start to wake up to the conventional nature of language. The name is extrinsic to the flower itself, yet its name can only function if we take it to be, magically, intrinsic to the flower. The flower is there. Some appearance is there that we agree can be called 'a flower'.

The appearance is fresh, open and free of defining self-substance; it is part of the field of appearances. These are not something, though the attribution of a name can wrongly be taken to indicate an entity with its own inherent identity. When we tell an appearance that it is the appearance of something and that that something is a sunflower, we are obscuring the openness of appearance by the imposition of our concepts.

The appearance in itself is pure and free of inherent existence. What we see is light, only light. You cannot see anything but light. This is pure perception. But when appearance, what we perceive, is obscured by what we imagine with our reliance on concepts, reification, judgement and identification, then we have karmic perception, karmic vision. All the habits and tendencies which have built up in our mind-streams, streams flowing in the great river of becoming, very quickly flood over the bright object leaving a patina of silt. It is this mud that we take to be what is actually there.

Due to this confusion when we think we are describing what is there, what is actually occurring is that we are inventing what we see. We are describing our own inventions as if they were 'just there' and as if we had nothing to do with them being 'just there' as we take them to be. Fusing the subjective into the objective creates a sticky mix as the excess glue causes diverse opinions floating by to become attached to the object and then to be presented as if inherent. The mind is the mother of all experience and when appearances are taken as 'just there', as motherless facts, then the darkness of assumption engulfs us. The world as we know it to be is not the world as it is. What we experience is in large part the product of our own activity.

If you simply sit with a flower and relax into the out-breath and allow your attention to rest on what is in front of you without being inflected by any of the strong thoughts, feelings and sensations that come and go, then you have a chance to see the thoughts as they arise without melding with them. We start to see that they have no existence or self-substance. Thoughts become substantial thoughts through our belief in them. Our attention pulls them out of the chorus line and into a starring role for a brief moment but then they rapidly, almost instantly, vanish. They vanish like rainbows. They don't go somewhere when they dissolve. They dissolve into space just where they are. They are not something that can go from A to B. Emptiness offers A and A shows its emptiness. The thought that seems to obscure the openness of the mind is not other than an aspect of the display of the mind. Emptiness shows the potential of emptiness to show the empty appearances as the expression of emptiness. What shows is received by open awareness without processing or without any attempt to make sense of it. It is what it is and what it is is the radiance of emptiness. Immediate, clear, inconceivable, inexpressible.

The domain of direct perception and the domain of concept

The domain of direct perception and the domain of concept are not the same. They are not fundamentally oppositional but they do need to be seen as they are rather than merged into our habitual sense of the world being composed of entities with inherent qualities. Direct perception accesses the revelation of the display of emptiness. Concepts transform this seeming revelation into an array of separate substances.

So much of our education and our habitual operation is concerned with creating narratives about the world through the use of sophisticated concepts. When we slip from the spacious receptivity of allowing the unmediated unfolding of occurrence into the domain of conceptual elaboration, these concepts bring about a forgetfulness of spacious awareness. The details of things seem to express their substantial essence and the ego's focus on these 'real' entities helps to confirm the 'real' existence of the ego. This makes intangible pure appearance unavailable for us. We mistake attribution for essence so that the compounded form is taken as a given and the role of the mind as source is ignored.

For example, the thing-ness of the flower is attributed by the mind. The flower is most fully seen when it is simply purely seen. Once naming of the flower occurs it is located in our field of knowledge. Having established the flower as an entity, we weave this 'object' into the realm of our own interpretive interests. However if we relax and open to the experience itself we find a 'something' which is actually nothing – uncatchable presence which is not the presence of something else. With this we see the absence of inherent self-nature in both the object and the subject. The flower-ness of the flower as it shows itself is beyond speech and beyond thought.

In the Zen tradition they point to the occasion when Buddha Shakyamuni gave a flower to Mahakashyapa, one of his main disciples. Mahakashyapa just smiled. The Buddha took that as a sign of his insight into the truth. In a sense, there is nothing to say. However, once we get into our mode of politeness, of *"Thank you very much. That's very beautiful."* then it is easy to lose the freshness of instant presence. Our over-invested focus obscures for us ever-present awareness, the infinite hospitality our mind offers to all that occurs.

THREE STAGES OF UNAWARENESS

A traditional Nyingma way of describing this loss of what cannot be lost is to see it as the **first moment of unawareness** in which relaxed spaciousness is oblivious to itself. This gives rise to a moment of precise appearance which is mistakenly apprehended as the appearance of something.

With this loss of panoramic vision, awareness inseparable from infinite openness is 'replaced' by a consciousness of something. Non-dual integrity cannot be opened to by self-regarding ego consciousness. Consciousness is a patterning of mental activity leading to dualistic apprehension of objects. This is the **second stage of unawareness**. It is how the field of display appears when its foundation, the field of openness, is disregarded. Now subject and object chase each other round and round like two hamsters on a wheel.

This activity develops as the **third stage of unawareness:** the naming of everything and the attribution of separate identities. This is a process of ever-increasing differentiation of the world as you develop more and more vocabulary about it and engage in increasingly nuanced conceptual activity of comparing and contrasting.

The ability to manage these details of subject and object are important for sentient beings in samsara. There are two aspects to this. Firstly, we couldn't communicate with each other without them and so they function as an aspect of compassion. However they are also the cheese in the mousetrap of samsara:

without attention to these details we find that there is always more to think and say. Events can be gone over again and again as we try to make sense of what has happened in our lives. These enquiries can be fascinating and can help us to understand how the patternings of our life have developed but they cannot point the way out of such patternings. Engaging in such dualistic inquiry weaves the impenetrable walls of our imprisonment in unawareness.

Fortunately, we have encountered buddhist dharma since this points out that the relief we are looking for is already here if only we relax and open. In the moment when we are relaxed and open to all that is arising, this very openness, non-judgement and non-interference directly illuminates appearance as appearance of the open empty ground. The ground itself does not appear yet it 'shows itself' as reflections. These empty appearances are open and so can be filled with projections. Only once they are wrapped in concepts are appearances taken to be signs of some 'thing'.

THE EXPERIENCE AND EXPERIENCER

It is the creativity of our mind that creates the world we know. From the dzogchen point of view, each individual being is the centre of the world they know. This is not narcissistic inflation but points to the fact that the world is revealed as knowable, as experience. Each person has their own unique experience.

Who is the experiencer? Within duality the experiencer is our subjectivity, our egoic consciousness which makes sense of what is occurring. The experiencer cooks the experience to make it palatable according to its own pattern of likes and dislikes. The experiencer feels that the experience is happening to them and so each moment of experience is taken by the ego-self to be a confirmation that it has a separate existence. The ego-self focusses on 'what' is happening, on the substance of events, evaluating them in terms of advantage and disadvantage. It is so preoccupied with what is happening –

and for it so many, many things are happening – that it does not consider how 'all this' could be experienced by me without me being overloaded. Experience is a flow of apparitional moments. It is not made out of stuff. We turn it into stuff by the way we apprehend it.

When we take a break from apprehending, for example in our sitting practice, the quality of flow becomes more obvious. The flow is actually ungraspable. What we grasp and conceptualise about the flow is what we, the grasper, have projected on to the flow. Moreover we, the projector, the knower, also invent our own existence. Existence is a mental event without inherent existence. Emptiness is the basis of our knowing yet the dualising ego experiencer is blind to this. Within duality the stream of experience arises in a two-fold manner: as what is experienced and as who is experiencing. Both are actually empty of inherent existence. To see this directly opens the way to relaxing into your own unborn awareness which reveals the flow without being part of it.

SELF-ING

From this point of view the self is not an entity or an essence inside of us. We don't 'have' an existent self, rather there is a process of self-ing in which 'we' identify with many different shapes and appearances. It is as if they are us, and indeed momentarily and situationally they *are* us. We have no identity apart from these moments of identification. The self is not someone or something in particular. It is a flow of radiance interpreted by reification. This misinterpretation, troublesome as it is, lacks the capacity to establish even one existent. The thingness of the thing is an illusion generated by interpretation. This contrivance is one of the myriad ways the ground shows its potential. This potential is the source of all that is taken to be samsara and nirvana, constraint and freedom. When the clarity of the mind is obscured by dualistic consciousness, we encounter appearance merged with conceptual interpretation.

Some of you have been here before, in this building in Frankfurt where we are meeting. You come in through the front door and you know what it is like. You come up the stairs, you see the little shop and you come into this room. You recognise it. This knowing of what is here is actually the knowing, or coming to mind, of your concepts of being here. This construct appears to you as a given, as an accurate perception of how it actually is. You have a conceptualised perception of the room and this gives rise to the thought: *"It is like this."* The flow of phenomena is being packaged by concepts. The impermanence of appearance as it appears is now veiled and becomes a screen on which we project our stabilising ideas of what we know it to be.

On the basis of the arising of these patterns of thoughts there arises the felt sense of: *'I know where I am.'* But these are thoughts *about* something. We think we are having thoughts about the room, but we are having thoughts about thoughts. The thoughts don't reach the room itself, they only have contact with other thoughts. We are convinced that we are thinking and talking about real things out there, but our thoughts are thinking about other thoughts. Our memories are remembering other memories. Our words are talking about other words.

Although empty of inherent existence, these patterns have affective consequences. With certain patterns we feel happy, with other patterns we feel sad. *'I feel sad'* is a patterning of experience. When I feel sad my experience of my body shifts, as postures, gestures and tone of voice all shift. Then when I start to feel happy my spine straightens. I feel able to engage with you. And then I feel sad again…

This is our life. It is movement – patterning and shape devoid of definitive essence. This fact can be most troublesome for our ego-self as it puts its very existence into question. If I want to maintain a stable sense of self the fact of its groundlessness is something to be denied and ignored. However, if we follow the dharma and seek liberation then this fact is very helpful.

The emptiness of our mind itself, its openness, its not being something, allows us the freedom to manifest many potential forms without being defined by any of them. In believing that we are 'something' or 'someone' we gain the feeling of security that 'having an identity' gives us, yet we also gain a restriction in the moves available to us. In being 'me' I have a limited repertoire of what I can say and what I can do: *"I can see that other people live their lives in different ways from me. I don't know how they do it. I couldn't do what they do because that's just not how I am."*

Our freedom arises from our non-definition, from our fundamental indefinability. Our immediate presence is simply present as presence with no defining features of its own. However the ego, lacking form which has an essence and being in denial or horror of that, is striving to formulate an essence. When we look at others they seem to be defined by their appearance and habitual ways of functioning. We don't feel like that because our experience of ourselves is unpredictable, haphazard. We are a work in progress so it is easy to think: *"I have to work out who I am. What is it that I want to do with my life?"* Such questions seem to be pathways to clarity and certainty but the very posing of them brings an unravelling to what we have been constructing. In this way, we find ourselves engaged in the endless work of self-construction.

Life can appear as a problem to be solved and if we take it up in this way and review our progress we always seem far from the goal. So either we avoid the question and settle into complacency or we reformulate its assumptions. However if we approach our life, our presence here in this moment, as a mystery to live then we might find that it is an amazing theatre of the mind with endless possibilities of summoning forth self-liberating illusions.

From the point of view of tantra this whole world is the play of imagination. When we use our imagination to visualise a mandala we start by imagining a clear blue sky, the symbol of the emptiness of everything. From this open blue sky, rainbow light emerges and transforms into a seed letter which then transforms into the palace and the gods and so on. Creativity is the breath of space. The unformed-ness of the mind shows infinite forms. At the end of the practice the mandala dissolves along with ourself, and everything we have imagined settles into its emptiness. Then out of emptiness, as the radiance of emptiness, the world arises, the world of familiar appearances, the world of getting the kids to school on time and getting to the bank before it closes.

In meditation we relax and open and simply stay present with whatever arises. That means not to pull arisings towards us and try to incorporate them as part of ourselves and not to push them away as if they were dangerous or contaminating. By allowing the mind to show itself however it is, the anxious centripetal pull of the unstable ego-self starts to relax. We start to see that these thoughts and feelings and memories just come and go like clouds in the sky. The mind gradually awakens to itself as it is, with the clarity of being the sky untouched by clouds as they come and go. I am the sky open and empty and I am also the rays of illumination spreading through it. I am also the heat they bring to their contact with appearances.

The integrity of these three aspects of openness, illumination and contact (Tib. *ngo-wo, rang-zhin, thug-je*) is the inseparability of primordial purity and immediate presence. This permits the arising of the limitless modes of our participation as circumstances and individual formations act in synergy. It is not that there is only one self or even no self but that we show as infinite self-ings which are situational shapings. For example, Padmasambhava is well-known as having eight main forms, forms which he showed in different situations and at different times. We too have many different forms. We have the form of somebody running down the street late for work. We have the form of someone waiting in a cafe for a friend. We have the form of being in bed with a lover. These are particular configurations of our potential.

ENJOYING THE PLAY

The actual continuity of ourselves lies in our emptiness, the dharmakaya union of awareness and emptiness. Awakening to this frees us to enjoy the arising of these many different forms. These are the *sambhogakaya*, our modes of enjoyment. We enjoy because enjoyment is free of seriousness. Seriousness leads into consolidation and the taking on of burdens. The more we see that we are labile, changing and moving, the more we see that reliability is dependent on objectification. Playfulness and connectivity are the qualities of inter-subjectivity.

Buddha's teaching on impermanence loosens up our assumptions and helps us to renounce the fantasy that we are in charge and know what we are doing. We start to trust that presence and genuine contact allows an intuitive participation that is fundamentally ethical. Wisdom is to see that all is illusion while compassion is to bring that clarity into our being with others in such a way that it helps them awaken from the dream of substantiality.

Public talk given in Frankfurt, Germany on 14th October 2015.
Revised by James Low in 2022.

Anxiety, awareness, ease

Anxiety is pervasive and so normal that it is almost invisible. We tend to experience it consciously when we feel its impact on our body, our voice, and our mind.

None of us know when we're going to die and yet we can't live without making plans. All the ideas that we have of our future may well come to nothing.

All the books that you read on psychology, all the exams that you take, all the hopes that you might have of enjoying a good career – these ideas may be blown away like leaves in the autumn wind. Death may arrive without warning. The day you get your final diploma you might celebrate with a little wine and fall down the stairs....

Our existence is underpinned by anxiety, yet its presence is often ignored. The fact of death is a deep source of anxiety which remains hidden by our extension of ourselves into our imagined tomorrow. Our commitment to our plans for the future supports our fantasy that we can fulfil our hopes and dreams. We wish the freedom to do as we please and have an anxious need to know and do everything. Due to this we ignore the signs warning us of serious, if not mortal, danger.

For example, although western culture is now largely focussed on the future, it is still influenced by the myth we inhabit, a fallen world. One version of this myth indicates that in the Garden of Eden there was no anxiety. Anxiety developed due to the breach of the prohibition God gave to Adam and Eve: *"You can do whatever you like except one thing..."* And of course that one thing, eating the fruit of the tree of knowledge, became so very tempting!

This is similar to the story of Bluebeard. When he marries yet another young woman he says, *"You can go everywhere in the castle, wherever you would like to, except for this one room."* But this forbidden place becomes more and more attractive in her mind as anxiety about restriction agitates her. She needs to act in order to find out, yet when she opens the door she finds...death.

These are two examples of the unsettling anxiety arising from the need to know. At this moment societies the world over are conflicted about whether the anxieties arising from climate change should be denied and ignored or acted on. Either option is full of difficulty and the main choice is between delayed and intensified disaster or facing a plethora of problems demanding material and psychological resources that we may well find we lack. These anxieties arise from our being forced to know what we would rather not know. Similar anxieties arise from knowledge of the past acts of colonialism, slavery, genocide and contemptuous disregard for the value of others.

Rules and prohibitions give shape to our lives yet also thwart our desire for freedom: freedom to know, to speak, to act. If you follow the rules you'll be okay, so don't try to look outside the frame. Outside our social frame lies death, unimaginable death, the great disruptor of our fantasy of self-knowledge and the will to power. Day by day we encounter facts that stab at our assumptions, especially our assumption that we are good kind people. Many western countries developed their economies on the basis of exploiting others. Many of these economies continue to be engaged in the export of weapons, of bombs, landmines and military drones that we know are used to harm the defenceless. The tension between troublesome facts and reassuring fictions is difficult to sustain. If self-thriving is based on self-deception then the repressed but ever-returning anxiety of being in bad faith is never far away. Egoic power rests on the freedom to impose rules on others while breaking them oneself.

There are many kinds of anxiety. For example there is situational anxiety arising when events beyond our control impinge on our plans. As an example, we may find ourselves caught in a traffic jam and so are becoming late for a meeting. This is uncomfortable, we're not certain what will happen and we don't want to let people down or have them think badly of us. This kind of anxiety usually does not linger long, vanishing as the situation changes – as long as we have the capacity to let the anxiety vanish with the event. If you go outside in the rain you get a bit wet but when you come inside you dry out and it is as though you never were wet. Life flows easily when we accept our own fluctuations – wet/dry, relaxed/tense. happy/sad – and don't make one polarity more valid than another.

Psychotherapy can help patients learn how to release situational anxiety so that it does not accumulate and energise itself by predicting future difficulties. For this we need to distinguish between event arousal where we mobilise towards the actual situation and act on it, and ideational arousal where we mobilise on the basis of an idea. In the first case the event has a beginning, middle and end and so does its associated anxious arousal. In the second case, arousal can easily continue for a long time as its focus is an idea and ideas can linger and insist whatever the actual context.

Habitual anxiety develops with our tendency to worry about our ideas of situations and to explore them again and again. There is no end to worry for it is an anxiety–maintenance procedure dressed as a problem-solving procedure. Worry generates a sense that the world is not very safe: *"I can't trust the transport system," "I can't trust my own plans."* We can become over-vigilant, looking for new instances of the difficulties and dangers we assume to be global.

With this orientation we often adopt worry as a means of trying to predict problems and solve them in advance. Worrying can feel useful and creative, both practical and efficient.

Unfortunately worry tends to lead us further and further into the forest of our anxious speculation.

Most problems in life are quite simple. You sit with a piece of paper and write down the various options, think them through, and then make your decision. But if you start to worry, you pick up one possibility and run around with it then put it down and pick up another and then another. This creates a huge amount of turbulent movement in mind and body without producing clarity and effective action.

The concrete problems in our life are linked to the space and time that we inhabit – something has to be done, usually in a particular way and by a particular time. However worry floats free of the concrete and is often increased by the necessity of making an actual decision. Instead of the decision being the end of the matter, worry allows us to be anxious before, during, and after the decision is made.

ANXIETY AND IDENTITY

Although anxiety is clearly an embodied experience expressing itself through our postures, gestures, facial expression, breathing, skin tension, tone of voice, rapidity of speech, semantic content and so on, it tends to dislocate our embodied self from its actual environment. This deprives the anxious person of the grounding available through attending to the precise details of how they actually are.

Even with seemingly external material factors which easily arouse anxiety and worry, such as poverty, sickness, violence, war and climate catastrophe, the anxiety often lifts us into a mental realm where concrete solutions are hard to establish. Hierarchical cultures tend to offer less choice and freewill to those at the bottom. Restricted by limited education and the stereotyping whereby one is seen primarily in terms of ascribed group membership, the seeming givenness of the structure easily feeds feelings of hopelessness and apathy. Lack of entitlement to citizenship, healthcare, reasonably paid work – all thin the sense of self necessary for the ongoing struggle to find a viable niche in this uncertain world. Some degree of control over how our social identity is formed is necessary for our ego-self to maintain the illusion of predictable stability. The more others can impose an identity on us, the more limited are our opportunities to influence the patterns of social signifiers which impact so profoundly on our sense of self and our place in the world.

Yet even when we are able to focus on our embodied presence it can be difficult to gain a sense of stable identity. Our body as it actually is exists only in this moment in time and in this specific location, and yet in states of anxiety we go off into the imagined past, future, and present travelling with our currently imagined identity.

The human capacity for imagination is enormous. We imagine that we have definite reliable knowledge about ourselves, others and the world around us. However our capacity to avail ourselves of this knowledge and use it effectively is inflected by our moods of hope, fear, joy, anxiety and so on. Moreover such moods often operate outwith our consciousness. They suffuse us and seem, at least for a while, to be part and parcel of who we are, and so when our perceptions and interpretations of events are mediated by such moods we can still believe that we are accessing the world as it actually is. Such commitment to the seeming truth of our interpretation alienates us from our being in the world in the immediacy of our ongoing interactions. This projection of our fleeting ideas and wishes is so convincing for us that the actuality of phenomena scarcely impinges.

For example, patients with dysmorphophobia can formulate their fixed belief about something being wrong with their appearance in terms of being too tall, being too thin, having the wrong shape of ears and so on. With this definite knowledge the person then approaches the world with the certainty that other people also see and are completely fixated on these details of this problematic appearance. This definite knowledge becomes their principle interpretive schema as they pay selective attention to factors in the phenomenological field and use this distorted perception as evidence to confirm their hypothesis. Thus somebody might believe: *"People do not like me because of the way I look. I try to make friends but people turn away from me."* It is then difficult for them to see that the actual reason people turn away is that self-preoccupation makes them unavailable for contact.

However we need to remember that there can be certain secondary gains with this kind of narrow fixation. The unpredictable flux of daily life gives rise to many reasons to be uncertain and tentative and this can lead to a diffuse pervasive anxiety. But if one can settle on a key focus of concern this allows a crystal to form out of the solution, a crystal with a definite shape that the solution lacks. Romantic love, nationalistic fervour, obsessing about a hobby like rock-climbing – such fixations can also provide relief from general anxiety even although they are usually accompanied by further fears.

Such habitual anxieties are often maintained by our effort to manage the fluctuations of our own central identity while acknowledging that other people are free to interpret us according to their own schemas.

I will never know what you think. Why? Not just because you might be very polite and not like to say... but because you cannot say what you think. None of us can say what we think for as soon as we speak we are already describing the past. The situation described and our thoughts about it have passed. Language cannot catch the moment, it merely plays with echoes. New thoughts are already appearing. The immediate is uncatchable. We think about and talk about representations of the already absent.

This is why you can be in therapy for many years and never resolve your issues. For example, in one session you may describe something about yourself that seems to be true. But then the following week you go back to therapy and say, *"Well I was thinking about it some more... and it's not quite like that..."* There is always more to say about our sense of our elusive ever-changing self.

Questioning the basis of your own identity can be interesting or troubling depending on circumstances. Moreover both options feel different from having your identity questioned by someone else: *"Are you valid, legitimate? Do you have a right to be here? To belong here? Do you have a right to exist at all?"* This kind of questioning, implying or clearly stating a lack of acceptance, welcome and inclusion is likely to increase many aspects of anxiety. If how I look is taken by you as a sign that I don't belong, then how can I shift your belief which is grounded in your sense of being normal and entitled? If you are the normal one expressing the truth of how it is, then your belief *de facto* makes me abnormal and less than you. Moreover if your view is backed up by the state, the police, religion and so on then you, the definer, are forever safe on the inside and I, the defined, am the uncertain outsider with only my anxiety for company.

THE ILLUSION OF SELF

We are unstable – feelings shift and change. Being interactive creatures, relational beings, we are constantly influenced by what happens around us... and 'influence' is about fluency...it's about flowing. We are swimming in the river of life with other people. In fact we are like little currents flowing in the great river of life. We are not standing on solid ground and yet we are required to make solid statements about ourselves. We are required to present ourselves into the world as something that is reliable – that we are stable: twenty-four hours a day, fifty-two weeks of the year. *"I am stable, I know who I am, you can trust me!"*

We are not a fixed entity that can be known. This is a simple truth that should not be turned into a problem. Our evaluations of who and how we are are easily altered by our situationally variable capacity to participate in what is going on. We are co-emergent with circumstances. Moreover we do not know what other people make of us and if we ruminate about the many possible attitudes they might have about us, then we are likely to further unravel our own sense of ourselves. Given this unpredictability it is not surprising that for some people it can seem safer to fixate on their own self-defined problem and use it as a consistent focus of their tendency to worry.

To be a social being able to survive in the world requires the capacity to maintain a persona, a mask, a presentational self behind which we can hide the messiness of our fragile fleeting actual selfing. Our constructed persona floats on the surface of our life like a little bubble. The waves, tides and storms of our moods shift and turn, their momentary forms often ignored as we struggle to keep our bubble of seeming self-entity intact. Sometimes we are expansive, sometimes we contract. Sometimes we are hopeful, sometimes not. Sometimes our minds are clear and sometimes there is a lot of confusion.

In fact our experience is ceaseless fluctuation: our body is full of sensations coming and going, and our thoughts and feelings are always changing.

As we attend to this ceaseless movement, it becomes clear that the narrative of our social persona, so effortful to maintain, is a cover-up, a deception, a lie. The stories we tell about ourselves are indeed just stories, mere fictions. Actually who we are is not something which **can** be known because fundamentally we are part of a field of revelation diversely unfolding. We are not like the bud of a flower gradually opening to display the fulfilment of its potential. It's not that we have some essence inside us, some deep defining core-identity which gradually emerges to show itself in the world. Rather we are co-emergent with circumstances. Free of fixed defining essence, we are participants in an interactive matrix of collaborative responsivity.

My sense of having and being a fixed self is a delusion. The fundamental root of our anxiety is our mistaken belief in a personal individual self-identity. If I am 'me' and belong to 'me' I should be able to define myself as the one I want to be and be able to live on my own terms. So much suffering arises when these deceptive notions become axiomatic, unexamined and determinative. Trying to maintain a self-structure that is founded on false propositions is a thankless task, an ongoing struggle to maintain a fantasy that is being exposed as groundless by the transient actuality of our experience.

UNGRASPABLE PRESENCE

The truth of this actuality, its very source, is beautiful, deep, and unchanging. This is the essence of how we are. Yet believing that we are a who and a what, someone named, knowable and known, we unintentionally hide the ungraspable yet livable truth of the openness of being. 'Being' is the presence of the intrinsic absence of something-ness. All seeming 'some-things' are actually devoid of inherent existence. They are no-thing, no-entity and are empty of self-defining essence. Now this might sound like a cause of anxiety but in fact it is the truth that dissolves the basis of all anxiety. As the sun dispels the morning mist, so the clarity spreading from true pure perception causes the delusion of individual substance to vanish. With no one to grasp and no-thing to grasp at, there is relaxation, freedom and bright presence.

We can now start to look at the buddhist view of dzogchen, the great completion, which points out the non-dual integral actuality which is the truth of all the complexity, confusion and anxiety we encounter. We have a mind. This mind is not a thing. It is ungraspable. Yet it is present as clear presence which illuminates its own open ground as well as all our transient experience.

The empty open infinite ungraspability, the bright illuminating ungraspability and the ceaselessly self-arising and self-vanishing relational ungraspability are the three inseparable aspects of the truth of life and the heart of the buddha.

To see the ground of our being is to see that there is nothing that can be seen. This ground or source or basis is not an object of knowledge. It is not something other than its illuminating awareness. This non-duality is open, empty and ungraspable. To 'see' this is to be freed from the need for hungry looking for what we need in order to be complete. We are already part of the whole. We are complete – not in 'ourselves' as something deemed to be separate but in our inalienable participation in the never-dividing, never-fragmenting whole. The whole is for ever empty and it is for ever full. To open to the presence of the empty ground is, paradoxically, to be with the fullness of instant occurrence. Moreover, the clarity of receiving the instant presence of the showing of the potential of the whole does not establish a fixed observer position. We are not clear due to looking but by receiving the showing of the ground. Moreover this showing includes our experience of ourselves which is in fact simply movement within it. All that we do and say is the playful non-dual display of the ground source.

STILLNESS AND MOVEMENT ARE NON-DUAL

The open aspect is still and unchanging while the other two aspects, illuminating display and relational patterning, are modes of movement. Stillness and movement are not the same and yet they are not truly different. They are non-dual. Non-duality indicates that actuality is neither just one thing nor many different things. For example, if you look into a mirror, you see a reflection. You don't see the mirror. It's impossible to see the mirror as 'mirror'. The mirror shows itself by showing something which it is not, i.e. the reflection. The mirror is the capacity to show something which it is not and yet which of course it also is. When you look in the mirror, the mirror is filled with your reflection. The mirror does not stand in relation to the reflection in it. You can't take the reflection out of the mirror. They are neither two nor one – they are non-dual.

To take another example, we wear clothes. We can take our clothes off, since our clothes are, in a sense, an ornamentation added to our body. They are not the same as the body, but when we wear our clothes we inhabit our clothes and it's as if they are an expression of ourselves. Yet at night we take off our clothes. Body and clothes are dual, not non-dual. However we can't take the reflection out of the mirror. The reflection does not clothe the mirror. The reflection and the mirror are not two things. The reflection is the showing of the quality of the mirror. The mirror is empty of self, of fixed content. It is the emptiness of the mirror which is the basis of its infinite generosity, its capacity to let the other arise as self within it, while remaining free of both self and other. The mirror shows the reflection of whatever is placed in front of it without prejudice. If you put something very horrible in front of the mirror, it shows that, and if you put something very beautiful, it shows that. If you turn the mirror away from something beautiful towards something ugly, the mirror doesn't sigh, it doesn't get sad, it doesn't have a temper tantrum; it just shows what is there. The mirror itself is still and unchanging as potential. The reflection is an aspect of movement whereby a specific pattern of potential is momentarily revealed.

THE SOURCE HAS NO PREFERENCE

This might seem very wonderful – yet then the question arises: *"If this is true, if this is how it is and how I am, how come I didn't know it?"* The ground or source of everything, and that includes us, is ever open, ever fresh. It gives rise to both clarity and confusion. Neither is 'real'. They are not things, or states, or essences but modes of revealing aspects of the potential of the empty ungraspable ground. They are illusion, appearances without individual defining essence. To see this within non-duality is clarity. To be blind to this due to the miasma of duality is delusion. The truth of non-duality is beyond the capacity of language and concept to depict accurately. Therefore what I say now is an offering of images, re-presentations of the unsayable, the ungraspable. Hopefully it is illuminative – but it needs to be held lightly.

THE FOUR ASPECTS OF IGNORING THE SOURCE

Confusion arises from the open ungraspable source as a magical illusion displaying the sudden deluding sense of the existence of something which can be grasped. The flow of non-dual appearance continues like the flow of reflections in the side-view mirror on a car. Yet suddenly within it, there seems to be something. Moreover for that something to be known there is necessarily an apprehendor of the 'something'. In the dzogchen tradition this is known as 'One Self ignoring', (Tib. *bDag-Nyid gCig Pu'i Ma Rig Pa*), the ignoring which is the sole entity, the first autonomous thing. The One Self is itself the ignoring of the ground, its ground. It is (in its falsity) by denying what it is (in its actuality). It is in fact an unborn empty moment of imagination, of delusion, of falsity, of invention, yet in its seeming truth, it 'is'. Holding on to this moment as an indicator of something generates our sense of an entity enduring through time. In fact time is born with it.

What is it that continues? A fiction, an illusion like a rainbow – yet as an over-invested reified illusion it is deluding and so a chain of falsity comes into apparent 'existence.' This is/I am – these are creative concepts operating like a magician creating the illusion of something out of nothing. And yet when they are taken to be descriptions of something, the fleeting phenomena and the stabilising concept become as one. This fabrication, this lie, this deceptive theatre, is the basis of existential anxiety. There is a belief in something which does not exist. It is only the power of belief that generates the seeming existence of that which does not exist. The familiar binary of fact and fiction arises when fact is not accurately seen as a mode of fiction. All is fiction, imagining, believing. This is the father, the activity of taking the flow of empty appearances, the children of the open empty mother, to be the presence of entities for ever separate and multiplying.

The ground source is open and empty, and awareness of the ground is free of being something as such. The actual ungraspable is light, bright, fine, precise, intrinsically valid without requiring dualistic validation. This has not vanished. It is unchanging. Although clarity and delusion arise together as the play of the open ground, now this play is taken as the existence of diverse somethings. This is known as 'co-emergent ignoring' (Tib. *lHan Cig sKyes Pa'i Ma Rig Pa)*. The open source offers everything including its closure which is delusion, concept and solidification. These are mere empty reflections in the mirror, but now the mirror and its reflections seem separate. They are co-present, 'born together', yet, seemingly, clarity is dulling due to the patina of the perception of 'things' superimposed on the openness of empty appearances.

This thickening is an accumulation (Tib. *'Du Byed)* of memories, associations, constructs which further veil the ever-open ground from which they are inseparable. It is as if the ground is something other than what appears and that this appearance veils the ground from the observing self which is other than it. Self and appearance are the display of the ground, a display that is blind to what it is a display of. The seeming entities that stand apart from the ground are like formations of ice appearing from water but being taken as other than water.

This thickening is reinforced by conceptual patterning as each momentary formation of the open potential is seized hold of as a 'something' and identified by its membership of a system of naming and classification. The immediacy of fresh appearance is dulled by being taken, for example, as an instance of a 'tree' which is then further refined as an 'oak tree', and then as a 'young oak tree with spring leaves'. By now the ground is fully ignored in its openness (Tib. *Ka Dag*) while its fullness (Tib. *lHun Grub)* is mistakenly taken to be the presence of nameable, knowable stuff. This is called the 'naming everything ignoring' (Tib. *Kun Tu brTags Pa'i Ma Rig Pa)*. Now perception is no longer simple and pure but is bewildering in its fixation on endless entities. This strengthens the developing ego identity: I see stuff. The seeming 'reality' of stuff as separate entities confirms my 'existence' as the separate entity I know as 'I, me, myself'. Yet, since appearance is inherently empty of substance, the mistaken belief in 'the real existence of self and other, of me and everything I find myself in contact with' generates further deep anxiety. I am having to reinvent myself moment by moment, identifying myself with a stream of rising and vanishing experiences: I am tired, I am thirsty, I am walking... How 'I am' emerges with circumstances yet I am burdened with the deluded and deluding ongoing activity of asserting my enduring substantial predictable essential existence.

From this arises our experience of inhabiting a body in samsara, the turning wheel of becoming. Having been born we find ourselves to be a fish, a bird, a woman, a man, a some-being some-where. Our environment arises for us as a series of options or choice points. We have to react or respond to the shifting situations we find ourselves within. Each time we choose an option and act, we establish tendencies, patterns, habit formations in our egoic self-reflexive mind-stream. Believing ourselves to be real and inherently separate from our environment, we seek to gain what we want and avoid what we don't want. But assessing another person for their potential to make us happy over time is very difficult. We change, they change – and what once seemed hopeful and viable starts to seem limiting, frustrating and unappealing. We shift from desire, to boredom, to anger. As the Buddha said, suffering arises from getting what we don't want and not getting what we do want. What is actually in front of us and what we take it to be are often rather different. This is the experience of 'obliviousness to karmic cause and effect ignoring' (Tib. *Las rGyu 'Bras La rMongs Pa'i Ma Rig Pa)*. Our actions have consequences beyond their immediate effect, for the patterning of what we experience is dynamic and unfolds through the intention and intensity of our participation. Our life is our own habitual patterning being revealed through our behaviour yet we do not recognise it and this dullness adds another layer to our ignoring.

This is the dullness (Tib. *gTi-Mug)* of not getting it, of not knowing what is going on. It brings the anxiety of playing catch-up, of trying to join the dots and see the whole picture. Dullness is blind assumption. Sometimes it is defensively confident in the narcissistic style of dictators and sometimes the underlying anxiety is more evident, arising as confusion, fear, mistakes, self-doubt and incomprehension. This dullness supports the narrow view that forms our own life. By not looking, not seeing, not feeling, not knowing what is occurring as history and as present activity in the world, our prejudices remain invisible to us and we are party to exploitation and disregard for the actual complexity of interdependence.

Each of these four aspects of ignoring what is actual, brings their own flavours of anxiety, uncertainty and hesitancy. The anxiety of believing the false proposition of the reality of existence leads to the anxiety of denying the intrinsic open ground and turning to the artifice of imagining self and other to be entities. Our imposter-self, which is a non-self, is taking the wrong way. We, this hollow self-image know this but we don't turn back. We travel on apart from the flow, seeking to become someone. We are in bad faith with our potential yet we choose to continue to live a lie. From this we find ourselves, our emergent selves, engaged in the work of conceptual elaboration as we seek to control and direct the patterning of self and other in this seemingly fragmented world. The cause of this fragmentation is our own mental process, but since we are committed to our idea of the autonomy of self and its isolation from objects, we cannot see this. Hence we have to keep acting on the world 'out there' to make it conform to our wishes and to the shifting patterns of our hopes and fears 'in here'.

With this we exist as ego-selves in a world of different species of ego-selves. Some we dominate and domesticate, some we live in fear of. We act to optimise the welfare of ourselves and perhaps those we love. We have our own hierarchy of values and this informs our choices and organises our planning. Act, react, act again. Life is ceaseless activity. There is so much to be done and so much of this seems necessary if not important. When we hear of the buddhist teaching that everything is empty of inherent existence, it sounds like nonsense. Life is real, life is hard, you've got to stay ahead of the game. If you don't take opportunities and threats seriously and strive for your own welfare you may not survive let alone thrive. This anxious need to be busy colours our days: tidy the house, please other people, be a good partner or parent – it never ends. And so we are entrained in karma, in activity and are too busy, too tired, too preoccupied to attend to the open spaciousness within which we live.

EFFORTLESS SELF-LIBERATION

We do not need to remove the habit of ignoring. It is not something bad that we have like a disease. It is a mode of participation based on identification with ideas. Our mind itself does not rest on ideas. Our ego-self does rest on ideas. Our mind itself is not improved by 'good' ideas nor harmed by 'bad' ideas. Involvement is effortful, although due to habituation this effort may be invisible to us. Awareness is free of effort. Appearance&experience arises effortlessly moment by moment as the unborn showing of the radiant potential of the ground. Like an illusion, like a mirage it arises without a doer or a maker. It is not done or made or compounded, it is effortlessly arising ('object side') instant presence ('subject side') non-dual, unborn, devoid of inherent existence.

Staying present with this, as this, the falsity of ignorance is apparent. It is a mistaken identity which vanishes when its baselessness becomes clear. Ignoring is self-clearing, self-vanishing, self-liberating when ego-self is not indulged and so takes its place as part of the flow. Then, with all illusory obscurations released into the flow, all entities are transparent and awareness shines forth.

Habits have their power through repetition. What is required is that we attend to the freshness of the moment. Its instant presence is an aspect of the ground. Rather than my body being a thing apart that I have to control, I can open to seeing how it is moving and from that come to see that moving is what I unnecessarily conceptualise as 'my body'. Moving is moving – just this. It is inexpressible in its immediacy. To talk of 'movement' is already to set out a particular kind of some-thing. This is why we need meditation as a moment in which the four aspects of ignoring can be allowed to vanish. They are held in place and operationally activated by the dualising mental activity we identify with as being ourselves. Therefore we simply sit and let experience come as it comes and go as it goes.

Non-involvement and non-interference allows our habitual arousal to relax as flow, revealing its actual openness which is intrinsic. As our reliance on concepts diminishes, we find ourselves less preoccupied and thereby free to enjoy the innate spaciousness of our source.

ATTEND TO HOW YOU ARE

However before we can access the intrinsic we need to start to recognise the dualistic artifice we habitually identify with. At first it helps if we can see that our bodies are always moving in space. Even if you're sitting very still, your body is moving; if it wasn't moving, you'd be dead. Breath is going in and out of your lungs. This involves shifts in the diaphragm, shifts in the nostrils, and if you touch your pulse, you can feel your artery going up and down according to the pulsation that is going through it. This 'body' is itself ceaseless change.

When we are small, we often want to be big; when we are big, we don't want to get old; when we are old, we don't want to die. No-one can stop the movement of time and this brings both dissatisfaction and anxiety. The body is the pulse of time. The body is rhythmic, the rhythm of breathing, the rhythm of the heart, the rhythm of all the hormonal cycles and so on. The person I refer to as 'me' is movement. 'I' am moving, arising and vanishing moment by moment: pattern after pattern of presence free of enduring substance. Generally this goes unnoticed as I try to stabilise myself as something, to formulate my identity so that I can reliably present myself as always being the same. However, as we looked earlier, this is a lie, a fabrication, a self-deception of and by the selfless self. Ignorance is the fictional creator of fictions. Imagination generates a world that does not exist yet so seductive which is this illusion that we believe it to be real. It seems obvious and undeniable that 'it exists'. Yet both 'it' and 'exists' are imagined. They are transient ideas fossilised by belief. What we take to be the self arises from deception and is itself self-deceiving and other-deceiving.

The most reliable thing about anyone is that stories can be told about them. The stories form a kind of cocoon disguising the ceaseless change that occurs within. Yet even the telling of the story is sound moving due to the throat moving. We cannot truly be caught by a story for we are movement and cannot be nailed down except by a lie. Saliva forms in the mouth, irritation forms on the skin when an insect bites, our knees hurt so we stretch and turn and move around. Posture, gesture, gait are all inseparable from specific environments. Our body is not a fixed thing but it is part of the ongoing conversation that is our 'existence', an existence that does not truly exist, being nothing other than the flow of experience of the non-duality of self and other.

The body is movement, feelings are movement, sensations revealed through proprioception are movement, thoughts are movement, memories are movement, plans and intentions are movement. Like rainbows, like clouds, like birds flying across the sky, events are arising and passing moment by moment. None of us can stop time. The good things we want to keep, vanish. Moreover the bad things we want to get rid of will also vanish. We don't even have to struggle to get rid of them.

The fundamental point is this: to look clearly and honestly at your life and your world and see that all that you are is constituted from movement. When this becomes clear to you, you see how ludicrous it is to spend your whole life trying to stop movement. All through your life rhythms have been playing around you and whether your life goes well or not generally depends on whether you can dance to these many different rhythms. For example, when you go to school, you have the playground and you have the classroom. These environments have different rhythms. Some children are very at home playing in the playground, but then when they come into the classroom, they want to continue playing. The teacher says, *"No, sit still, listen, write, do what you have to do!"* But the child feels, *"I can't hear this tune, the music I want is in the playground....so sweet....I want to dance."* People who can only hear one tune get a lot of trouble because in all situations they just hear the same tune, their tune, and so they clash with the music of where they are.

Health, both mental and physical, is the capacity to bring forth from the vast repertoire of one's own rhythms the specific rhythm which will fit with the rhythm of this arena of the world at this moment. We have the potential for this, we have the capacity, so what is it that gets in the way of our manifesting according to circumstances? Generally it is because we limit ourselves by the fixed beliefs we hold about ourselves. We see how other people live, but we think, *"Oh, I couldn't do that."* We see the clothes they wear, but we think, *"I could never wear that!"* We hear the things they say and we say, *"Oh, I couldn't say that!"* I couldn't wear that or say that because I am me. Being me means yes to a few things, and no to many, many, many other things. These other things are done by people with two legs, two arms, two eyes, one nose! Now we check ourselves... two legs, two arms, two eyes, one nose! *"Okay so I am almost the same. Maybe I can change. I am going to try this, but oh, I am not so sure. This doesn't feel like me..."*

I start to feel anxious, how can I let myself become someone who I don't believe I am? This is my problem, how will 'I' do it? Well 'I' won't be able to do it, because I have already defined 'I' as somebody who doesn't do it. If you want to be free you have to let go of being the you that you know yourself to be. From this perspective knowing who you are is bad news. When somebody is dead we can write their obituary, we can sum up their life, but as long as we are alive, we don't know how we are going to feel or what we are going to do. One morning you wake up and there is a new tune in the air. Often it is a tune of spontaneity you have not heard since you were a caterpillar in your youth. Now after years in the cocoon the butterfly is ready to take off. The cocoon can't fly. So let's hope the butterfly is free of the cocoon and happy to be a butterfly – then flying is easy.

How does this happen? In a moment of self-forgetfulness we arise anew. I am not who I thought I was. I think I'm this, I think I'm that, I'm being like this, I'm being like that. How I am thinking and how I am being are changing in their 'how-ness', in how they emerge. Unfortunately this is easily disregarded by my commitment to my what-ness, to my being an enduring someone. This self-reflexive, self-defining fixed motif has maintained the illusion of my predictable self. However, suddenly, for some unknown reason, I might find myself doing something else and being someone else. This doesn't fit my existing image of myself, so I am at a choice point: either I go with the new and fresh or else strive to be more of the same.

FRESH OR FAMILIAR

Psychotherapy can help to bring about such moments of decision. If the therapist can be a warm supportive presence free of agenda, then they are not of themselves reinforcing the patient's belief system. Of course the patient's perception of the therapist is mediated by their assumptions and tendencies and they often transfer patterns from the past in to their felt sense of who the therapist actually is. When this transferential or projected image of the other dissolves there can be a moment of freshness in which one sees the other as other rather than as a creation of one's own self-confirmatory patterning. In freeing the other from our interpretation we also have the chance to free ourselves – at least momentarily. A therapist's training should help to free them from their stale knowledge of who they take themselves to be. This can create an ambience which supports the patient to simply show how they are rather than to identify themselves as someone already known.

Moments like these bring us to a choice point. We can either step into the fresh and see how it is, or step back and try to reconstitute ourself as the person we know ourself to be. Breakdown to breakthrough, to open up, to open out, witnessing the self-vanishing of the props that kept the old story starring on the stage in the drama of 'my life', or breakdown with a frightening sense of groundlessness, a collapsing of structures of self into bewildering not-knowing generating an anxious need to pull oneself back together again. To choose the former is to start to experience a profound deconstruction of the fantasy that you are 'who you thought you were'. To choose the latter is to re-engage with the endless task of self-construction accompanied by the pretense that you truly exist as a reliable entity.

When you look at a musical score you see notes written on paper. If you are a musician, when you see the notation of a phrase you know what to do with your fingers. Each time this pattern comes on the score you make a particular sound. The same notes occur again and again. However the sound of these notes is heard as part of a movement of sound and the notes that are before and after this particular instance of the sound create the context in which the 'same' sound is different due to the difference of context. Our life is like this. We play the notation of ourselves again and again yet according to the context it has different resonances. We are manifesting as a transient formation in a transient field of disclosure: here for a moment and then gone. That is to say, neither ourselves nor our environment are a fixed territory which can be secured. To live this is to experience that the musician and the music are fresh and fully revealed in each moment.

When the carapace of knowledge falls away, it reveals the fresh tender skin that is so alive, sensitive and responsive. The fixed rhythm of our habitual moves is replaced by an ever-expanding variety of moves, of moods – a co-emerging polyphony without end. Instead of a self struggling to keep to its own rhythm and not be led astray by other people's tunes we find that events are calling us forth and as we freely respond we get closer to the source of the response. As self dissolves our ungraspable bright awareness shines forth like the rising sun.

FANTASIES INVITE BETRAYAL

So now we can perhaps gain a clearer sense of what anxiety is. Anxiety is the feeling tone of trying to make stable something which cannot be made stable. There is no 'something' to get hold of and control, not then, not now, not ever. For example, people often get anxious in a relationship: *"I want you to love me but I feel you don't love me anymore. I don't know what to do."* Love is very unreliable. In the old days people had arranged marriages because they understood very clearly marriage is about land and cows and children! Keep the heart out of it. Most of us don't have any land, we don't have any cows, and though we might want to have children, the basis for having them is a hope rather than a fact: *"I love you, and I will love you forever."* I know who is going to win the football championship because I can tell the future! So I can say with full confidence, *"I will love you forever." "Oh thank God, I have been waiting for this, because I am going to love you forever too!"* Isn't it beautiful? Well, in England the divorce rate is now over 50%. Feelings are not very reliable, as we know.

When you are a child and Christmas is coming, you see lots of adverts on the television for cheap plastic toys made to look wonderful. The child is convinced by the advert that the toy they want will be exactly the same as in the advert. Then Christmas comes, they get the toy but after a week they don't want to play with it because it is not the same as in the advert. It is not what they thought it would be.

The excited hopeful feeling that the child felt on imagining what they would get could not be fully replicated with the actual toy. The magic was gone. Where did it go to? Back into the potential of the mind. All the qualities of all the objects and all the people in the world are the qualities of the mind. If you have faith then dying for you your country can seem glorious. If you have faith then torturing the enemies of the state can seem noble and patriotic. If you have faith then this particular person is the most beautiful and wonderful person in the world. Looking through the eyes of loyalty or love you see a truth that is hidden from others. Rational, sceptical eyes cannot see this beguiling bright inspiration radiance.

One of the reasons that our identity as human beings is so unreliable is because we are enthusiastic. 'Enthusiasm' indicates that the theos, the god, comes into us. Similarly 'inspiration' indicates that the spirit comes into us. That is to say some divine or ungrounded presence fills us and in this merging we imagine that we taste the truth. But spirit, like the breath, is coming and going, here and then gone. The divine cannot be caught, the breath cannot be caught, life cannot be caught, love cannot be caught. These are not commodities to be traded, for there are no commodities only delusions.

A mood takes us over for a while, and then it's gone. Afterwards we cannot imagine how we could have been caught up in that story. *"How could I ever have fallen in love with someone like that? I see them so clearly now. I don't know what happened to me. When I first met him all my friends said, uh uh, not for you....but I knew in my heart that I was right. Oh, how stupid, how wrong I was, I'll never make that mistake again."* It's like that, we are unreliable and others are unreliable too. Why? Because we are movement like the wind. We shift so quickly for there is nothing stable in the personality.

IMAGE LEADS US ASTRAY

However this ceaseless unpredictable movement does not condemn us to chaos. The ground or basis of movement is stillness. Stillness is the actuality of our awareness. If I have a mirror in my hand and I turn it around to display the room, as the mirror moves many different reflections arise and pass. The mirror itself is not changing. The mirror's quality is to be open to what is there. The potential of this openness never changes. No matter what arises in the mirror the potential of the mirror to show reflections is not marked or limited. Now, if you take a blank piece of paper, it too has a lot of potential. At this stage you can draw or write anything on this piece of paper. However, once you start putting marks on the paper the infinite potential of the blank piece of paper is lost. The potential of the paper is vulnerable to circumstances. Once marked it cannot be unmarked.

Although our unborn awareness is like the mirror, our personality is like paper, taking on mark after mark until its open potential is fully obscured. As we develop through life we become what we take to be 'ourselves'. When we were small, we could do and become many many different things. But by the age of twenty, our life is starting to take shape. This shape is not actually authentic yet its repertoire of familiar patternings comes to feel like me and gives some density to my existence. Moreover in the minds of the people around me some shape or representation of 'who they take me to be' is also being formed. They become used to their sense of me according to their habitual interpretations. They think that I am a set of particular knowable patterns. If that is not confirmed by my current behaviour they may ask, *"Hey James, are you okay? You look a bit different."* They are letting me know that they need me to be who they think I am.

So as a personality, as an identity, the James-ness of James is held in place by factors not all of which belong to 'James' as he takes himself to be. There is a social obligation to be reliably oneself: my 'self' is not mine! This demand is very restrictive and does not allow much room for happenstance and this also can be a cause of much anxiety.

CONSCIOUSNESS AND THE SENSE OF I

When we are managing our identity, examining options, making choices, trying to increase happiness and reduce suffering for ourselves. And for those dear to us, we are employing the aspect of mental functioning known as consciousness. Consciousness is dualistic; it takes an object, it focuses on something both apprehendable and comprehendible. The operation of our consciousness leads to our saying things such as, *"I like apples more than pears."* This statement rests on the identification of apples as objects different from pears as objects. This is followed by comparing and contrasting and the allocation of status in a personal hierarchy of value. A lot of quick and often habitual mental activity lies behind the simplest of statements. The more precisely we define and identify objects in the world, the more precisely we can identify objects in ourselves – memories, plans, regrets and so on. Our developed subjectivity brings a highly selective attention towards the rich variety of entities displayed in the ever-changing field of dualistic disclosure.

For example, I see people in this room, I hear the sound of someone talking next to me as they translate what I have said, I taste the traces of my lunch in my mouth. In each case I am experiencing specific 'somethings'. Subject and object are arising together. In experiencing the object, there is a reflexive sense of me, myself, confirming that I am the experiencer, I am the one to whom this is occurring. If in active mode, I am the one who is making this happen. However this 'I' has no true independent inherent existence. 'I' is an empty signifier. In a limited dualistic way, 'I' is like a mirror, because it can take on any content. Actually it is more like a sausage skin since you can stuff anything into it! I am happy, I am sad, I am thirsty, I need to have a pee – anything can be referred to in terms of 'I' because I is empty. The value of the signifier 'I' for me is that by using it I can claim many identities and experiences as 'mine'. I am thirsty. True. Now I drink. I am not thirsty. That means a statement such as 'I am thirsty' is a lie in absolute terms since I am only thirsty in relative terms subject to the play of causes and conditions. *"You said you were thirsty. I gave you something to drink. Now you are not thirsty. Now you don't want anything to drink. Why should I believe anything you say! Last night you told me you were tired now in the morning you say you are not tired! You're just like a puppet, something pulls your strings and you do this, you do that."* This indicates the dynamic interdependence of self and other, subject and object, subject and subject.

This is us: this is our life. We fabricate a story of stability and apply it to 'something' which is completely unstable. So who is the one who says I? To employ the term 'I' as referring to 'myself' is to use it to organise 'my' experience or rather to organise experience so that I can take it as mine. 'I' is not referring to something deep inside 'me'; it is not a personal essence, but a signifier working in the world in myriad transient formations. I can be fused with my experience: so if I'm tired, I'm just tired. I can also be conscious about saying I'm tired. So I might say, *"I'm tired"* and then start to think, but why am I tired? In that case the second thought has the first thought as its object. I'm thinking about thinking, and each thought appears like the subject when I speak it as it or think it as it, but it then appears as the object for the next thought. This is consciousness functioning as the interweaving of our self and our world as we take them to be.

There is no autonomous self, no stand-alone individual represented by the term 'I'. I am because you are. I alone has no past or present or future. I alone has no content nor is it a container: the sausage-skin of self does not exist as something that could hold true content. The idea of I operates as both a reference point and as an 'owner'. The felt sense that an experience is mine installs the idea of self as something apart, something possessing the functions of owning and doing. Yet both subject and object are part of the flow: they show and go in their specificity. Only in abstraction do they endure as seemingly eternal ideas far from the actual. However, as presence 'I' alone is the dawning of awareness, open, empty, naked, available yet ungraspable. Open empty I is nothing at all – even if you look again and again, you will find no personal essence underpinning it. It has no owner and it does not own. Yet it is also the basis of all that can occur, it is the immediacy of potential revealed as the diverse richness of this moment. Moreover, here I am, present in this, as this, of this – yet without being truly a someone somewhere. I am this apparitional play, this *fata morgana,* this undeniably ungraspable mirage.

It is sometimes possible to make this insight central to our work in psychotherapy. For example, it might be appropriate to help some of our patients to be more mindful of the way in which they formulate their fantasy of an enduring self with enduring characteristics. It might be a great relief for them to see how they themselves restrict themselves and deny themselves access to their intuitive spontaneity. If we are to help someone else open to their potential, we firstly have to open to our own ground. When we observe how we identify with a pattern and how this becomes the moment of self-creation, we can see the cloud of self forming out of the open sky. This is not a matter of abstract speculation or the imposition of an interpretation.

We need to focus on the concrete and be present with phenomena as they arise and pass in their ungraspability. For example, at the moment I am moving as I am speaking. I am conscious of this and I am also aware of the field of experience within which the event and my consciousness of it are occurring. Dualistically I can catch what I am doing, I can define it and I can tell you what I am experiencing – this is the work of consciousness. Yet in the immediacy of this occurrence, consciousness and its objects are both revealed as empty reflections in the mirror of awareness. There is panoramic seeing without a seer doing the seeing. This is awareness or presence. I am not observing myself but rather awareness reveals without observing. Awareness is never an object. It is not aware of itself but is present as itself although it has no self to be present as. I am the non-revealing revealer free of bias and intention. I am open: all this and just 'me' in this moment. Awareness is not subjective agency but the luminous field within which subject and object show as self-arising self-vanishing display. This is a tricky area on the edge of language since the word 'I' can be used to refer to my conscious individual self or to my unborn open awareness. They are different and yet not intrinsically, since neither exists as an entity.

If we were practising ballet, at least one wall of the room would be mirrored and we would be observing our bodies in different postures. We would be working with the fact that our proprioception is often inaccurate and misleading. That is to say, I may believe that I have a clean balanced line, but when I look in the mirror I can see that my right shoulder is too high and the extension of my arm is crooked. In this case observing myself helps me to correct my fantasy about myself.

Similarly when people are learning yoga they need to have someone to help them again and again achieve a balanced position because the somatic memory, the kinesthetic memory, is often inaccurate in terms of actual posture. We experience movements of thought, of feeling, of sensation arising as pattern after pattern. Some patterns we say are perfect, some we say are off balance. This is the evaluative judgement of consciousness working with learned criteria and it may well frequently be inaccurate.

However in the moment when I am simply present with myself in the unfolding of the becoming of this instant of 'myself', I am not apart from myself observing myself, but neither am I merged in it or identified with it. Awareness is non-dual with whatever occurs, just as the reflection is in the mirror and the mirror is showing the reflection it offers hospitality to. This is a generous selfless hospitality free of bias to either subject or object. Each aspect of the field is welcome as it is and free to come and go.

This hospitality is a key quality of awareness as described in the dzogchen tradition. Awareness is not an energetic formation; it is not transient or situationally altered. It does not arise due to causes and conditions although what it shows arises due to causes and conditions. The mirror and the reflection are non-dual, awareness and occurrence are non-dual. Just as the space of the mirror instantly shows what is there without having to build up the reflection, awareness effortlessly shows what is occurring. Nonetheless the patterns which are revealed can be seen in the relative terms of historical causes – and of course this is the more familiar arena of psychotherapy where our focus is on the work of consciousness rather than on the play of awareness.

PSYCHOTHERAPY

If both therapist and client can be present in open awareness this can greatly facilitate the work of psychotherapy. In particular as therapists, if we relax into the intrinsic clarity of simple presence before a therapy session, our availability is no longer a limited capacity of our ego-self, a capacity that is easily influenced by events in our own lives. The hospitality of intrinsic clarity is effortless and unrestricted and as such does not interfere with the revelation of the patient as they are.

Many of us are used to effort, to artifice, to intentional interventions and perhaps to formal diagnoses and treatment planning. We may feel we have to do something, to engage in a process of enquiry, perhaps of analysis, and most probably of change. This orientation keeps us in duality, burdened by what we take to be our tasks and responsibilities. However being caught up in a professional identity may be another veil to the open space of co-emergence. Therefore avoiding both wary self-doubt and hubristic over-confidence we could lighten up, relax and trust non-duality.

The mind is very subtle, you can't catch it: you have to learn to be with it in its non-duality. So it's important to develop an appreciation of how you are which is subtle, graceful and non-restrictive.

When someone presents with anxiety or depression, it can be helpful to consider them as patterns of energy, patterns of experience. The more the patient fuses with the experience and takes it to be indicative of who they are, the more difficult it is to help them. Although to say, *"I have depression"* is less dense than to say, *"I am depressed."* Both these statements can feel like the truth of the patient, their limit and definition, and therefore something to be taken seriously and honoured. However, on the basis of what we have explored so far together, we might relax and hear such statements in a less reificatory way.

The patient says, *"I am really depressed, I can't do anything. I feel terrible."* We need to hear the intensity of this as rhythm, as energy. The insistence present in the semantics, in the tone, in the physicality of expression, are all conveying how the energy flow of the person is compromised. The life energy, the prana moving in the subtle channels, is trapped in fixed sections where it vibrates in limiting and intoxicating ways. This trapped vibration with its repetitive beat is reinforcing the sense that this is the truth about me and is my permanent state of affairs.

"I feel terrible. Dum dum dum. I feel terrible, terrible, terrible, de de da. I feel terrible, please pity me, da de da de da." This is a tune, a vibration in space and time, an expression of energy. It feels like me, yet not recognising this self-validating feeling as a vibration I take it as a consolidating definition of myself: *"I am depressed. Listen to me. Get off my back. Why do you keep asking me to do things? I'm really depressed, just leave me alone. This is me, I'm at my limit."* Suicide often occurs as the depression lifts giving the person the energy to act. They often feel so fused with the experience that for them it is the absolute truth and limit of their existence. This is all there is and there is no way out. Depression becomes essentialised as the core definition of what and who they are. However, the actuality is that every moment of depression is a second-by-second manifesting event. It is the arising and passing of experience in space and time. The seeming permanence lies in the conceptual interpretation and not in the actual phenomena.

If this experience is happening to me, for me, as me, who is the one who feels, 'I am me'? If we can see through our mesmerising self-perpetuating narrative and look directly at what is occurring then we see movement not stasis. The surface of our ego-self is like blotting paper. It is very absorbent and what is absorbed fuses with the paper.

However awareness is like the mirror. The mirror shows the image right inside itself without any barrier yet not being absorbent, it remains fresh, open and unaltered. The awareness-mirror is never conditioned by experience. The ego-self is always conditioned by experience. Thinking about something is the ego's activity, its principal way of resourcing itself. However you can't think your way out of severe depression and you can't think your way into awareness. The door to awareness is meditation and in particular the meditation of non-meditation in which we simply open to the transient presence of whatever is occuring. The needy ego-self is never free of hopes and fears and this keeps it primed for involvement.

Non-meditation begins when we cease to identify with the ego-self nexus, and remain empty and open with the self-arising/self-vanishing display.

The prime function of this approach to meditation is to release us from our biased identification with aspects of appearance. With this we cease to feed ego formation. Ordinarily we register that something is occurring. It impacts us and we react with identification or dis-identification and some qualities of this involved reactivity are absorbed by the ego. Our sense of self is altered by these adaptations of expansion or contraction.

In particular, we can carry the impact of trauma in our body. For example, the impact of a fear-inducing event on the sympathetic nervous system can establish an unhelpfully high level of adrenaline as normal. This feeds an ongoing hyper-vigilance and hyper-arousal. With this comes a selective attention directed towards potential problems and provocations in the environment. Through this we subtly re-traumatise ourselves by our fearful separative stance and so maintain the high level of adrenaline we are used to. This is activity generating a fabricated and unnecessary sense of enduring identity. If this dualistic activity of anxious observation were not on-going, the adrenaline level would go down opening up new arenas of experience and identity.

When the effects of an experience are incorporated as an aspect of my sense of self, this fusion makes it difficult to separate from and let go of what has been incorporated. As we looked earlier, the ego-self is like a sausage skin – it can fill with joy, with pain, with hope, with regret – and that filling can then be taken to be an essential ingredient of our identity.

Our identification with our ego-self as being who we really are is the reificatory basis upon which we are bound into an attachment to patterns as indicators of defining essence rather than as transient phenomena.

Intentionally focussed meditation can help to develop our capacity for mindful attention. This can then be utilised to observe the patterns of ego formation maintained by the selective inclusion and exclusion of factors from the field. From this we can see that the ego is not the enemy, being merely a self-perpetuating nexus of energy devoid of inherent existence. The key task is simply to recognise that what we call 'ourself' is a patterning of energy and not an enduring substance that can sustain an accurate definition of 'who I am'. It is actually a patterning of my communication with the world, a patterning that has become habitual and limiting.

Seeing that 'our' ego is a reading of our organisation of our energy of connectivity with others, we can start to recognise that change is continuous. The meditation of non-meditation – free of intention and agenda – reveals that there are no fixed entities to be altered or got rid of, rather both self and others are rippling patterns in the ever-changing flow. The experiences that occur in therapy can be helpful for gaining a direct taste of this. Therapy lets us see what gets in the way of our opening to the other and to the wider potential of ourselves. Whether we see this foreclosure in terms of transference and counter-transference or in terms of interruptions to contact, our aim is to open wider and deeper pathways of connectivity. Neurosis is self-enclosure, an echo chamber where preoccupation with pre-formations blocks attention to the immediate and the actual.

When we spend our life inside ourselves going round and round in the labyrinth of our mind trying to work out who we are and what we should do with our life, we are following a tragic path of lostness. Other people are not who we think they are, so if we want to relate to other people, first of all we have to open to them, receive them and try to be with them as they present, moment by moment.

Revelation of occurrence free of interpretations and projections that impute inherent existence is freely available – we have merely to avail ourselves of it. By being present as part of the unfolding field of experience we have optimal access to the dynamic presence of the other. We start to receive how they show – simple, direct, immediate. Then our response arises as part of the non-dual display in harmony with the potential of this moment. To be silent or to speak, to be still or to offer energetic engagement – our non-dual presence will intuitively, spontaneously, display as transient patterning within the bright ungraspable field. Trusting the simplicity of this frees us from spending a lot of time in our skulls trying to work life out.

WISDOM

Life is dynamic and interconnected and is intrinsically beyond being something that could be captured by a theory or a set of principles. Presence is present with each moment. So where and how are we? Here and open, or locked inside 'ourselves'? The ego is finite in its capacity to receive the world – it gets shaped and overwhelmed and then cuts off. But awareness has no limit – it just lets experience flow through.

To be present as awareness is not something esoteric, it is the actual ground of the phenomenological richness of our life. The whole is undivided and reveals itself all at once. Just turn your head and look around the room. As you turn your head new aspects reveal themselves instantly, completely, moment by moment by moment. Thus-ness, this-ness is immediately here, self-revealing its ungraspable display of which we are always already a part. Life is not a problem to be solved by thinking – you do not have to work it out, and in fact you can't. Life is revealed fully through participative immersion and not by grasping at fabricated 'facts'.

When we practise, we sit in a relaxed way, breathing in and out. We are here, aware and simultaneously part of the experience that is occurring. We meditate with our eyes open without separating outside and inside. We are not trying to achieve something. Our presence is simple and without agenda and by resting in it, as it, we are the unchanging welcome that is non-dual with whatever occurs. The occurring is the showing of the unchanging – it is not other than its own open empty ground or source or basis.

How can it be this simple? It just is.

So why have I been trying so hard to sort myself out? You have been deluded by the myth of separation: you have taken the real existence of yourself for granted and starting from that assumption, which is shared by all the beings you encounter, you have created your own factory. This factory makes work for other factories.

Each of us works away sorting out the constructs that we encounter and in that activity we create further constructs for others to sort through. Psychotherapy can offer a space in which to see the vapidity of the veil of ontology and let it fade and vanish. Or it can be an arena in which the veils are multiplied and thickened, where we work hard to make sense of what has happened and its consequences for how we are. This investigation of cause and effect is located within the paradigm of duality: *"This happened to me. I did this."* Then therapy is just another factory producing stories about life, stories which veil the actuality of life from this life-moment which I am.

Whatever occurs, however it seems, is actually self-vanishing experience – direct, clear, just this. Nonetheless if you conceptualise it and enter into judgement about it, then self and other will be taken as inherently existing and you will inhabit the troubling delusion that the whole can be fragmented – indeed that the great all-inclusive whole is just another idea and that each fragment is its own autonomous whole.

Experience is the display of the breath of awareness. Yet if it is not seen in its non-dual integrity, it appears to be split into experiencer and experience, subject and object. By simply sitting with the undivided field, awareness, although inherently free, is released from our habitual over-layering and revealed as empty of defining self-content. We are present, open, aware, yet uninvolved.

This level of availability can be very helpful for psychotherapists because when you are sitting in this way with a patient, you don't divide the field. This ambience can help the patient to deactivate their tendency to anxious defensive splitting. In this non-dual field of experience, everything is happening together. Now free floating attention and free association occur simultaneously. The pulsation of speaking and listening, receiving and responding, is like the flow of waves in the ocean. The field is 'healing' itself of imposed divisions and so communication becomes unimpeded.

Presence does not rest on anything and so is free of need. It is not improved by happy experiences nor is it diminished by troublesome experiences. It is with them but not involved and not affected. By staying with what arises now, and not identifying with the subject polarity, subject and object are seamless in their co-emergence and are evidently non-dual with their open empty ground. The temptation to separate off from the open ground and to identify with the ego consciousness will continue for as long as this temptation is taken to be real and powerful. Yet by relaxing all tension in body, voice and mind, limiting fixations are unharnessed and are free to arise and vanish. We are not applying an effortful technique but are simply releasing the energy bound up in our habitual striving. With this the therapist is the presence of the integrity of the three inseparable aspects: open and empty; instant and diverse; and this precise patterning of the energy of collaboration.

This offers a deconstructive generous availability, welcoming the patient as they are with a spaciousness that helps to ease them out of the fixity of their over-determined identity. The patient's story will tend to entangle us and pull us towards our theories. However the patient's presence, fully attended to and openly received, will allow the free-flow of non-artificial connectivity.

This is the prime factor in healing. It is not so complicated. Yet the social organisation of training and validation tends to introduce distracting complications as trainees are required to show that they have developed the capacity to think about the patient and the interpersonal skill required for upholding a professional identity. Yet, paradoxically, most of what we have learned while training as therapists and perhaps now employ in our work is not truly helpful because the deep and vast work is done by self-forgetfulness, by becoming a simple availability free of agenda. The plasticity of the field is the potential out of which both therapist and patient can emerge offering each other the non-dual welcome we have all been seeking even if we did not know what we were looking for.

This is something we can experience for ourselves. When you go home, you can find some music you hate and put it on and dance to it. *"I can't dance to it, I hate it."* Yet you know that other people do dance to it; it is danceable. *"But not by me!"* In that moment, the dynamic of how you limit your potential is directly revealed.

NON-MEDITATION

For therapists not to impede the self-healing of the whole they need to let their limits dissolve again and again and again. Our job is to be available for the other as the other needs us, without reifying the patient or their needs. Let the flow flow, sometimes rough, sometimes smooth. Sometimes patients' limits require confronting and sometimes they need sweet acceptance. According to their lived circumstances you might tell them jokes, sing a song, make some drama, or offer some self-disclosure. Availability is freedom from self-restriction and the choreography of expectation. We dissolve the rigidity of our fixed definitions. Not dissolving these patterns of energy into nothing at all but into the bright unformed potential. For example, if you take an ice cube and let it dissolve, the water is freed from its imposed shape and can now be poured into a thousand different shapes. We don't do anything horrible to the ice cube when we let it melt, it is not an act of violence, it's just letting it relax so it can show its myriad possibilities.

This style of meditation as aimless non-meditation avoids all artificiality and employment of techniques such as observing our breath going in and out. It's not about visualising deities or mandalas. It's not about body scanning. These are all methods of working with energy. Here the focus of the practice is to open to openness, the fundamental uncloseable openness of your own being. Because this openness is infinite it has no shape. It is not something other than us which is going to swallow us up. It is the ground of our being, our presence and so we don't have to be afraid. Non-heroic fearlessness is a beautiful quality in therapists. Not to be afraid to make a fool of ourselves for the sake of our patients. Not to be afraid to make mistakes. Our movement is delicate and connected and non-harmful. Most importantly, no event is final and reparation is part of life.

Sit in a relaxed way letting your spine carry the weight so that your muscles can relax. Relax into the out breath. Here you are – so don't interrupt your presence. There is nothing more to do.

Who is the one who is sitting? What you take to be your body, your voice and all the various contents of your mind are transient. See how they come and go. I can see that they are not me, yet they are if I identify with them. Relax and avoid the effort of identifying. Avoid the contrivance of doing and making. Simply aware, we find that awareness is simplicity. Life is going on. We do not interfere, neither seeking to improve nor avoid. It is as it is. The still acceptance of this allows a simple seeing free of interpretation and evaluation. We have no list of tasks. We are simply open to and present with whatever is occurring. Whatever happens is the object of meditation. There is no need for control or imposition. Experience is occurring like a procession of reflections in the mirror. Without making any choices, without adopting or rejecting, allow experiences to arise and pass. The open state of the mirror is neither held apart from experience, nor merged with it. Non-dual integration is free of bias and judgment.

This practice is not something you do, it is not an act of will or intention. It is not about struggling to make a particular something happen. If you find you are distracted and caught up in something, don't worry, relax and release your involved consciousness as part of the flow. With this, you are open with what is here. Relaxing and releasing are not activities you do, rather they occur simultaneously with the dissolving of the tension generated by holding on to something. If you enter into judgement about your experience, you will find yourself back in the dualistic state of individual subjectivity. In this meditation we are not trying to learn anything from the experience, but rather we simply open ourselves to the intrinsic clarity which is the luminosity of experience.

In our culture we have been encouraged by teachers and parents and so on to try to make sense of what's going on, to find out how things work. This has given us the sense that we have to do something to our experience, as if it were a raw material to be worked on in order to add value to it. From this familiar point of view, to sit and just let the mind be as it is, however it is, without control or involvement may seem like a wasted opportunity.

Cultures, in their honouring of fire, tend to indicate that the cooked is better than the raw. Yet if we always cook everything how will we know what the raw tastes like? Unlikely as it may seem, the buddhist dzogchen teachings indicate that our familiar striving to cook according to approved received recipes is in fact the unnecessary activity that hides the fresh door to liberation from delusion.

Mental activity structured as subject in relation to object creates artificial divisions in the field of experience. By relaxing we find ourselves in wholeness, the unaltered integrity of the three aspects of how we are: unchanging openness, inclusive clarity and self-dissolving participation.

The openness of our mind is like space. This space is the ground or source of everything we experience. If you start with an assumption that your mind is some 'thing' inside your head, it will be very difficult to see the actuality of how you are. If you are out in a park and you see a tree, both the tree which you experience and your experience of the tree are occurring within the bright field of your awareness. Awareness is not a thing. It has no shape or colour, no fixed location. It is not to be found inside or outside and yet is everywhere with everything.

Our addiction to concepts leads us to try to define awareness, to nail it down and make it apprehendable. However all this effort cannot catch the mind itself. Rather it catches the ego-self inside the web of imagined entities it seeks to acquire.

Open awareness is ungraspable. Beyond conceptualisation, it is the ever-present basis of our life. This openness reveals the second aspect, the field of experience, the bright presence of awareness, which is neither inside nor outside. All-inclusive, it is beyond all polarities and dualities. With this as the field we move and live in, there is no anxiety.

The most fundamental anxiety arises from duality, from being a self seemingly cut adrift from the field it is actually part of. The individual self is living a fundamental lie. It has no existence separate from the field of experience yet it claims to have its own autonomous existence. This fraudulent claim, this imposter identity, carries with it a profound anxiety that no amount of technical adjustments can resolve. Only by the ego-self releasing itself from its fantasy of separation and taking its place as part of the whole can this deep anxiety dissolve. The ego-self has never been other than an inalienable part of the whole. One small lie, the self-deluding idea of a separate self, gives rise to an ocean of sorrows. From one brief moment of true clarity the sun of awareness is revealed and its warmth dries out that sad ocean.

The function of meditation is to support us as we continue to relax into openness again and again, relaxing and opening into the openness that is always there. Let life move as it does, without judging or managing events. The judge and manager claim an illusory apartness, whereas our non-dual presence is authentic instant participation free of duality and its consequent burden of accumulations.

So relax and trust the clarity that is inseparable from presence. Then each moment is self-liberating and without residue. If you open to this openness, you will find that this clarity rings true and has infinite value compared with the pseudo-clarity generated by analysis of events that have already passed.

Once the ego is seemingly born as an autonomous entity, it starts to interpret the richness of the non-dual field as an endless array of entities. Some seem attractive and this provokes desire. Some seem unattractive and this provokes aversion. Then we have the fear, anxiety and suffering of getting what we do not want and of not getting what we do want. This is especially troubling when the object of interest has both pleasing and displeasing aspects. We often attempt defensive splitting so that the good aspects will not be contaminated by the bad. It is this effort that gives employment to the judge and the manager and condemns us as ego-self to engage in a never-ending task of adjustment of self and adjustment of field.

However with this meditation, we find our way to letting the mind come as it comes. We simply sit. All kinds of weird experiences occur: fearful thoughts, wild thoughts, self-destructive thoughts, boring thoughts and so on. By offering hospitality to whatever occurs without editing or retaliating, our fear of them thins and fades leaving us with the uncontrived confidence that all arisings will vanish by themselves without contaminating our awareness. By keeping our ego-selves out of the driving seat, we find ourselves present as awareness that sees all events as the energy display of openness. This reveals our intrinsic freedom to participate free of identification. Now whatever arises can be our ally in our non-dual availability in the service of universal benefit.

Today we have covered a lot of territory. I hope it's of interest to you and I wish you good luck with your studies.

Teachings based on a talk given to psychotherapy trainees in Milan, Italy on 14th November 2013. Substantially extended and revised by James Low in September 2020.

Finding freedom when you feel trapped

This was a small talk given for the benefit of people in prisons.

OUTER PRISON AND INNER PRISON

There are many different kinds of prison in life. Clearly there are outer prisons where we are held inside a locked environment and we lack freedom to move. Metal doors, stone walls, iron bars certainly constitute a powerful kind of prison. But we also have an inner prison of our own thoughts, feelings, memories, hopes and fears, which trap us in very habitual and often punishing ways of thinking. And then we have a very innermost prison, which is the core beliefs we have about ourselves, perhaps believing that we are unlovable or that we've wasted our lives. Such negative beliefs seem to sum us up and put us in a very, very small box.

MEDITATION AS A WAY TO FREEDOM

One of the functions of meditation practice is to free ourselves from these inner prisons, even though we may remain trapped in the particular constricting physical environments. Because we have to live with our own mind, we live with our thoughts and beliefs, and these very powerfully determine what happens to us. In the course of the day, there are some events which are pleasant, some events which are not so pleasant. Pleasant or unpleasant, all events are very transient. They are impermanent. They are here and then they're gone. Nobody can stop the flow of time, and yet strangely our own mind grasps on to negative experiences. Somebody says something cruel or we are blocked and not allowed to do something that we want to do, and it starts turning and turning in our mind, and we suffer more and more. The event is gone, but we continue to persecute ourselves by not being able to let go.

So, a basic function of meditation is to enable us to let go of immersion in our thoughts.

TAKING REFUGE

In order to do this, traditionally, we take refuge. Taking refuge means finding a refuge other than the things that we habitually rely on. On an outer level, we can get lost in alcohol, drugs and crazy behaviour of all different kinds, and we need something to separate ourselves from the impulses that take us in. But at least you know, if you're lighting a cigarette or if you're opening a bottle of beer, that there's something *outside* which you can see: "*Oh, I've decided I don't want to do this, but still I have the impulse to do it.*" When the impulse is just happening inside your mind, it's more difficult to recognise.

So basically we take refuge in the idea of freedom. In the Buddhist tradition, this is called our buddha- nature, our potential for being fully awake, for being free, our capacity to be completely open so we don't get trapped in restrictive circumstances.

We can simply sit in a quiet, relaxed way. It's best if we can allow our skeleton to carry our weight; so the weight of our head is going down our spine. Then our muscles relax, and we can breathe more easily. If you are wearing a tight belt, you can loosen that up. You don't need to sit cross-legged; just sit in a chair, if that's comfortable.

We have a sense that, '*In the world, there are many people who suffer, not just me. In the world, there are many people in different kinds of prisons, some in prisons run by the state, some in the prison of their own body, if they're very disabled. We all live with limitations.*'

There's a kind of solidarity in this thought. This is not to normalise suffering nor to diminish the sense of our own pain and restriction but rather to see that this world itself is not generally a state of much freedom. In the Buddhist tradition, this is called samsara, which means we revolve round and round and round, from one kind of limited situation to another limited situation to another limited situation.

Things can only revolve if there is space for them to revolve in. So the revolutions of habitual thought are occurring inside the very space of the mind. So when we take refuge, we take refuge in the spaciousness of our mind, which is the basis out of which all the thoughts, feelings and sensations arise, and within which all our perceptions – through our eyes, ears, nose, mouth and so on – occur.

Space is primary, and it's when we forget space that we become trapped – trapped in old habits, trapped in negative beliefs and so on.

So, first we just sit quietly and take refuge, or relax, into the natural spaciousness of our mind. Even when your mind is whirling, this whirling thought, this physical arousal, the hot sensations in the body – anger, envy, despair and so on – these are movements. They arise and they pass. What is it that they arise in? Our mind. What do they pass out of? Our mind.

What is central is to find a more direct and immediate relationship with our own mind.

MEDITATION PRACTICE: CALM ABIDING

The first part of the meditation is to calm ourselves. We do this by focusing on the flow of the breath as it leaves the nostrils, on the sensitive skin that's just inside the nostrils. Breathing in, breathing out, in a slow, easy way. The mouth is slightly open. Our tongue is turned onto the hard palate just behind our upper teeth. Our weight is resting easily on the skeleton. We make a clear intention: '*I'm going to follow my breath.*' And as the breath comes in and goes out, that's all we're paying attention to. Everything else is irrelevant. There's a kind of freedom in this.

However, of course, for many, many hours and many years we have been following our thoughts, following our sensations. They hook us and pull us this way and that. So when we do the practice, it's not surprising that we find ourselves drifting off, getting carried away. As soon as we recognise this, we very gently bring ourselves back to simple attention on the flow of the breath. And we do this again and again.

If you have plenty of time, you can sit first of all for, say, fifteen minutes and then extend it for half an hour, for an hour. Do that several times a day. This practice is called *shiné* in Tibetan, and it means 'staying calm, being peaceful'. This is our goal.

So we'll do a little bit of this, just to begin. So breathing in and out...

[Meditation]

ENERGY AND SPACIOUSNESS

Just continue in that way. There's nothing else to do. It's a great relief, a holiday, from habitual preoccupations. There's nothing to think about, nothing to worry about. Just this very simple task. But of course we then recognise, *"Oh! Actually I prefer excitement. I prefer distraction. I prefer the sense that something is going on. Just being peaceful, there's not much there, nothing much to hold on to."*

What is that movement of wanting to hold on to something? This grasping that says, *'I need to construct my self out of the contents of my mind, trying to get the kind of contents that I like – the sort of thoughts that make me happy – and trying to get rid of the kind of thoughts that I don't like, that make me feel sad or despairing or hopeless or suicidal'*? This is a very busy orientation. Always something to be done. Always some new kind of work to be done.

Why? Because we're not at ease. Because we see ourselves as activity.

According to the Buddhist tradition – and in my own experience I've found it very useful – we are not just the energy of our manifestation, of how we come into the world, of how our body moves, of the kind of things we say, the thoughts and feelings we have. These are all energetic, unfolding forms. They change in time; they change with situations. But we're also an awareness, an awareness which is different from thoughts and feelings and sensations. It is simply a clarity, a clarity which reveals and shows whatever is occurring.

So we want to relax into the clarity, into that openness, and allow whatever comes to come and go.

A PRIVATE GARDEN OR A PUBLIC PARK?

If you think that *your* mind belongs to you – *"It's my possession, and I should be able to organise it the way I like."* – then you're turning your mind into a garden. If you have a garden, you try to plant some flowers and make them grow nicely. But snails come and start to eat the plants. Greenflies come on to the roses. Birds come and shit on the plants. The neighbour's cat comes in and shits all in your special flowerbed. You can't protect the garden. If you try to cover over the garden, then maybe nothing will get in to attack the plants, but the plants not going to do very well. Plants need free, fresh air to survive, just as we all do.

So it's better if we consider our mind like a public park. In the park, dogs run around; people are chatting; someone's sitting with a can of beer, getting a bit drunk in the afternoon. All sorts of things are going on. So when we sit in the meditation, whatever comes, comes; whatever goes, goes. It's just a park. If a terrible, horrible thought arises, this is not an x-ray of my soul; it's not telling me who I really am. It's just something wandering through the mind; it comes and goes. If a beautiful thought comes, and you think, *"Oh! I need to have thoughts like that all the time"* you can't hold on the thought; it's going to vanish anyway. It's just something wandering through the park.

So we relax this personal sense of having to live my life on my own terms, of *'It's up to me, it's all up to me!'* and just allow experience to arise and pass, arise and pass. And we stay relaxed, open, available and fresh.

As we more allow thoughts and feelings to go, we're not being annihilated; we're actually being enriched.

This is quite a paradox, something we probably wouldn't imagine to be the case.

By doing less, we have more. The more we try, the less we end up with because actually we can't hold on to anything in life. The more we grasp, we just get exhausted, and at the end of the day, our hands are still empty.

If, however, we begin with openness and emptiness, every experience that occurs in the course of the day is fully there and then gone. This fresh, open awareness of the mind is not contaminated by bad thoughts or painful situations, nor is it improved and given more value if the thoughts and situations are sweet. They just come and go. So in this way we have more space and more equanimity. And this is the goal of the practice.

MEDITATION PRACTICE: LETTING IT HAPPEN

So now we just sit in a relaxed way. Our gaze can be a bit open, into the space in front of us. Breathing in a relaxed way. Start by relaxing into a long, slow out-breath. And then just sit with whatever occurs. We sit like this for five minutes, and as you get used to it, you can extend the period of time. It's a period where you're present, you're here, you're alive, you're vital. But you're not on duty. You're not having to do everything, because everything is happening, as you start to see, by itself: '*Oh! Energy (manifestation) and spaciousness are not two different categories; they are not in opposition. They are inseparable.*'

So in our spaciousness, we allow everything, and we open to everything and we experience everything.

It's very simple, very straightforward. You can do this if you're sitting in your own room, in your cell. You can do it if you're standing in a queue. You can do it if you're having to do some work. In any situation, just open ourselves to what is there.

And what is there, by itself, in the first instant, is simple. *We* are the ones who introduce judgment. Judgment is an unnecessary addition; it's an ingredient that this dish doesn't need.

Part of the nature of our own suffering is that we expend too much mental energy trying to make sense of things which have already shown us what they are. There is sound. There is light and colour. There's the immediacy of the world. If we just stay with things as they first appear without wrapping them in the coverings of our own intelligence, of our own interpretation, then life becomes much simpler. Doing this won't make us stupid; in fact it makes us more able to work with circumstances as they arise.

So this is the basic practice: staying with space, watching energy moving through space, so that our mind is like the open sky and the world around us is open like the sky and these two skies are moving together. Whenever we collapse into solidification – into taking up a position, going into opposition with what's around us, full of likes and dislikes – relax into the out-breath; allow this transient structure to dissolve itself, as it always does, and stay with the space.

Then at the end, with whatever benefit we've gained from the practice, we share it out with all other beings: *'May all beings be happy.'* There is so much in the openness, there is more than enough for ourselves, for all the people we know. There's more than enough for everyone. Our nature is infinite. The nature of the world is infinite. Releasing our fixation on the finite, over-defined sense of who we are, there is love and happiness for all.

May all beings be happy! May you be happy!

Teachings given for the people in prisons, June 2015. Edited by Barbara Terris.

Being at ease with yourself

I'm going to talk about being at ease and what gets in the way of our being at ease. Some of it will be from the psychotherapeutic point of view, some of it from the buddhist, point of view. They are not, in fact, so very different in their orientation.

OUR ANXIETY

Anxiety! We have a huge capacity to think about ourselves and the things that happen around us in ways which wind ourselves up.

From the buddhist point of view this is due to the way we conceptualise the world, that we consider ourselves as a thing amongst things. As soon as we're born we are introduced into patterns of identification. Even before we are born our parents have all kinds of fantasies about who is growing inside the mother's womb. Names are thought about, often plans for the future are thought about. So the infant, who is developing, is being wrapped into a whole conceptual matrix. After birth these projections continue more and more. So, the baby is being welcomed into a world which has particular lineaments, with particular shapes and patterns and organisational structures some of which support freedom, but many of which are designed to promote social adaptation.

ADAPTING

When we look around we can see there are many things we might not agree with in how society is structured and yet we've got to find a way to survive. In order to do that we have to learn to adapt, to develop our plasticity, so that we can make the accommodations that are necessary to fit in. This does not always work out well. Even if the family that we grow up in is very harmonious, even if the school we go to is supportive, there are going to be tensions, because always we are faced with choice.

The human condition is marked by excess and lack. We have an excess of creativity, that is to say, we imagine all sorts of scenarios which are not actual.

We may imagine living a different life. It is very common for small children to have imaginary friends. So too is playing all sorts of 'let's pretend' games in which a simple object gets transformed into many other potential objects. Part of going to school is learning to rein in one's imagination so that what is being presented as the given-ness of our situation is encouraged to take precedence over other ways in which we could imagine it as being. This is often a big problem for children, for example when they move from primary school into secondary school. Becoming a successful student means accepting that your value in the world will be established by your capacity to fill yourself with other people's ideas. Bringing up too many of your own ideas can result in your being seen as distracted.

That is to say, social alignment involves paying attention to patterns which have already been established by other people. In this way children start to notice a conflict or tension between the family patterns and the patterns established as normal in the school environment. Inside that they try to work out what is right, what is wrong, what they like, what they do not like. Some children are drawn towards identifications which put them at the heart of things. Others are drawn towards identification that can make them marginal. How should we live? Should you encourage a child to be more mainstream? Should you support them in pursuing their own particular trajectory of desire? These are the difficult issues for parents because there is the sense of *'Oh, I'm helping to mould this person and to shape them so that they get the best possible interface with the world.'*

ADAPTING TO WHAT?

Of course all this would make sense if the world had a definite shape, if it were configured like a giant jigsaw puzzle, and the young person had to fit in by taking up a particular shape. But of course we don't live in a world like that. We live in a world where there is always change. New possibilities are arising. Cultural patterns are changing, the economic situation is changing, the political situation is changing. What then should we be adapting towards? If there is an ongoing tension between being true to myself and paying the price of belonging, to what am I supposed to belong? The is a difficult question to answer, especially in our modern fragmented culture where there seem to be few established patterns of social alignment. When you can pretty much do what you like how do we then decide, *'How will I be?'*

This question, which is a very profound and very helpful question, can be side-stepped by merging with preconceived ideas received from other people. My life is going to be formulated around getting a good job..., making a lot of money..., finding a way to impress other people..., finding a way to sleep with lots of people... There are many solutions that people come up with about what the meaning of their life might be.

IDENTITY AND IDENTIFYING

Do these solutions remove anxiety, stress, confusion, disease, being ill at ease with oneself? Perhaps not. Why not? Because the tension which arises is between my conceptualisation of myself – of my identity, largely based on what I have identified with – and the notion that there are requirements. Who sets these requirements? Whom should I follow? In whom can I believe? Who can I trust?

Nowadays many people find it difficult to trust in political parties. Many people find it difficult to believe in established religions. Who knows? Does anybody know?

Perhaps then I should trust myself? As we get older we may, however, look back and think of the many mistakes and confusions we've been caught up in, and we might well think, *"I can't really trust myself but I can't really trust you either!"* That can be pretty scary!

So we can see that there is a pervasive hesitancy which lurks around in the world. So, how can we be decisive if we don't really know how things are going to unfold inside or out? We are changeable creatures. We have fluctuations of mood, fluctuations of intention, fluctuations of interest and taste. Probably in our houses we've got objects, ornaments, bits of clothing, books and records which we collected at some stage in our lives but which are now less and less relevant to us. We might look back and wonder, *"Why was I ever into that?"* It seemed a good idea at the time but that time has gone. If that was me – and it really did feel like me – it doesn't feel like me now, and so what is the me-ness of me? If I'm such a fickle creature, if I'm taken over by my fancies, if I'm actually quite whimsical, yet am educated to believe that I am a rational, autonomous agent, somebody who can sit down and think about life and make plans and notice when things get a bit off target and then revise and regroup and move more in the proper trajectory towards my goal – if we've been educated in that vision of ourselves – then the actuality of our whimsicality is very scary.

The Freudian unconscious is now generally known and understood as explaining that there are aspects of ourselves that we will never clearly know and yet which are operative inside us, that we are strangers to ourselves because we are estranged from ourselves.

Is that established as a definite fault-line? Are we always cut off from the wholeness of our being? Whether one imagines that in terms of some historical sequence – such as that we were once in the garden of Eden where everything was simple and then we were expelled, forever exiled (many cultures have originatory stories of that kind) – or we see it as something internal – that aspects of ourselves are being repressed but there are also streams moving inside us that are beyond our cognisance – we cannot know ourselves.

That is one reason why it's helpful to have friends, because they can let us know when we are getting lost since we ourselves don't see what we're up to.

On one level that is quite terrifying. If I am in charge of myself, but I don't see myself clearly, am I a drunk driver in charge of my life? Can I ever sober up? What would be the method of sobering up? Is there anybody sober? Is there anybody who's got a clear idea about what they're up to? Yes, we can all access theories which explain the meaning of life, eastern religions, western religions, ancient philosophers, modern philosophers... there are so many interesting thinkers who come up with their own conceptualisations of what we're about.

What all of these do is to offer us narratives, which are more or less coherent and which we may find to be more or less fitting to the particular, current topology of our existence. The contours of our existence, our felt sense of who we are, change through time. At certain periods we're drawn in one direction, and then we're drawn in another. So if we're seeking reassurance that we're okay by searching for parallel patterns in the world, then that would indicate that any alignment, any harmony, is always going to be just for a brief period of time – since the outer and the inner shapes change.

What appears to be meaningful can become meaningless. And that can indeed be a very terrible thing. For example, in Britain fewer and fewer people now attend Church and from the 1920s onwards both religious and lay people have explored the question of loss of faith. How could it be that you are educated in a particular system and which seems to encapsulate you, hold you in its warm and comforting bosom, then it fades away? How come you can no longer believe in what you once believed? This is a very profound question.

People experience this also in love relationships. They meet someone, they feel attracted to them, they feel they fall in love and in that moment they see some profound, even ultimate value in the other person. Things go well for a while and then the problems come: *"If you're behaving this way to me then you are not who I thought you were. I fell in love with you because I thought you were who I thought you were. Well, that means I fell in love with my own projection, with my own idea about you! Now that I have woken up to the fact that you are not like that, that you are not like my fantasy, that you are some other ordinary bugger wandering around in the world, I don't know whether I love you anymore!!"*

That's very difficult, isn't it? Reality is the enemy of fantasy. We all know that. Nevertheless it is still a painful thing to see how so many of the deep feelings that we have are conjured up on the basis of our fantasies, of our mental constructions which we project out onto the world. That we see our fantasies as being actually existing in the world in a self-existing way.

If you fall in love with someone you feel that you have some privileged truth about them. Even if you introduce that person to your friends and they're not quite as certain about them as you are, you still feel: *"Well, that's because they don't really understand my beloved. He really is nice!"* – In your fantasy!!

Our projection, our narrative

Now, from the buddhist point of view this is just a subset of a very normal structure of misconception. For example, here is a glass of water. It's very obvious that what I'm holding in my hand is a glass of water. The glass-ness of the glass is in the glass. That's obvious. It just is a glass of water. Well, not necessarily. Because if it were a glass of vodka and I had drunk quite a few full glasses of vodka, I might be inclined to smash the glass and stick it in your face! In which case, I would be holding a dangerous weapon. Normally however, because we are very nice polite people, we think of it as a glass for drinking from. Nevertheless people do use glasses as weapons, something which the Accident and Emergency wards in hospitals all over Britain can confirm.

So the glass-ness of the glass is held in place by our concept of what it is. The glass-ness of the glass is the meeting place between the potential of what is in my hand and the particular form of conceptualisation that I have and bring to bear on it. If, for example, this glass were a precious family heirloom and a child of about three grabbed it, you might say, *"Ohho, careful with that! Look here, let me give you this shiny red plastic one instead. No, don't touch the crystal glass. It's a horrible, horrible thing!"* You would try to swap the glasses around, knowing that the child doesn't see the value. We see the value. We see the value on the glass because we know, *"This is my great- great-grandmother's glass. It's been in the family for a hundred and fifty years..."* That value is not in the glass. That is in **your head.** That is **your** narrative that you're projecting onto the glass. Therefore the anxiety about whether or not it is going to break is your own production. The glass is not intrinsically valuable. The value is in your projection.

The world is our projection. The world is our interpretation. That's quite a strong idea. What it means is that moment by moment when we encounter situations, these situations are not self-existing. Now, that flies in the face of science, as we learn it in school. We learn about matter, that matter is neither created nor destroyed, that it gets moved around into particular shapes, that when it's in a particular shape it manifests as something which can be known, apprehended and employed in a way which is harmonious or disharmonious with its nature.

Here in this room there are bluey-purpley chairs that we're all sitting on. These are plastic moulds sitting on metal legs and are designed to be cheap and cheerful, which is very appropriate for public buildings like this. When we make use of objects like that, we do expect them to support our weight. We have expectations that the world is safe on the basis of our knowledge about it: *'Because I can interpret the world correctly, I know how to behave.'* That is to say, there is an object out there which, once I know about it, I will be able to use properly.

What I have been suggesting earlier is a rather different view. It's saying that we will *never* apprehend whatever is out there, because the movement of our mind towards the objects of the world is the process of the co-creation of the world. It's not that there is a chair there before we see it. But rather that we have been educated to perceive the chair in a certain way. If there was a bunch of five-year- old children in here they would do all sorts of different things with these chairs. Some might make a castle, others a boat, or a den, or a tower, or a tank... These objects would be incorporated into the children's imaginations and be expressive of that imagination; they would become part and parcel of the field of imagination of the child.

"Well, we are not children anymore, we have put away childish things and now we see things for what they are!" This is not true. What we have done is entered into a more prosaic, conservative and tedious diminishment of our imaginative capacity in order to have the prediction not only that we know what a chair is, but that other people will know that we know what a chair is and therefore other people will see that we are 'normal'. Children of five are not very concerned about being normal unless they feel edged out of their little group in school. But *we* are very concerned to be normal. *We* are very concerned that other people won't think we're too weird. Because there's a price for being weird and it's not nice. If you're normal then it's very nice because you can hide. You must have seen these nature programmes on TV and there's a big herd of deer all fleeing

together and there's a lion coming *"Grrrr"*. It grabs one on the outside. It doesn't grab the one in the middle. That's the same for us in life. If you're in the middle of the herd you look normal: *"Don't pick on me. I'm just like you. I'm normal. Pick on them! They're weird!"*

So this is a generalised fear and anxiety which is around. And it comes about from our betrayal of our own imagination.

Now, very often we see imagination as a kind of fantasy-construct: that we are going to create something which is untrue. A novelist or a film-maker sets out to construct a storyline which we can believe in but which is not actually true. We cannot go and meet the characters that are in the novel, but by reading the novel, by offering ourselves to the novel, it is as if these characters become real. This is what Aristotle referred to as 'suspending disbelief': that if we're too sceptical, if we're too suspicious, if we're keeping our distance, we will be afforded a particular kind of clarity – because with that separative perspective we'll see things in their proper place – but we'll be a bit lonely and cut off.

We can really enjoy giving ourselves to something, being carried away by a good movie, falling into a wonderful novel and getting so interested in what's going to happen next. 'Suspending disbelief' allows us a fusion into another world. Now, as adults we accept that we have got to hold our lives together in various ways, that experiences like going to the cinema or reading a novel, are a kind of holiday, a time-out from the grim, fixed realities of ordinary life.

But maybe there *is* no grim, fixed reality. Maybe *everything* is imagination. It's not that the grim, fixed stuff is out there. It's that the grim, fixed stuff is in us! Once we fall into over-fixated thoughts, self-attacking propositions, limited conceptualisations about our identity, the ground that we are standing on becomes narrow, predetermined, over-determined. We are preoccupied by accumulations of past experience which come to be a seemingly substantial basis for our sense of who we are: '*I am who I think I am.*' That is reinforced by '*I am who I think that you think I am.*' I am full of thoughts, memories, hopes, plans and fears which act as a kind of lens through which I look at the world. I believe in these mental constructions as the guarantors of the truth of the situation.

WE APPROACH THE FRESHNESS OF THE WORLD WITH OUR STALE ASSUMPTIONS

Life is about managing your life as you find it. We can't just get a new life. We're stuck with what we have. In any case whatever new life we would like is impossible because we're full of old thoughts, old beliefs, old assumptions. "*Assumptions are the mother of fuck-up*", as the saying goes, but in any case assumptions are a way of making life quick and easy. We can buy a pre-prepared meal. We can store it in the freezer. We can come home one night, tired, and stick it in the microwave and eat it. Easy. It's just food. It probably doesn't taste great but we're cold and hungry and it's alright. That's what most of our mental activity is. Out of the freezer of our memory-bank into the microwave of our current moment of agitation we tuck in to the stuff and with a big or small spoon according to the situation.

Where then is the freshness? The freshness is there in the phenomena themselves, in what is coming in through our eyes, our ears, our nose, tongue, skin. The senses are always of the moment. The senses are not existing in time. Our interpretation of the data which is given in the immediacy of the sensory moment, yes, that is based on the past. We approach the freshness of the world with our old assumptions. That is like whenever we go to the market to buy fresh vegetables, we carry them home and pop them in a pot that's already covered with mould. If we do that then how can our food ever taste fresh?

So how do we shed the past? We are made up of the past. We went to school, maybe we went to college later; we've learned so many things in our lives. Some people experience traumas, suffer brain injuries and experience amnesia. They have to spend a lot of time coming back into a working relationship with the world, slowly building a new memory bank to help them function. Certainly we are our history, in some ways, but what I would suggest is that our history exists like ingredients in a kitchen. Herbs, spices, salt, pepper, all kinds of things can add flavour. You don't open every little jar and tip them all into a big pot. If you have tomatoes, would you use a lot of sage? Or cinnamon? Perhaps you might use oregano instead, or basil. It might go better with the tomato.

In terms of relating to other people, if I want to connect with you, if I'm wanting to prepare something that you might be able to eat, that will be palatable for you, I need to pay attention to how you are. Therefore *your* tongue is the determinant of *my* spice. But if the spices and herbs are controlled by our assumptions of what is true, by our memory, by our own tongue, we're essentially cooking for ourselves.

And, as we know, sadly a great deal of human communication is simply serial monologue. One person says something, the other person replies but it's like ships passing in the night, because there's no real contact. If you really listen to someone else and you're touched and moved by them, you have to respond to what is there, to how this person is in the moment, not according to your sense of who they really are.

　—Oh, cheer up, you'll feel better tomorrow!

Why would you say that to somebody who is sad? We don't know how long they will be sad for? It doesn't matter whether they feel better tomorrow. Today they are sad.

　—But I don't know what to say if they're sad. —Why not?

　—What should I say?

That will not be answered by any 'should'. If you see their face, if you see the sadness around their eyes and you let that in through your eyes and your heart opens, something will come out.

—I don't know if it would. I get lost. I don't know what to say!

"I don't know what to say." It's as if every human communication had to pass through central command, a cognitive centre where things get processed according to our template. We all have some idea about what is good and what is bad. Once you have that installed, it's nice, because then you know what to do. The more there is a central command predicting and organising on the basis of reassuring me that I know what I'm doing, I will be doing a violence towards *you*; because I will be delivering you something on the basis of my need to feel competent. Rather, I have to find a response, that is to say, I allow the response to arise through me towards you.

In power-differential structures like counselling and therapy it's very easy for the person who is in the seat of power to keep all their clothes on and get the client or the patient to, figuratively, take their clothes off. Therapists can take up the position of interrogator, pinning the patient in a being of supposed light. *"Because we know best and are the source of light we are here to illuminate the darkness that you wander in."* [ironic]

But of course we are all in dark. And we are all light. The darkness is actually our accumulated knowledge. We are hidden from ourselves by our knowledge about what is going on. 'Knowing' and 'knowing about' are not the same, but they tend to be fused again and again in the ordinary conducting of our life situation. To 'know' is to see and receive, that is to say, it starts from the relationship with the world which is passive-receptive. Not an active agent, not a kind of phallic invasion which is going to do something to the world, but: *"Oh, this is what is there!"*

I can only receive if I have space inside me. It is my openness, or emptiness, or lack of preoccupation, which is actually the basis of my hospitality to you. Maybe you have visited someone's house, they invite you round, and they have a white carpet and a white sofa and then they give you a glass of red wine? There's a kind of anxiety that goes with that, isn't there? You're not going to relax. Some environments allow you to be yourself and if you make a mistake, it doesn't really matter. Life goes on. But other environments are more anxiety-provoking: *"Oh, I see that they do things in one particular way."*

That is not hospitality. Hospitality means there is a space for you. That is to say, I am available because you can avail yourself of me. Now what does that mean? If someone avails themselves of me, is that on my terms or on their terms? All of us exist as a huge potential, a potential which is often hidden from ourselves by our own conceptualisation of ourselves, but also by other people's conceptualisation of us.

STORIES WE TELL OURSELVES

Working in many different clinics, seeing all sorts of different people, couples, families, therapeutic communities, I would say that of most of the – let's call them 'patients' – whom I have met, make twenty percent use of me. Occasionally you meet someone who gets eighty percent of you. I'm trying to say: *'You could have more. Take more!'* But they want to go round and round and round and I want to say, *"Just shut the fuck up!"*

—But it's very important! I'll tell you the same thing again.

Why? Poking about in your poo is not going to tell you much about your life. It's going to tell you about what you ate. It's going to tell you about your history, about the past.

—But you'll only understand me if you know about my childhood.

This is not true. What it means is: *'You will only know about me if I tell you a lot about me.'* Now I know your story and you know I know your story and telling it was a hell of a story. All this makes it pretty difficult for me to do anything to help you because we can easily get into a confluence, a flowing together into a trapped agreement that life is hopeless. But actually in the very moment that somebody is telling the same trapped, repetitive story again and again, there is freedom. Somebody is speaking.

   —Who is the speaker?

   —Me!

   —But who are you?

   —I'm the one that's speaking!

   —But who is the one that is speaking? —Me!

This gets very solipsistic, an unbreakable circle. *'I am who I am. And I'm the one that's doing it. I'm just being me. What more do you want?'* It's almost impenetrable; it's like a heavy, thick waterfall, you can't see what's behind it because of the flow of conceptualisation, held in place by the fearful notion that *'I am who I am, I know who I am, and I'm me.'* But everyone in this room can call themselves *'me'*. At least I am called 'James'; maybe there are two or three other people who are also called James here in this room? That's not so bad, I can share my James-ness with a few people. But if everybody here is saying, *'I am me!'* ... Anybody here find that difficult?

   —I am me.

   —No, I am me, you shut up! I am me! You are you!

If we are all *'me'* and *'I'm just me'*, this is the great drug of forgetfulness. This is the answer which is designed to annihilate the possibility of enquiry. This is the answer which is always popping up so that the question, the deep question, *'What does it mean to be alive? What is this existence?'* is never asked and never answered.

Here we are, breathing in, breathing out, we hear sounds, we see things, there are smells, there's a taste in our mouth... Experience is arising. Who is the experiencer?

If we come up this from the level of narrative, we can tell our story in infinite ways. And of course we all do that. If our parents are alive, we tell them one story about how we're doing; we tell our friends another story; we might tell a partner something different. If we've got kids we tell them a different story from what we tell our boss at work. Our one life, our 'just being me', is more like a diamond with many different facets. As we face other people we present different aspects of ourselves. Nobody will ever see the whole of us. Even the people in history that we know as the most evil foul people, they had friends. They had partners, they had kids. Somebody loved them.

Examining in this way we realise that we can never ever catch the whole truth of someone else. Similarly we can never catch the whole truth of ourselves.

One of the things that makes us ill at ease is that we live in relation to ourselves but we live in relation to ourselves in a gesture of getting hold of ourselves, appropriating ourselves, apprehending ourselves, catching bits of ourselves and formulating ourselves in different ways to different situations. *'But if I'm that multiple, there's probably more.'*

THE CENTRE CANNOT HOLD

Yes, we live as excess. We are creative. There is no end to any of us telling stories about our lives. Giving commentaries on what has happened in the garden, what sorts of birds are there at the moment, what's happening to the price of milk and so on. There's endless things to comment on. As new aspects of the world impinge on us we find ourselves moving into opinions and responses that we had never imagined we would be doing. We are ungraspable. Other beings are ungraspable.

—But does that mean that I don't know who I am?

—It does!

—But that's terrible! You have to know who you are! Otherwise you're lost! How would you go on in the world if you didn't know who you were?

—Oh! I don't like this anymore. Can I go home now, please?

This is the sort of anxiety that arises when we have what's referred to as a 'mental breakdown'. It's often exactly on that point. The centre cannot hold. This centrifugal force has us dispersing out, fragmenting, and we are all over the place. We are not all of a piece anymore, we can't work out what's going on. Before we were adding and subtracting bits of ourselves. We think, *'I've got bad qualities, I've got to get rid of them.'* And then, *'I'm quite good at this, I'll do more of that.'* Trying to build up a kind of Lego profile of all the little ingredients of ourselves, juxtaposing them into socially acceptable patterns. When that starts to fall apart... [gesture: speechless]

Actually there can be a freedom in that, because the patterns which gave us the reassuring image that we knew who we were, starts to fade away. We don't know who we are. Is that wrong or bad? No, but if we are going to hold ourselves together we do want something to cling to. So why do we have to hold ourselves together? Because we don't want to fall apart.

That would indicate that the basic hypothesis that we have of ourselves is that we are some kind of entity, that we are a thing, a thing operating in a world of things. Things need to hold together, otherwise they don't work. All the bits have to be in the right place functioning together. This involves planning and control and the effort of maintenance. This mechanical model of the human condition is increasingly common now as we move into an android culture, where people are programming the telephones and not really acknowledging that they are being programmed as they program – that we come into a reciprocal relationship with the binary oppositional structure of the mathematical programmes that derive these incredible apps and so on that we make use of. We're caught into a binary world of yes/no, right/wrong, good/bad. Either this or that. If it's this, it's not that. If it's that, it's not this. Then you supposedly know where you are. Are you a boy or a girl? Are you young or are you old? Are you happy or are you sad?

But we are not like that. We are complicated. That's why when we try to tell a story about ourself, we meet someone new and we want to introduce ourself, we are caught up in the beginning of an endless story, because there is always something more to say. Whatever we say about ourself...

"Well, I was thinking about what I told you yesterday. Was it really like that in my family? Yeah, my dad was a bit difficult and so on, but actually we had some quite good times. I used to play golf with him and so on..."

It just endlessly mushrooms out, because this is our life. In a single second this whole world is revealed to us. We come into a room–everything is here! We walk out the door, there is the church and there is the sky and the trees. It's all already there! We get the whole shebang, just like that, in a second. We don't have to sit and work it out bit by bit, painting by numbers. We always get excess. There is so much, and yet we feel a lack. *"Something is missing in me. I'm not quite right. If only I was more like you. You seem to be able to do everything. You're so confident. Why am I not like everybody else? Oh god, the years are going by and this is as good as it gets."*

IDENTITY BELONGS IN THE HOUSE OF COMMUNICATION

What is the lack? The lack is the self-abandonment of our being, which comes through grasping at our notion of identity, which is always a betrayal. Whatever you say about yourself may be situationally true, but it cannot be intrinsically true. It is a momentary construct. That is to say, self- knowledge belongs in the house of communication, or the house of compassion. It is relational. Our identity is relational. We come into being with other people. We present ourselves according to how we feel towards the other person, warm/cold, attracted/not attracted, looking up/looking down and so on. There is expansion and contraction and this is dynamic and changing. It is not fixed. Identity is a world phenomena or a field phenomena.

Our identity is exactly the site that marks our participating in the world with others. It is being in the world with others, but what is this being itself? What is the ground or the basis out of which I reveal myself to myself and to the other in the moment of coming into being with them? Where does this come from?

This is being. We are here as a presence, a presence which is there prior to any gesture that we make of communication. Say, for example, you go to a party. You meet some people and you find that you can talk easily to them and have a nice chat. Then you turn and you look at someone else and you wonder what on earth you can find to say to that person.

That is not a sign that you are not a nice person. It's a sign that our connectivity with others is energetic, it comes from the belly. It's an embodied phenomenon. It's not about having social skills, because if you apply your social skills, you are just going through the motions; you may be having a pleasant enough conversation, but there's no juice in it. The juice is the gift of life, and shows that we connect with some people more than with others. That is to say, it's not a conscious egoic decision; it's not a sign of our agency as social participants. Rather, it is showing that the world is revealed to us in the given-ness of what happens when we are in proximity. We open or we contract. We don't decide which to do. It just happens like that. Of course, we can learn to manage it if it's a bit extreme, but...

IDENTITY IS BASED ON EDITING

So we have two main roads that we take at this point. I will describe them in terms of the traditional buddhist categorisation of the five elements. These five elements are earth, water, fire, wind and space. Water, fire and wind are moving elements. Earth and space are stable. Space is ungraspable, but it's very stable. It doesn't change. It is the infinite space within which phenomena are occurring.

What tends to happen in our upbringing is that space, because it is so subtle, is discounted. We turn our mind more towards what is manifest: the earth, the water, the fire and the wind. The three moving elements are the turbulence of our life; sometimes exciting, sometimes anxiety-provoking. When the turbulence gets a bit much, we seek something to cling on to. That's the earth element: *'I want to secure the territory. I want to know where I am. I want to know something definite about myself. I am this!'*

When I was a child I learned that I was Scottish. That became very important. *"I'm Scottish, I'm not English!"* I didn't know what that meant, but anyway I would say, *"I don't like the English!"* I grew up in Glasgow so, *"I don't like the people from Edinburgh!"* I had never been to Edinburgh but, *"I don't like the people from Edinburgh!"* Moreover I grew up in the West End of Glasgow so, *"I don't like the people from the South and the East!"* I grew up in one street and I didn't like the people in the other street! In fact, I didn't like my brother either! So, *"I am me and all the rest is shit!"* That's a very common way of establishing identity.

Freud described this process as 'the narcissism of small differences' Since it is so difficult to define yourself it is much easier to say what you are not. By excluding all these other factors in the field, that are almost but not quite like us, the residue is myself. However you never quite finish excluding all the others so you never have to actually give a true vertical account of who you are. Which is just as well, because we are not. We are 'being' and 'becoming'...

When 'being' and 'becoming' are aligned, then we have 'belonging'. Belonging is the feeling of participating in the shared field of activity. However, if we ignore 'being' (and I'll say a bit more about what I mean by that term shortly) we just have 'becoming'. So moment, by moment, by moment we are becoming this or that. And then we are having to hang on to these fragments, these moments of experience, extrapolating them from their context, and trying to build up a picture of who we are, what we like, what we don't like, what our plans are... There is a solidity in that. So we cleave to the earth element: The world is full of 'things'. There are some people I like; these are my friends. There are some people I don't like; these are my enemies. There are foods that I like, there are foods that I don't like. There are some kinds of clothes that I wear, some that I don't. We push away what we don't like and we try to bring towards ourselves what we do like.

In that way we live by maintaining an identity which is based on editing. We bring our prejudice, our predilection, into the emergent field of experience, moment by moment, on the basis of our selective attention. Strangely, the curious thing is that other people choose something different! Why do they do that? *"It's because they're daft! If I was you, I wouldn't do that, but there again, I'm just me. So you do you. Bad luck! I'm better off being me."* Thinking that way, what you do doesn't need to bother me. Going to a restaurant you look at the menu and you choose something. Other people eat other things, but this is what you like. This is what we are doing all the time. Moment by moment this infinite menu of the world is in front of us, but, *'Waiter, you know what I like. Just give me my usual.'*

No wonder we are ill at ease and alienated from ourselves. If – as I am suggesting – our self is a potential which is called into being in its richness through the widest possible participation, when I narrow my gaze about how the world is and exclude a great deal of what is here in front of me, then I'm also excluding a great deal of myself. Many potential aspects of 'how I could be' remain dormant because I am always in this repetition compulsion of the reinstalling of my imagined notion of who I am.

In that sense I'm making a differentiation between identity as a construct – just as we have passports or identity cards which show officialdom who we are. When we go through passport control, this little booklet lets us come back into the country. If we don't have it, if we have lost it, then we have to get through a lot of hassle. But if we say, *'Look at this photo and now look at me; we are the same.'* then the important document confirms and blesses us as being a proper citizen of the country.

That is to say, our identity is outside ourselves. Our identity is part of communication with the world. It is not an X-ray of our soul. It's not a true definition of who we are. It's merely a set of conventions, which we move around and shift according to the different environments that we encounter in our lives.

Prior to that there is being. What is being? Being is what is here. It is just being here. Indoors or outdoors, you sit and you just allow life to happen. Thoughts are coming ... sensations in the body... the senses are open ... you hear sounds, smells and so on... And they are passing... and they are passing... and they are passing...

Experiences are occurring, many different experiences, some you would take to be pleasurable, some you would take to be unpleasurable; but the whole gamut of experience is occurring. Usually you are being the busy manager trying to protect yourself from the things you don't like, trying to hang on to what you do like, but if you just relax that for a moment then you are the experiencer. It's all going on and you are just experiencing it.

Who is that experiencer? In the tradition, this is the basis for meditation. Meditation is about gradually dissolving the glue that binds subject and object together.

Because as subject and object are turbulently turning and we sit in our subjectivity – which is our sense of a personal self, me being me, me being who I am, who I know myself to be, taking us into the domain of our narrative about ourselves – when that is glued onto the unfolding patterning of the arising object, then I'm endlessly busy. Twenty-four hours a day I'm adjusting and maintaining and because of that arousal, that busyness, there's no sense of the space within which it is occurring.

For example, you entered this room the chairs were already laid out so you might think, *"Right, this is where we will be sitting. There is a seat in the front, so James is probably going to sit there facing the rows of other chairs. Okay, I'll sit near the front so I can hear easily, or shall I sit near the back where I can hide more..."* Whatever is your fancy. However the room has quite an interesting shape and a lot of the potential of the space is hidden by the way the chairs are laid out. If you came in early before the chairs were arranged you would become more aware of the potential of the space. The chairs could be done in a spiral, in a circle, in a square, in an oblong, in an ellipsis... You could set them up any way. Lining them up in these serried rows creates a particular mood. The room is set up for a talk and we are going to get a talk so that was jolly sensible. But we didn't see the space!

It's just the same in your mind when the furniture in your mind is installed, you don't see the space, because you are following thought, feeling, sensation, round and round and round... without ceasing.

Theatre is only possible on the basis of an empty stage. It's the empty space which allows the elaboration of the drama of life. Once the drama starts you see the actors moving around the stage furniture. You are captivated by the activity and the space is invisible. Even if you go to the ballet there is all this gorgeous movement in space. Without space they wouldn't be moving, but what we see is bodies and movement. We see shapes.

It's the same with paintings. Unless we learn to look at art we are captivated by what is figural. We are aware of there being background but actually, without the background you wouldn't have the foreground. If you're looking at Rembrandt's paintings, his backgrounds tend to be very, very dark indeed. And you have these faces or bodies looming out of that with their intensity – out of the dark. Without the dark you wouldn't have the intensity of the figure. The figure and the background go together. The ground here is always the space.

Likewise for our mental life. Space is the basis. Thoughts move through time and space. Feelings arise in time and space. Sensations in the body occur because there is a space to receive them. When you can release the fixation of attention on the ever-occurring movement of life, you start to see the space within which the movement is occurring. The fact is that movement is ceaseless. Since you wake up in the morning until you go to sleep at night, there is always something happening. Meditators change their sitting postures, you find yourself scratching, fidgeting, you get some little pain in your back, you suddenly remember something important you need to do tomorrow... We are like some market square with all sorts of messages passing across. That doesn't stop.

MOVEMENT IS ALWAYS MOVING: YOU CAN'T STOP IT

Therefore, on that level of your existence, you will not find peace. You will not find peace. Movement is moving. It doesn't stop. However, the space within which the movement is occurring, is *never* moving. The space is always still.

One of the big problems in mental health is that people try to stop the movement. *"I've got these negative thoughts and I want them to stop!"* You can spend a lot of time trying to do that and you can learn all sorts of tricksy methods of doing it but such techniques tend to lose their potency after a time. The key thing is: *'Who is it who is caught by the thought?'*

What is it that gives a thought the power to catch you? The power is not in the thought. Thoughts arise and go by. It is our proclivity, our tendency, our susceptibility that makes us drawn towards that thought at this particular time. Just as if you go shopping in a big store and there are many kind of shoes, many kinds of T-shirts. Your gaze is drawn towards one of them. Other people are drawn to something else.

—Oh, these shoes! Fabulous! Exactly what I've been looking for! I must have them! Other people were not looking for these shoes.

—Why not? They're fabulous!

For you, maybe! That is to say, they are not intrinsically fabulous. They are fabulous for you according to your interpretive matrix. In fact, they may not always be fabulous for you either. The glue, the potency, the power is not in the shoes; it's in your incorporation of the shoe into the patterning of what is desirable. The other shoes are organised into the patterning of what is undesirable. This is a mental activity.

—Oh no, but look how well the shoes are made!

Nobody else is running to get them. It is like this for you! Each of us lives a life of unique sensibility. Each of us is shining, radiant, uniqueness. This is vital, this is alive, this is shining forth moment by moment, unrepeatable.

Why then are we so dull? It's remarkable. Life is vibrant, sparkling, alive. There ain't nothing but this. You, alive, having experiences. There never was anything other than this. What kind of experiences you get is determined not by what is out there – because most of what is out there you've never seen, you've never tasted – it's determined by the furniture in this little box of yourself.

Why do we hang onto that furniture?

—Because it's me!

What I'm suggesting is that if we want to be at ease with ourselves we have to realise that what we take ourselves to be is better seen as a range of ingredients. Why? Because if you appropriate your narrative about yourself as something fixed and determined, it will be very difficult to change.

On the telly you can see programmes like 'The strongest man in the world.' They have a big parked bus and the strong man has to pull it with his teeth. The most difficult bit is to get the bus moving. Once the bus is moving, it's easier. So, if you want to change something, change something that's already in motion.

—But I've had these thoughts for a long time. I wake up in the middle of the night and they are always there.

—Are they there just now?

—No.

—They weren't there, they're here, then they go.

—They were there, they are not here, they'll come back... They are moving. If they're moving, you can move them. They are not fixed like a bus or a building.

—But they feel like it. And I tell you how bad they are! It's been so difficult, my life. You don't understand. So hard.

—Mmm, I think I'll refer you to a colleague.

We stick ourselves, we jellify ourselves. We are the solid, glutinous mass. We cover our world in aspic. Why? Because we want something. We want to know something definite. This is how we cheat ourselves.

We are a potential which unfolds in a situation, and the basis for that unfolding potential is open spaciousness, the unborn mind itself as it would be described in buddhism. Or the dharmakaya, the mind of the buddha.

That doesn't mean that it's completely random and unstructured. Of course we have patterns, but patterns are dynamic formations. We recognise patterns, but the recognition is not the thing itself. If you are in the countryside and you see a beautiful bush or beautiful wild roses you might think, *'Oh, how lovely the wild roses are!'* That knowledge may allow you to look at them for two seconds and then it travels on. But if you open yourself and look and you go forward and you see the incredible pink and the white and the delicate, delicate formation, you receive it. And it's not just a wild rose. You are transformed in that moment of looking. William Blake would call it 'clearing the doors of perception.' The 'doors of perception' are not covered by the muck of the world. They are covered by our knowledge, our assumptions, our sense that we are powerful agents who know what is what. Freeing ourselves is to allow ourselves not to know, what the poet John Keats called 'negative capability'. To be able to stay open and at ease and allow the unfolding of the world.

No need to worry, because – to use the image of jars of herbs and spices that I offered you earlier – we have a lot of knowledge. You are not going to lose that knowledge. The question is whether you use it in a way that fits the situation. Because if you use the knowledge as a lens to see through, it will restrict your vision, giving you more of the same. If you use it defensively to define and fix in an attempt to exert power over the situation then you get a kind of drying that goes with that. We become sclerotic because we become rigid. The more rigid we become, the more fearful we become, because we're frightened that something will hit us and we will fragment.

Actually, our being in the world – when we allow it to be – is very flexible, very soft, very dynamic. We are like seaweed in the ocean, moved around by events. *"But I don't want to be moved around. Why is it that everything gets to me?"* Many people come and they tell me, *"I suffer from over-sensitivity."* How lucky! Every graveyard is full of people who are no longer sensitive at all!

How to deal with this? Well, you could enjoy it! Turn your sensitivity towards things which are beautiful. Avoid situations which are difficult. In the summertime, take off your shoes and socks and walk barefoot. You may have to practise at first, perhaps on soft sand. After a month of doing that you can start to walk on pebbly beaches and it's not so sore, because the skin has thickened. In that way we need to shift our interface. It is not, of course, about accumulating thicker skin. It's more like a camera lens, which shifts the speed of the shutter according to the amount of light. As a system, as a living system, we have a huge, immediate movement towards and away from things. If I run towards you and try to stick my finger in your eye, you turn away. Just like that. We can trust our quickness. We don't need to build up a big defence if we can move. And we are always moving. What traps us is our sense that we are not moving, that we are fixed, that we are entities, that we are things, that we are our own possession.

'I have to take care of myself.' Now that's a strange grammatical construct. *'Well, I am myself, and I have to take care of myself. So in order to take care of myself I can't **be** myself. So I **am** myself but I'm not myself, because if I was just myself I couldn't take care of myself!'*

On one way, of course, that's true. A baby is itself, pissing and shitting whenever it wants and crying in the middle of the night. They can't take care of themselves. As the baby starts to get bigger they learn to know that they need to have a pee before they go to bed. They learn to wipe their bum and so on. They learn to manage themselves. All this we have done. We are used to the notion of the dualistic construct. There is 'me' as a thing and there is 'I' as a subject. *'I am going to look after myself.'* I look in the mirror and what do I see? *"Oh my God, have I really put on all that weight? Right!! Health! In the spring I will definitely change my diet, get more exercise. Take better care of myself. I am in charge of myself. I am managing myself."*

Now, on one level of course, this is true but it's not the whole story. It sets up a huge amount of anxiety, because, *"If I'm going to take care of myself, why did I eat that extra biscuit? I didn't need the biscuit, I didn't even really want the biscuit. I ate the biscuit. Who ate the biscuit? I ate the biscuit, but it wasn't really me because I had already decided I wouldn't eat the biscuit. I said, 'They're looking at the biscuit but I don't need it so I'll leave it on the plate.' and then somehow there I was eating it!"*

So how am I going to take care of myself when I don't know what I'm doing? This is the problem of the egoic fixation on *'I am in charge'*. We are working with circumstances; there are external circumstances and there are internal circumstances. Some of our internal circumstances we might call 'impulses' and the impulse arises and moves through us and we find ourselves pouring another glass of wine.

—Why am I drinking? Look at the time! It's already so late. I have to work early tomorrow. Mmm, but that's nice.

I am divided against myself. That would be the normal interpretation. But that presupposes that I am the first person singular. If I am the first person singular, if I am a whole circle, surely I should know myself by now. Surely if I make a decision I should be able to carry it through. Otherwise, come on!

But we can't. And people berate themselves and torture themselves and even kill themselves on the basis that *'I can't bring myself under control. I can't bring my eating under control...'* Health services spend lots of money on gastric bands because people can't control themselves.

WELCOME THE RICHNESS OF OUR EXISTENCE

What I am suggesting tonight is that that's because the whole paradigm of control is unhelpful, that actually we need to make friends with the complexity of our existence. We need to collaborate with the richness of the potential that we can move in all sorts of different directions. In order to do that we need to relax and open and trust that the spaciousness of our being is infinite enough to contain all these many tendencies. And that by allowing them to be there they take their proper place. It's when we put on the blinkers and we make a firm decision that we assign a lot into the shadowland. But then suddenly it surprises us from left field and we are taken over by our impulse!

If, however, you open yourself to yourself and you know: *'I have many voices, I have many sub- personalities, I have many aspects or many facets. Yes, they are not always in harmony; sometimes they are in conflict but if I give them a place at the table, if they all know that they'll get something to eat, then they calm down.'*

Remember the story of Sleeping Beauty? The father and mother are so proud of the birth of their beautiful daughter that host a big party and invite everyone to celebrate. Everyone apart from a spiteful fairy whom no-one liked. No-one wants someone like that at a party. But she turns up anyway she puts a curse on the baby. Then the story unfolds.

It's always dangerous to exclude. You have the return of the repressed. Whatever we don't want to know about ourselves doesn't just fade away. It moves under the carpet. It moves behind the walls. It will manifest sooner or later.

So in order to be at ease with oneself, one actually turns and welcomes the richness of our existence as an unfolding, dynamic participant in a world which is beyond control but not out of control. It's not in my control but neither is it chaotic. It is patterns in which, if I'm present, I can find the balance. I find the fulcrum point and by my own flexibility and dynamic nature I take my place; sometimes expanding, sometimes contracting; sometimes full of happiness, sometimes full of sadness. Each of these is valid. Why should we not be sad? Why should we not be lonely sometimes? Loneliness is a flavour. It's a colour on a pallet. What does it taste like? It's not poisonous. If you believe it's poisonous you can start to feel persecuted. Actually, what is this sadness? *'I am alone.' 'I am unloved.'* What is that feeling? I am. It's all present, the being is here. The current flavour is 'unloved'. What is that? There's a place for it. If you give it its place it will vanish, because 'being unloved' is a movement of the mind, a movement of sensation and feeling.

OFFERING HOSPITALITY TO WHATEVER IS ARISING ACTUALLY AND PARADOXICALLY ALLOWS IT TO GO

If you sit in meditation you will find your thoughts are always changing. Feelings are always changing. Sensation in the body is always changing. It's only when we are immersed in our narrative, which is clunky and solidifying, that we stabilise notions about ourselves. *'I'm hopeless.' 'I can't do that.' 'I don't know how you do it, I couldn't do that.'* We sit inside that narrowing definition and because we know this about ourselves we avoid the situation that give us a chance to try. *'Oh, I wouldn't be as good as you. I'm not going to do it, because you will laugh at me.'* How much of our life have we diminished out of this fruitless anxiety, endlessly comparing and contrasting. It doesn't matter what other people can do. If we block our own life force, if we hide the richness of ourself from ourself, we are also hiding it from other people. And we do it out of embarrassment, shame, guilt, pride ... because we are not sure if we will get it right. So the evaluatory, judgemental approach, which, in a sense, can only be applied to real entities, becomes our imprisoning directive.

Where *are* these real entities? *'I'm like this.'* How do you know? Again and again in the practice of psychotherapy we see people imprisoned in core negative beliefs. Out of the family matrix or events that have happened in life, people come to believe that they are useless or stupid or unlovable and so on. That brief transient thought, repeated, rises with its semantic glue and appears to tell the whole truth about someone. *'I can't.'* The libido or the prana or the chi, the life energy, collapses on the basis of such a transient thought.

The key point, in our mediation or in our therapy, is starting to trust that we can be more present in the moment: that the accumulations of knowledge and information that we have from the past can be re-framed or re-identified as potentials or tools or resources that we can call upon if necessary. We will only know if it's necessary, however, if we see what's there.

Imagine owning a toolbox with different kinds of spanners and screwdrivers. You look at a screw and you decide if it has a star head, a slot head or a Phillips head and then you select the appropriate screw driver to fit. The screw comes first, not that you especially like using a particular screwdriver. *"My father used to use it all the time and then when he was old he gave it to me. It's the best gift he ever gave me so I always have to use this one!"* No, you don't. Look at the screw. If it doesn't fit then use one of the many other tools you have in your toolbox.

So the royal road to happiness and relaxation is not to believe the stories you tell yourself about yourself, but to look at the world, to look at your unfolding potential. Don't come to a premature conclusion. Don't mobilise on the basis of assumption and prediction. Just see what is there and feel your response. Allow the full reception of the situation to evoke the widest possible range of responses in yourself and – you find yourself being right there in the moment!

It's that easy, yet it's difficult to do. Why? Because we won't let go of what we know.

To be at ease in ourselves with others, let go of what we know and be available for what is. That is our ongoing work.

Public talk given in Devon, UK on 28th November 2014. Edited by Barbara Terris.

Seeing identity and buddha-nature

The topic is identity – national identity, political identity, religious identity and personal identity – in relation to the buddha-nature.

"I" IS AN EMPTY SIGNIFIER

Generally speaking, the more specific we can make an object, the fewer elaborations can be made about its identity. We may say 'chocolate ice-cream with nuts' and there is a shared sense of what that is. We can still imagine a few things, but the mind doesn't have much room to move around that concept. If we simply say 'ice-cream' there are many more possibilities: flavours, colours, ingredients and so on.

This is the same with identity. If you say *"I am German"* this could mean thousands of things, hundreds of thousands of things. Many and various people can unite together and say, *"We are German."* It might mean something completely different for each of them, but somehow all these different ideas of German-ness can be inserted into the notion of being German.

This is the power of the empty signifier. We have words like 'love'. *'I love you'* could mean anything. There are many words which are very difficult to find out exactly what they mean. But of all the possible signifiers the one which has the greatest possibilities of expansion and contraction is simply 'I.' 'I' functions for us because of its emptiness. 'I' as a linguistic term and as a sense of feeling-tone is able to accommodate a very wide range of associations. I can feel lonely, I can feel happy, I can feel expansive, I can feel shy... All of these are possible for us to express and identify with because 'I' by itself has no determination.

Day by day, hour by hour, in fact second by second, the content of what we take to be 'I' is shifting and changing. 'I' can be filled with aspects that seem to be internal – with sensations, with feelings, with memories that perhaps only I have access to – but 'I' can also be filled with the colour of the autumn trees. 'I' can be filled with the early evening darkness and the light reflected in a puddle of water on the road, the pathos that that evokes. Things which are outside and things which are inside feed in and generate the sense of an individual self.

From the buddhist point of view this is very important and very significant because the continuity of 'I' is the emptiness of 'I.' If a particular content of 'I' was to get stuck – if 'I' was always going to be sad for example – there is some echo of *'Oh, I was not always like this.'* So I can compare and contrast.

Usually we are caught up just in the flow of significations which marry with the signifier 'I'. 'I' is filling and emptying, filling and emptying moment by moment. And yet, when we speak of ourselves it is as if we are expressing some definable identity. One might say *"I like being by the sea."* Not really. Sometimes. In the summer. When the beach isn't too busy.

When we make these general global statements they are usually not quite true. The more we finesse what we say, the more we customise it to fit ourselves, the more we see that this thing which I say is true about me is situational and conditional.

On a more general level a term like 'being British' or even the notion of 'being European' or even 'being a human being' is very generous. It is willing to accept all kinds of associations. When we hear that people have behaved in a way which is very cruel we might say *"That is inhuman."* That is to say, human beings don't behave that way or shouldn't behave that way. And yet they do. So human beings can be non-human, can be inhuman.

There we have the problem of category. We imagine that the category of 'human being' indicates something: two arms, two legs, walking about, causing trouble... But some of the time humans are inhuman. How is this possible? Because the category starts to get twitchy when you try to put things into it that extend it too much. Despite all the unbelievably nasty things which human beings do, we still hang on to an idea that human beings are good. We approach our impressions of the behaviour of people with our categories of reasonable/ unreasonable, compassionate/selfish and so on. And if what the human beings are doing is basically inside the parameters of our favourite categories, we say *"That's what human beings do."*

You can watch a video clip on YouTube of somebody having their head cut off with a blunt knife and you can say, *"This is inhuman!"* Somehow using a blunt knife or axe is worse than using a sharp one, or the sharp blade of a guillotine. So maybe we have to say that a definition of inhumanity is using a blunt knife.

This is how we start to see that we are playing games with concepts. The tool by which I move towards the world and make sense of the world is primarily useful to me because it's not overdetermined. The indeterminacy of the language allows us to occupy it in a particular way while at the same time enjoying the feeling that we are saying something very precise and meaningful.

'ME' IN HERE AND 'YOU' OUT THERE

Why is this important? Well, from the buddhist point of view, especially in the dzogchen view, the ground of our being or the basis from which everything that we see, hear, smell, touch, and know, all arises from this ground that is beyond the reach of language. Language emerges out of the inexpressible, the ineffable. Ignorance is the loss of simple, relaxed, open presence in the ground. When this arises there is a kind of mixture of anxiety, a sense of instability, and this manifests as grasping, as clinging on, as holding on to something as a means of gaining reassurance.

This is how duality arises. Duality is subject and object. 'I' hold on to 'that'. I am James. There is a grasping, a holding on to a particular formulation which appears to be definitive or at least accurately referential to me. Now that I feel *'I am me'* I can ask *'So who are you?'* Then we start to multiply our words and concepts and give names to everything.

In the Old Testament this process of naming is described as an act of the wisdom and generosity of God. From the buddhist point of view, however, it is the mad stumbling of the ignorant. We name things because we don't see what they are. Whatever we encounter is the radiance of our own mind but what does that actually mean? We are sitting here, we are aware of being here, and generally we are aware of being here in our body: I am inside me looking out at you; you are inside you looking out at me. This is normal and deluded. So what is actually happening? I experience my feet on the cushion beneath them. I experience a sensation which I interpret to be the pressure of my buttocks on the cushion I'm sitting on. That is to say, there is a flow of experience which I identify as 'I, me, myself'. And simultaneously there is a flow of experience which I identify as being 'you'. You arise for me as experience. I experience different peoples' shapes, the colour of their clothing, their posture. This arises for me. What is happening for you, I don't know. I only have access to the 'you' for me. The 'you' for you belongs to you! That's why it is never a good idea to talk about other people, since we're always just talking about ourselves. We never reach anyone else. We think we have an accurate perception, but we have an interpretation.

For example, from where I am sitting I see people's faces, shoulders and so on. It's not possible for me to see anyone's back. I impute that you have a back, I imagine that you have a back, but I don't know. But that fact doesn't worry me, because I'm not only imagining your back, I'm imagining your front as well. I am constructing you. In Tibetan this is called *'du she'*: *'du'* means to gather together and *'she'* means to know. When we open our gaze we see light and colour. With this as a basic raw material we massage into it our habit formations, our identifications. That is to say, you appear as human beings to me because I have access to the perception of human beings. If I was a mosquito or a bird I wouldn't see you in this way. I would have different associations. Most small birds are rather wary of human beings. Most mosquitos are quite happy to meet human beings. Both engage according to their own interpretive matrix. This world is our interpretation.

We are used to being what we call 'ourselves'. We are used to seeing the sort of things that human eyes see. We are used to smelling the things that human noses smell. We know that dogs can hear things that we can't. We know that dogs are fond of smells that we probably are not so fond of. So the quality of the sound or the smell is something revealed through the bandwidth or aperture of the sense organ linked with the particular associations that arise. The implication of this is that there is no meaning already established out there. It means that a baby is born into a world of meaning, but rather the baby as it evolves is helped to find the way to find the world meaningful. The baby learns to allocate meanings. If the baby is born in an upper class German family then they will drink their soup without making a noise. If they are born in a Chinese family probably they'll make a little bit of noise, because slurping, which is a normal thing to occur, is given different interpretations according to culture.

The point of this, especially for meditators, is to start to appreciate that I am part of whatever is arising, that the world is revealed to me through my interpretive structures. Some of these structures we can relate back to our family background and some tendencies we just seem to have, they seem to flow through us.

From a buddhist point of view that would be a sign of a pattern, a karmic pattern, established from a prior existence, that the patterning of my tendencies that was arising at the time when in the intermediate period, the bardo, I became aware of my parents copulating, becomes determinant of whether I enter into the point of sexual contact or not. I am implicated, I am already in process. As I grow up in the family I'm learning and changing, I'm making choices. I learn things about the world, I know things about the world and the normal conclusion that we have, and that we are encouraged to have through our parents and school, is that the world is out there and you know some of the things about the world so you are becoming bigger and you can function with more independence.

THE UNRELIABILITY OF IDENTIFICATION

If I start to observe how I approach the world it's based on selection and apprehension. When you walk down the street some things catch your eye more than other things. It's quite unusual to have a completely even panoramic gaze at everything you encounter. Our disposition and our tendencies are already tilting us towards some features of what is revealed and away from others. Although I say *"I walk down the street"* – 'the street' – what I am actually doing is walking down 'my street', the street that is revealed to me at this moment with this degree of light, this weather and my mood. When I'm more relaxed and happy I might look around. If I'm a bit worried and preoccupied by something I can walk down the street and not see anything. Oh! The world is a revelation. And I am part of the process of the revelation.

There might be a song that I have some positive associations with and then some heartbreak occurs and I don't want to hear this song again. Some sound or place or person which appeared to be a road that opened up the world for me now is like a wall and I want to turn away from it.

111

This is indicating that what I take to be my identity is not something I have inside me, but is rather a potential which can manifest in many different ways according to circumstances. It is the same with national identities. Countries can be friendly in one direction and quite murderous in another. When we study history we learn about the Greeks and the Persians and the Romans and at every stage every country has some friends and some enemies. Friends and enemies means liking and not liking. This is the fundamental polarisation that we use to organise the experiential field.

Buddhism talks about the three root poisons or afflictions. There is mental dullness or assumption, which means primarily the assumption of reification: I am real, you are real. Flowing from that as soon as you have something real out there and somebody real in here, you have liking and not liking. On the basis of liking I say *'You are good.'* On the basis of not liking I say *'You are bad.'* *'You are my good friend'*, *'You are my bad enemy.'* This is very unstable. While we are fighting ISIS the Kurds are our good friends. When we realise we have to support the Central Government in Baghdad then the Kurds are our enemy.

This is life. As the Buddha said: *"Friends become enemies and enemies become friends."* This is why our world is so turbulent; because we speak as if what we said was the truth. But what comes out of our mouth is just a stream of lies. *"You are my friend."* *"You are my friend – yes, but for today."* That's a bit more honest. *"You are my friend at the moment because you are washing the dinner dishes and I don't have to!"*

We start to see that *'You are my friend'* is situational, contingent. We are using the word 'friend' as if it indicated something intrinsic in the other. You are my friend because 'friend-ness' pervades you. But our world is co-emergent. The friend-ness I see in you is put there by me. It's the same with enemy-ness.

And so our world is pulsating and fluctuating between expansion and contraction. We find ourselves being more available to those who we call 'friend' and less available to those who we call 'enemy' but neither are fixed identities. This is the play of identification.

Let's go back to the point earlier about the progression from ignorance through anxiety to the polarity of subject and object. Once we have a sense of *'I am the self inside me and you are the other outside me'* then I have to work out how you are in relation to me. What is your current value for me? Externally the currency markets have fluctuations of exchange rates all the time yet the values that we ascribe to other people are even more volatile. Maybe this is true for you. It's certainly true for me. Unreliability is one of my hallmarks. People like us to be reliable. This is a theatre of stupidity. If you were really reliable you would see a beautiful sunset and be indifferent. You would stand in some dogshit on the road and be indifferent. We are creatures of mood. Mood is primary. Mood is what we operate from. Mood is ungraspable yet it is everywhere operating.

So our identity is filling and emptying with different kinds of moods which are teased out and flavoured and coloured according to thoughts, feelings, memories, hopes and fears and so on.

I am unstable. This is why I can communicate. If I were completely fixed I could not communicate. For better or worse the table is not talking, *I* am talking. And the reason we can talk is because we can relate, which means I am available to manifest with you. I'm not pre-formed on the inside and then showing something I prepared earlier. We find ourselves being in a particular way with a particular person at a particular time. So where is the identity? You have a very pleasant evening with a friend. *"We must meet again soon!"* Next time you meet them it's not so interesting. Why not? They are in a different mood, you are in a different mood. What you had was a moment. Moments are there, full, but unreliable. *"But I like this person!"* The problem is that this person doesn't exist anywhere except in your mental construct!

BUILDING OUR IDENTITY OUT OF CONCEPTS

This is a fundamental buddhist view: The stability of the world is conceptual, not phenomenal. Moment by moment the phenomena which we call 'self' and the phenomena which we call 'object' are always in complex interactions.

This is not a problem, however, if the mind is relaxed and open. Relaxed and open is the quality of the ground, the ground of our being. However, when we fall into this delusion of ignoring the ground and imagining entities, the entities come into being because of concepts. We interpret the world not after the fact of the world but we interpret the world as our participation in the emergence of the world.

This is why the buddhist texts say, 'Wake up!' Your life is dynamic. It's not stable, it's not secure, you are going to die. What will happen to you is determined by how you are. Are you here? Moment by moment this experiential field is, to a large extent, patterned according to your mode of participation, though not totally determined by it.

When we start to meditate we start to become more aware of this. We are sitting quietly, not trying to do much. But all kind of thoughts and feelings and sensations are arising and passing. I don't know if the same things are happening for anyone else; they are happening for me. 'My thoughts.' But I didn't make them. The ego is a thief. The ego has nothing of its own. Everything we have we got from the world. The body grows from getting food from the world. We take nutrition when we are inside our mother's body and later from her breast. We learn a language that already exists. We are taking.

—But what I take is *mine*! *I* am speaking.

—Words you learned.

—Never mind. *I* am speaking

In that way we make ourselves more and more stupid as we become more and more intelligent.

We learn to steal more quickly and hide the evidence of our theft.

When I worked in a hospital, they had a slogan for the medical students regarding small operations: *'See one, do one, teach one.'* You see someone doing the operation, next day you do the operation and the following day you're teaching someone else how to do it. It's a little bit alarming in the realm of surgery, but it's actually how we proceed in life. You learn to go on your skateboard without falling off and then you show your friend how to do it. This is not an accident. This is the sign that the ego yearns for mastery. *"I know what I'm doing!"* *"I can do it!"* Small children spend a lot of time getting other people's attention to show what they can do.

Now the most powerful man in the world is constantly tweeting to his universal mama and papa to say, *"Look what I can do!"* This is very helpful for us, because to have so much money, to have so much power and to still be so fundamentally insecure is terrifying. We might imagine, *"Oh, if I had more money, if I had a bigger house, if I had a better partner then I would be confident and relaxed."* And it's this kind of longing which keeps us in the process of self-development and hunger to find better objects. But we never really arrive, at least not for very long

This is not a personal fault. This is a structural fault. We are the manifestation of the ego-structure. The root of the ego-structure is the patterning of mental activity which arises consequent on ignoring the ground of our own being. This anxious, hungry, very active formation which we find ourselves existing as is a desperate attempt not to be nothing. *"I exist!"* *"I am someone!"* *"At least someone loves me!"* *"I exist!"*

From the buddhist point of view – no! We don't exist. We manifest. That is to say we are patterns of shape and colour moving in space, dynamic and situationally emergent.

SEEKING SECURITY THROUGH CATEGORIES

What is it that we think we exist as? For example, *"I am James."* In Britain there are a lot of people who also are James. *"But I am my mother's James! I am her special James. That's only me."* Being 'James' is a relational definition. The 'James' is not pointing to anything intrinsic or inherent. Likewise whatever we take to be our identity – young or old, intelligent or not, male or female, black or white, gay or straight – these are all categories. And how do we cope with somebody who doesn't fit into the basic categories? That middle territory is sometimes not very welcoming. This is because we seek stability through category.

Categories are conceptual, however the actual phenomena of our life, the way experience arises moment by moment, is ungraspable by concept. Nevertheless on the level of an ego-self we want stability. We see this all the time in political formations. Many national governments have been intentionally destabilised by the CIA. Generally the state departments and the Pentagon and so on have a clear idea of who is friend and who is enemy. Why would one want Salvador Allende to have any power in Chile? Much better to have General Pinochet. He wears a uniform and so we know what that means. It means he's a regular guy. After he had seized power he did exactly the right thing: he promoted his friends and killed his enemies. The US government understands this; this is how 'proper people' behave. It simplifies the world. Like/not like. Good/bad.

This is at the heart of the Buddha's teaching: once ignorance arises you necessarily start dividing up the world. If we come into mahayana practice we start saying things like *'May all sentient beings be happy.'* Not only that, we also say, *'May all sentient beings be equally happy.'* We don't say *'May the capitalists have more happiness than the communists.'* Irrespective of the qualities I might perceive you are having and irrespective of the interpretive categories I might use, *'May all sentient beings be happy.'* May terrorists be happy. May torturers be happy. May politicians be happy. May everyone be happy.

"But I don't like torturers. I think doctors who save sweet little children should be more happy than torturers. They deserve it. Happiness and goodness should be distributed according to merit." Judgement however is always situational.

From the point of view of meditation this is very important. We see that here is a torturer, or in any case somebody who does things that we think are horrible. They may even enjoy doing these horrible things and so it seems reasonable to say that this is a bad person. Certainly, the behaviour is bad and any enjoyment in it is self-referential and devoid of compassion. So here is a person and we look at their behaviour and we say, *"Aha, this is a bad person."* We have the evidence. It is undeniable that what they do fits into the category of 'bad.'

Let's put that to one side for a moment and just stay with *'this person is.'* There is a 'person.' Who says so? I say! We all say. We all know. Why do we know this? Because we are wandering in samsara due to ignorance. The category of 'person' arises for the ignorant, not for the wise. This is not something you would have learned in school since our capitalist economy, being based on commodification, cannot tolerate nouns that are empty, nouns without an adjective.

THE FIVE SKANDHAS

So what is a person? In Tibetan they say *'gang zag'*, and in Sanskrit *'pudgala'*. *Pudgala anatman drishti* is the view of the absence of inherent self-nature in persons. This refers to what are called the 'five heaps' or the 'five skandhas'. 'Five heaps' means there are five aspects or five parts which are juxtaposed, placed together, to create a pattern that we then take to be a sentient being, a person.

The first is **form**, that is to say shape and colour. Actually it means shape and colour taken as 'something.' Essentially it is the establishment of a 'something.' Form would be, 'in my hand there is a watch'. Even before we say 'watch' and go on to say anything more about it, 'something' is there. So form indicates a basic 'something-ness.' And as we looked earlier this arises from ignorance. We have this double move of reification, of solidification, plus grasping. As soon as it's there I am holding on to it. My holding on to it invests it with its seeming separateness and intensity.

Next to that we have **feeling** or response, which is positive, negative or neutral.

Then we have **apprehension**: we take hold of this watch. Because I like the watch I look at it more. Because I look at it more it becomes more separated out from the background, it becomes a kind of Gestalt-formation and that is what I'm taking hold of.

Then **associations** gather around this watch. These associations are the construction or the elaboration of what is here. Things that we see bring other things to mind. When I looked at the watch a thought about my father came in to my mind. He used to say, *'Never buy an expensive watch! You'll lose it or you'll break it. Buy a cheap watch and when you need a new one you can buy another.'* That brings a further relatedness, a massaging of significance into the object.

The fifth skandha is **consciousness** or comprehension: bringing everything together into a formation. This functions as a normalising conclusion. I think: *'Oh yes, this is my watch.'* Then it recedes into being just a something; it's just my watch. Having created this particularity it reassures me about the seeming givenness – which of course is not given – of this world I inhabit.

In his first teaching the Buddha said that there is an absence of inherent self-nature in phenomena. For example when we look around the room we see people. Maybe some people you have seen before, maybe some people you have never seen before.

Some people might seem more interesting, others less interesting. Anyway these are all people: that seems like a starting point. If you like the person you might think: *'I would like to get to know you better.'* I start from the assumption that there is a 'you' to get to know. But as I get to know this 'you', 'you' come into formation with 'me'. As you start giving me the 'you' towards me, I then grasp with my crumbly fingers and form a 'you' for me. So now I am getting to know the 'you' that I imagine you to be.

Where is the person? The person is a process of construction. This doesn't mean that people don't have a presence. It means that they don't exist as entities. They are not held in place by an internal identity. Rather they are an infinite potential of identities which emerge according to circumstances, both emergent and co-emergent.

MOVING FROM IDENTITY TO BUDDHA-NATURE

Who then am I before I emerge? We use meditation to try to find that out. That is like the question, *'What was my face before I was born?'* To be born is to have an identity, to be someone. But the someone that I am is a set of concepts. I am a story that I tell myself and other people, and that story includes the stories that other people have told me about me. So who am I if I am not a story? Who am I before I tell myself who I am?

This is when we move from identity to buddha-nature. In telling a story about something we are constructing it. The Buddha said that all compounded things are impermanent. The constructs that we developed at the various stages of our lives have a sell-by-date. They lose their relevance. I can say, *'I used to live in India'* but that was thirty years ago. A lot has happened since then. At first when I came back from India I found it very difficult to adjust to life in Britain. Life in India was what seemed very true to me, but gradually the years go by and now it is something in the past. I can still say *'I used to live in India'* but now there is not much juice in it. The juice of the saying was the feeling I put into it: 'Oh, India!'

In that way we can see how these five skandhas or five heaps move around as potentials to keep creating pattern after pattern after pattern. They are like sandcastles in that they have no deep truth or self-definition in them. They are unreliable.

If we are troubled by suffering, if we see suffering in the world and would like it to end, we heed the Buddha whose third Noble Truth is, 'There is an end to suffering.' Suffering has an origin and it has an end. Suffering is not intrinsic, it is generated, it is fabricated. If you stop fabricating it, it will not be there. We make suffering for ourselves.

How do we do this? We look at the flow of experience, which is constantly changing, and we take the scissors of duality and try to cut out little bits, and stuff them in our pocket for later. Now I have something! Maybe but it's rotting, decaying, dying. So we keep cutting and taking and hiding, cutting and taking and hiding. This is suffering. It is never stable, never secure.

But there *is* something secure – the buddha-nature. This is the mind itself. The mind has two aspects: Unborn openness (that is to say, it's not a thing in that it has no shape or colour; it doesn't have an origin in time or an end in time) and the quality of the mind, of awareness, is the clarity that reveals the ceaseless flow of experience. This flow of experience manifests as the eternal conversation or dialogue or dialectic between subject and object.

'I, me, myself' is experience. I think I am the experiencer, but I am something revealed. The revealer of the experience is the clarity of the mind. The clarity of the mind is not the ego; it's not an intellectual clarity. It is the clarity which is present with the arising of phenomena. As the phenomena arise we layer them over with narrative. The freshness of the arising moment is being smeared with the faeces of the past. We do this all the time and we tell ourselves that the shit smells like roses. I can even pretend that shit is not just roses but tulips and daffodils and snowdrops as well!

The central task and the central point is to see that you cannot get out of samsara by relying on concepts. Clearly in talking with you this evening I'm using a lot of concepts. But my hope is to use concepts to deconstruct concepts. We don't need to accumulate more concepts to become Buddhists but we do need to become more suspicious of ourselves. I am in ignorance. If I believe what the Buddha said then what I think is true, is probably not true. So I can't fall asleep in speaking. I can't wrap myself in a duvet of concepts and dream my life away, because now I want so see what I am up to, what tricks I am playing on myself.

The practice is again and again to relax our excessive mental arousal so that there is some space for what is actually here, to reveal itself. It is quite a challenging idea, that when I think I am simply seeing I'm actually involved in complex imaginative interpretations. That is to say, I am so easily merged with, so easily confluent with, thoughts and feelings that I take them to be the messengers of truth.

When we start to do some basic meditation we become aware of the kind of thoughts and feelings that arise. We start to see that we are crazy, that the mind is full of weird stuff coming and going all the time. We see how our mind fills with things we don't want it to fill it with, but are difficult to get rid of. Our mind fills with things we'd like to identify with, but they keep running away and we can't hang on to them. Yet somehow I'm still here.The good moments, the good thoughts, the good feelings come and go and similarly the bad moments, the bad thoughts and the bad feelings come and go.

So who is the one who is here when all is passing through? Clouds are in the sky; the sky offers hospitality to the clouds, but the clouds are not the same as the sky. Even when clouds are in the sky, the sky is free of the cloud. If the sky wasn't free of the cloud then when the wind blows the clouds wouldn't move. But they do.

In the same way our buddha-nature is open awareness like the sky within which thoughts, feelings, memories and so on move like clouds. Some clouds are light and fluffy and others are dark and full of storm. But they all pass and the sky is there. From the point of view of the ego, we become excited when the sun shines and depressed when it's cold and rainy because we are addicted to clouds. What the Dharma says is: *"Don't worry about the clouds. If you become like the sky the clouds won't bother you."*

This is the difference between an identity based on selection and grasping, and the buddha-nature which is forever open to everything that occurs and is neither imprisoned nor diminished by anything.

Public talk given in Berlin on 25th October 2017. Edited by Barbara Terris.

The glue of duality

Exploring the terms 'apprehension' and 'comprehension'

Question: Will apprehension and comprehension both fit in the mental factor of perception?

Question: Why do we use the term *nampar shepa* for consciousness (Skt. *vijnana*) if it means to comprehend?

Question: When I am grasping at something is that dependent on my prior reifying of a transient event?

Will I never be free of this?

Question: Does being compassionate and including everyone not involve grasping?

Question: Can I 'grasp at something' without 'finding a place for it within my existing ways of making sense of things'?

Question: Do apprehension and comprehension begin to arise from the first level of ignorance?

Question: In one of your teachings you said, 'this is', 'this is a cup', 'this is a cup in my hand'. How does this relate to apprehension and comprehension?

Question: Is it possible to have grasping without comprehending when acting within our dualistic frame of reference?

Question: In dzogchen, are we trying to break free of the first level of ignorance, where an emergent phenomenon is made into something?

Question: How can this 'allowing' happen without grasping?

Question: Where does apprehension and comprehension fit into eight consciousnesses?

Question: Do apprehension and comprehension both arise from the eighth level of consciousness? Can we pinpoint one level of consciousness for them both?

Question: Where do apprehension and comprehension fit in the four levels of ignorance?

Question: Do 'making it something' and 'grasping it as something' happen simultaneously?

Question: When does direct perception, the first moment of seeing something, occur? Does it occur before the moment of 'making it something'?

Question: Can we have direct perception of a concept since it is also a phenomenon?

Question: Please suggest the kind of practice that should be done?

Question: Please explain the meaning of terms 'apprehension' and 'comprehension'.

You referred to both terms in the commentary on one of the texts:

"Consciousness is essentially a mixture of apprehension, of taking hold of something, and comprehension which is to be able to hold it clearly within our existing frame of reference."

In Tibetan the term *'Dzin Pa'* indicates to grasp, to hold , to apprehend, and the term *nampar shepa* indicates to be conscious of something, to know what something is, to comprehend something. To apprehend is to grasp 'something': the 'object' of grasping is the reified appearance.

- We make an appearance into the appearance of **something** without knowing that we do it. This is so usual for us that we are blind to the intrinsic inseparability of appearance and emptiness.

- We then grasp it as **something** as if it were an existent something before we grasped it, then

- We comprehend it by finding a place for it within our existing ways of making sense of 'things'.

This is how the dynamic or glue of duality manifests the pseudo-clarity of my understanding of how things are. My experience is mediated by concepts yet I feel that I have direct contact with substantial entities each with their own inherent existence.

Awareness or rigpa is our mind fully relaxed and open as the natural illumination of whatever is occurring. It is without bias and without prejudice being panoramic and all-encompassing. The essence of the mind is emptiness, its quality is clarity or luminosity, and, never straying from the essence and its quality, kindness is all-pervading. This kindness or benign contact is freely given and is not dependent on the qualities of the recipient.

With unawareness or ignorance of basic openness there is a loss of being at ease with all phenomena as they come and go. The first moment of unawareness is a grasping at something, separating appearance from its ground of emptiness. It is not that 'some-thing' is taken out of emptiness but rather that the fact of its intrinsic emptiness is not opened to and so is ignored. An entity, something existing in itself, seems to have come into existence. With this the work of maintaining this delusion begins.

This initial ignoring is not done by someone. It is a moment of the absence of awareness of the ground. This moment passes yet it is as if it has inaugurated something other than openness. This establishing of something other, something apart, generates the site of co-emergent ignoring. The co-emergent factors are: a) absence of non-dual openness, and b) the beginning of imagining the false, the real, the existent. When the as is of openness, is as it were 'veiled' by unawareness, the as is of imagining, of fabrication, occurs as the misrepresentation and misinterpretation of appearance. No one is doing this yet the opacity of unawareness thickens as the sense of someone and something. In this way the fiction of samsara begins as a story without a storyteller, which is a story about a storyteller and the story that they tell. The storyteller manifests as subject and the story manifests as object.

Subject and object are like twins. They are born together. Then, although subject and object are actually brother and sister or conjoined twins, it's as if they vibrate in opposition. *"I'm not you. Get away."* Like fighting siblings, they create more and more separation: clinging to 'I, me, myself' and clinging to the idea that the other is not like me.

The self's definition of self is based on exclusion of the other, *"I don't know who I am but I'm not you."* There is a kind of stupid clarity in this. Although each self needs to keep relating to others, the integrity of the self, the continuity of its specific identity, depends on the rejection of the other. If the otherness of the other is appreciated, this tender relatedness will seem to diminish and relativise the autonomy of the subject as ego-self. The unique specificity of my ego-self is taken to be someone, to be I, me, myself, and the falsity of this identity is always vulnerable to exposure in any interaction with the other. It can be influenced, collapsed in on itself, pulled out of itself – all of which highlights the self-deception underpinning the belief in autonomy and personal agency. Self arises in dependent origination with all that is other: on the basis of not being the other, I am self; on the basis of being self, I am not other.

The ego-self is inseparable from the other and yet it needs to deny this in order to preserve its existence based on being separate. As subject and object become more defined and differentiated the subject becomes conscious that *'I need you'*. If the connection with the environment of objects is harmonious this need may feel supportive, but when disjunction occurs the feeling can shift to abjection, rage and terror. With this, desire and anger emerge as powerful relational forces seeking to unravel the confusion inherent in duality, the dependence of autonomous self on other. Self can seem to resolve this confusion by merging in the other in a caring confluence that is warm and inclusive. However such fusion is impermanent. Self can attempt to resolve this confusion by annihilating the other, a hateful rejection aimed at final exclusion. Yet this antipathy is also impermanent. As the Buddha said, *"Friends become enemies and enemies become friends."*

This dualistic experience is very different from the uncontrived actuality of *kadag*, the primordial purity of awareness. Awareness is unborn, uncompounded and uncreated. It is intrinsic and unchanging. Its purity, simplicity and virginity has never been touched or soiled. This is because it is not an entity standing in relation to other entities. It is not a thing amongst things, and so its purity is unchanging.

The ego cannot contact awareness. Awareness is non-dual with all occurrence, whereas ego is dualistic and operates through dualistic consciousness. Awareness offers the immediate revelation of how it is, how the whole is in this instant. Consciousness tells the ego-self about something, something which it is not. We are conscious of the other. Even when we are self-conscious, we are conscious of a transient image of self, an image we take to be self.

Consciousness is always dualistic: I am conscious of something. Consciousness always takes an object. You're not just conscious; there is always a subtle object. For example, if you were sitting in a clean room and you are reading you're not aware of smell. But maybe somebody is cooking downstairs and there's a smell of chili coming up in the air and you go, *"Oh!"* Your smell consciousness arises with the smell; the object and the subject arise together. The consciousness of smell grasps at this fragrance coming in on the air and then your mental consciousness (Skt. *manovijnana*) processes this smell in terms of its concerns. *"Have I smelled this before?"* or *"This means mom is preparing lunch"* or whatever it would be. You elaborate your interpretation thereby making this occurrence more relevant to you. The smell is taken to be the smell of something. *"Ah, now I know what it is."* This comprehension follows apprehension as the fleeting scent becomes the signifier of something existent and knowable. I can locate this smell within the body of knowledge that I have about myself and my world. Perhaps another smell comes up and suddenly you feel a bit anxious: *"What is that?"* And then you look outside and somebody's doing something with their car engine. *"Oh, it's that smell!"*

In this way, the hopes and fears arising from the ego's anxiety about survival maintain the dualistic consciousness that pervades our experience as we scan events in the hope of gain and the fear of loss. Is this a friend or an enemy? Should I open to this or close down? This uncertainty pervades perception, the third *skandha* heap, which rapidly builds up a composite image of what is going on. In Tibetan this is called '*Du-Shes*' (Skt. *samjna*), a gathering of information with which to build up a picture of the something-ness of what is occurring. This is the basic apprehension or perception upon which consciousness (Tib. *rNam-Shes*) develops its comprehension.

Question: Will apprehension and comprehension both fit in the mental factor of perception?

Although many technical terms are used in the analysis of experience, our actual experience arises all at once. It is important to learn to use the technical terms but without taking them to have an existent referent. For perception to occur there has to be something, something which you take to be the object of your attention. The smell came into your nostrils: *"Oh, what's that?"* Our perception is both proactive, going out to the object, and reactive, having the impact of the object come to us and elicit a response.

This pulsation in perception reflects how our body is in the world – we breathe in and we breathe out. We spread our breath out into the world and the air comes into us. We are in a constant exchange. This is what we call life.

Question: Why do we use the term *nampar shepa* for consciousness (Skt. *vijnana*) if it means to comprehend?

In English, generally the word consciousness means my mental aliveness – the fact that I have mental experience in which I am conscious of something. When you go to hospital for an operation the anesthetist makes you unconscious. You're very happy to be unconscious because you don't want to see what they're doing. For the ego it is a wonderful thing to be conscious if what I am conscious of is pleasing to me. If it is not pleasing, then I prefer to be unconscious.

Consciousness is a limited form of experience because it is so reactive. And that reactivity or ego sensitivity brings our attention up and out. Generally, we're not settled in ourselves because we're always concerned about how others will behave towards us. The Tibetan term *nampar shepa* indicates knowing something, some shaped form, some entity. This unites apprehending something, the sense that there is a 'not me' that I can grasp and get a handle on, and comprehension, my sense that I know what I have got hold of.

Awareness is different. Awareness is like the ocean and consciousness is like a wave. The wave is always moving, going up and down, subject-object, subject-object. That's the world of consciousness. Yet the ocean itself is very calm. The wave is not separate from the ocean but due to our habitual grasping and need for identity, the unstable wave is taken to be me, *"Hey, get out of my way, I'm a special wave."* Everybody's trying to push away the other waves or pull them in. But waves are ungraspable, as is the consciousness of all sentient beings.

Our aim in meditation practice is to see that the water in the wave is the water of the ocean. The wave has no water of its own. Individual identity is a delusion maintained by the capacity consciousness has to make the impermanent seem permanent.

Question: When I am grasping at something is that dependent on my prior reifying of a transient event?

Our consciousness manifests a long history of reification. Our self is reified, our consciousness is reified, and all that we encounter is reified. This is the structure we are born into life after life. We do not carry the details of our experience of one life into the next. What is carried forward – or what appears as the substratum of our new series of experiences – is these three aspects of ratification. Consciousness is a mental event which appears subjectively to be an ongoing quality of our self. This is a false interpretation, an identification which hides the openness of our mind itself. Self and other are both imagined, and they are both imagined to have inherent existence.

It can be useful to make a distinction between mind and the content of mind. As a way of exploring this we can imagine that mind is like a pot and the content of mind is like the food inside the pot. So if you look in the pot and there's nothing there, you might think, *"Hey, this is not very interesting, there's nothing to get here."* If somebody has cooked something nice in the pot then, *"Oh! wow!"* and then you add your judgement and say, *"It's a little bit sweet, but also nice."* The content of the mind maintains duality because it gives your ego-self something to work with as you add in your patterns and interpretations. The mind itself is intrinsically empty and offers nothing for the ego-self to hang on to. Unfortunately for us as meditators interested in liberation we rarely experience the open emptiness of our mind. Even if our life is like a desert, we're like a camel that has had a drink in the oasis. We can walk for many days on the fuel of the past. We are a karmic camel and we can go for a long time living on these old ideas and old tendencies. That's why meditation can be quite frustrating. We don't get a clear view of the intrinsically empty pot because we are fixated on our ego pot where new traces of the past ceaselessly arise for us to taste.

Will I never be free of this?

The truth is that you, as you take yourself to be, will never be free of this, because subject and object are born together. If the person doing the meditation is the ego-self then it can't get free. We have to relax out of the ego-self because it is a non-existent false identification.

After India's partition, there was a lot of a lot of pain and horror in the Punjab and people had many memories of what had happened. For as long as they're thinking, *"All these bloody people, look what they did!"* it just keeps heating and heating and heating. Yet the day when someone says, *"Oh, my brother!"* to the person they have taken to be their enemy then the mood can be very different because when you can say 'brother' you are being inclusive and there is less basis for involvement with the memories of the past, even if they keep occurring. You're saying, *"I see you two-eyes, two-legs brother, breathing in and breathing and out. I am also breathing in and breathing out, my brother, my sister."* However as long as you think and say, *"Oh, your people did that to my group. I can never forgive!"* then everyone is in a prison of anxious identity. So, it is very important to observe how duality functions in our lives.

You see little children playing in the street and waving bits of wood. Mom says, *"Leave it behind, we're going home now."* The child say, *"No. This is my sword. I need to keep it."* With this you see how the mind has given an identity to this piece of wood through the magic of interpretation. The wood was just lying in the road. The child found it yet within one second, it's theirs.

Grasping at something, claiming an ownership of it, is activity generated by the three root poisons. The first poison is the dulling toxicity of being sure that I exist and that everything I encounter exists. With this basic dualism, I am then either attracted to or repelled by the existents that I encounter.

The toxicity of desire is the conviction that this entity is special and important and is something that I must have. This one person or item is given a status above all others. This is delusion.

The toxicity of aversion is the conviction that this entity is unpleasant or dangerous and should be avoided and pushed away. This prevents me from having a rounded view of what is in front of me. I then act according to my beliefs about the other and ignore the fact that we both manifest as transient patternings of illusion.

Question: Does being compassionate and including everyone not involve grasping?

If compassion is 360 degrees in all directions, then I take care of you and I take care of me simultaneously. Compassion is not top down, an offering to the needy as if they were inferior. We are all equal in having buddha nature. If I am helping someone whom I take to exist as a separate person then I am still grasping at the duality of self and other and attributing inherent existence to both. If I see that you are hungry and I focus on your hunger, which is an arising sensation, and I give you food then your hunger goes down. Have I helped you? Tomorrow you will be hungry again, yet in this moment I have made a gesture of connection and aid.

If this gesture is made in the full acceptance of impermanence then it helps us on the road to emptiness. There is no helper, no help, and no one who was helped – the whole sequence is an illusion happening in the manner of a dream. If we see this, then we awaken to our actual situation. Each person has to awaken for themselves, nobody can do this for us.

When we help other people we are involved in a dynamic activity. As long as we are in samsara all gains and losses are temporary. We cannot build an enduringly safe place for others with our activity. Compassion is connectivity, the great method for lessening the sense of separateness that all sentient beings experience. In the classroom a good teacher will try to help each student but they will also know that some students understand very quickly, some understand less quickly, and some understand only after a lot of difficulty. Sentient beings are differentiated by their own karmically generated current capacities. There are no truly existing children who are fundamentally 'stupid' and 'bad' and 'will never get anywhere'. Such limiting definitions do not truly define the child – but they do show that the judging, defining adult is trapped in duality and in reifying concepts. Compassion is connective and is about working with the energy of the potential in the moment.

If you are farming a field with a lot of stones in it, then you need to use a special kind of head on the plough so that it won't break too often. You have to take care ploughing. Also you

133

have to grow crops such as oats or rye that can survive in such a soil. Some crops don't mind stones too much, but for wheat it can be difficult. So the farmer has to know all about his or her land: is it well drained, is it alkaline, is it acidic? In Britain farmers previously got very excited about taking down all the trees and hedges so that they had bigger fields. But then when heavy rains came they washed away a lot of soil. If you don't see the big picture and you think, *"Oh, now I'm winning"*, then you forget dependent origination – on the basis of this, that comes.

Being in a hurry to help people is often not so helpful. I remember when I was living in Shantiniketan with my teacher and his wife there was a lady who taught in the university. Sometimes she had some mental health problems. On one such occasion she was getting a bit disturbed and Amala, Rinpoche's wife, said to him, *"I think we should bring her into the house and take care of her."* And he said, *"Fine, you invite her, you cook for her, you talk with her into the night because she loves to talk. Then it's you who tells her that she has to go when you have had enough. I'm not going to do that."* It's one thing to be sweet and say, *"Oh my dear, come, we will take care of you"*, but after some time, you might find that it's very tiring.

It is vital to be aware that our capacity to help others will vary. Our mind is unreliable and other people's minds change too. So help as you can, when you can, but without making grand promises. If we see that there are no truly existing people and that everyone is a pattern of energy, then we have to work with each specific pattern without reification.

Once when C R Lama was in Ladakh he was invited to give some initiations at a monastery that was quite high on a hill. He was carried up the hill and when he got to the top he took off his shoes and went into the temple. He performed the initiation and when he came out his shoes were gone. Everyone was running around looking for the shoes, very upset. But he told them, *"These shoes were very nice shoes. I was in Europe and people bought these wonderful shoes for me. However as for the theft of the shoes, 90% of the of the sin of the bad deed is mine. This is a poor area. There are sharp stones everywhere. So who would not want good shoes here? By leaving my shoes outside I created temptation for the thief. So the thief has 10% of the badness and I have 90%."* In this way we have to be aware of how complex life is. We can't just consider something as a good thing to do without considering the possible side effects.

This is made clear with the Buddhist concept of the Three Wheels: subject, object and the activity that links them. This structure is present in many languages as subject-verb-object or as subject-object-verb. The value of the object is not free standing, since it is linked to the status, mood and requirements of the subject. It can seem obvious that chocolate is good, intrinsically good, yet it is not good for someone with diabetes. It might seem good to their tongue, but it will not help them maintain stability in their blood sugar.

The teachings advise us that our awareness should be as vast as the sky, and our compassion should be as fine as milled flour, as precise as the point of a needle.

Question: Can I 'grasp at something' without 'finding a place for it within my existing ways of making sense of things'?

We already, automatically and habitually, see the world as full of things. It's not that we are consciously transforming light and sound into things. We're living in a world which is already solidified due to it being mediated by our own karmic constructs. When I see a bird flying in the sky, I can't imagine how it does this. I watch the little bird... it flies right into a bush, right into the branches of a tree and I think, *"Oh, how does he do that? His wings come in at just the right moment."* The bird is not having to think, and it didn't go to a flying school; it just flies. In the same way we see according to our karmic vision, the assumptive interpretive vision that brought us into the human realm. In each of the six realms the formative assumptions are unquestioned; in each case what happens seems completely true for the experiencer. Our karmic vision reveals to us that we are individual entities living in a world of separate real things. On the basis of this we add liking and not liking. We say, *"I've had enough"* or *"Give me more."* Our wish is that everything which arises for us should fit into our personal frame of reference.

For example, when I was young in the 1960s, there were certain kinds of music which felt like 'my music'. Then later there was punk and rap which I would sometimes hear on the radio and wonder, *"What is this? This is not music!"* I didn't feel an easy resonance with that kind of music. Similarly in a family, in a social grouping, we find that particular kinds of patterning seem normal for us yet when we look at other people we see that what is normal for me is not normal for them. Usually this difference is not disturbing for us because we can simply think, *"Oh they're different"* and leave it at that. Buddhist teachings encourage us to examine this more closely.

If each person has their own normal, and there is no normal shared by everyone, then the assumptions that our identity and choices depend on are merely conventional. They are true and valid for me because I believe they are true. They have no actual basis apart from my belief in them and so they're relative to all the karmic and cultural influences that have contributed to these beliefs. These cultural formations are not inherently true. They are just constructs and the value of a construct lies in whether you believe it or not.

The ego wants to feel secure in its knowledge. Many years ago when I was walking along the River Ganges heading towards Prayagraj at Allahabad for the big kumbh mela, I passed through little villages. I had only two lungies, so each day I would wash one by beating it on a rock in a certain way. The women in the village would come and say, *"No, no, you have to hit your lungi with a stone to wash it."* So the next day I'm in another village and I'm hitting my lungi with a stone to wash it and the women there came and told me, *"No, no, you have to beat it with your clenched fists to wash it."* In each village the women had a different way of washing cloth. Then we see that this is a relative truth, but in each village the people there believe that they know the correct way to wash clothes.

However we can't just throw away our grasping, because it is the glue that keeps our social formation together. Our beliefs and identities are not absolutely true but they are relatively true, and we need to employ them in our interactions given that we are living in a world of fabricated identities. In meditation, we can dissolve the glue a bit and gradually become free of relying on such identifications. Our meditation helps us develop wisdom on the basis of insight into the lack of inherent existence in people and in phenomena. We come to see directly that everything that occurs is inseparable from emptiness, from the open empty ground. However, if we wish to develop kindness and compassion we need to be able to relate to all sentient beings, each of whom believes in the truth of their identifications. It is not about destroying all identifications but rather about seeing that all identifications refer to illusory formations. Real entities are the product of delusion.

Thus in meditation we do not grasp at the thoughts and feelings which are arising, yet when we get up from the meditation and go out, we have to be able to relate to the fact that people's constructs are real for them. We have to work with their beliefs without believing what they believe. Other people may be convinced that we are basically like them. Disrupting this assumption is unlikely to liberate them. We have to offer authentic contact and communication – yet in the manner of a dream. Thus, compassion is to enter into interaction without getting caught in reification or reactivity.

Question: Do apprehension and comprehension begin to arise from the first level of ignorance?

It is indeed from the first level of ignorance that all of these aspects begin to arise. As soon as there is a 'some-thing' there is the beginning of some-one who knows that some-thing. The arising, which is actually transient and devoid of inherent existence, is apprehended as something. This starts the process of defining: what type of something is this? And thus comprehension, the work of consciousness, begins. Comprehension is part of the process of constructing the object as an identifiable and knowable and usable entity.

I don't know if it is still practised but in the old days, after the monsoon, people would put potassium permanganate down their well since it was known to kill off many of the bacteria that had come from things being washed down into the well. If you take even the tiniest crystal of potassium permanganate and drop it in water, all the water immediately becomes purple. It's like that – one tiny drop of 'this is', 'this exists', 'I am', and the whole world is suddenly pervaded with its colour! Everything is some-thing! It's like when the sun is going down in the evening and a red colour pervades the sky. It's just suddenly there, the sky is red!

Ignorance is suddenly there and then we are living in this world suffused or flavoured with duality. We are, in our limited identities, the fruition of the first moment of ignoring the actual ground.

Question: In one of your teachings you said, *'this is'*, *'this is a cup'*, *'this is a cup in my hand'*. How does this relate to apprehension and comprehension?

As soon as there is this very simple first sense of existence, there is an anxiety. Existence and non-existence are born together as mutually contradictory binaries. This anxiety of the insecurity of existence seeks reassurance. Its lonely vulnerability seeks a friendly other. If I say, *"Hello"* to you, you might wait to see if I say anything more. Maybe I only know *"Hello"?* Maybe I can only announce my existence? The lonely self has to reach out more clearly, so that the idea of self is calling out for a friend; it is calling to the idea of the other. I say, *"How are you?"* Now we have the Three Wheels. I want to know how you are. Now we're having a conversation.

One thing leads to another to another and we build up pictures in language, in association, in memory. We are all, from the position of the ego-self, creatively constructing these patterns. This construction occurs in the face of intrinsic emptiness. The construction of meaningful entities pleases the ego yet it covers up the inherent emptiness of all the ingredients used in the construction.

It is vital to be clear about this first moment of arising. This moment occurred long long ago and it also occurs in each and every moment we experience. 'This' arises. Is it the sky or is it the some-thing in the sky? In the traditional buddhist view a rainbow manifests from the sky. It is a quality of the sky. The sky shows a rainbow. The ocean shows a wave. If you truly see sky and rainbow together, without conceptualising them, it is obvious that the rainbow is a sky-showing, a sky revelation. The sky has the capacity to display many forms which are non-dual with it. But if you take out your dualistic scissors and cut around the rainbow, *"This rainbow is the best rainbow, this is the most beautiful rainbow"*, then where is the sky? The sky vanishes as the now ignored background while the rainbow is foregrounded and becomes very real. You take your camera, you're photographing it, you make an exhibition and you call it 'The Rainbows of the Himalayas'. This rainbow you have found is in fact your own creation because you have separated it from its non-dual source.

All entities are created by reification – this is the creativity of the basis manifesting in unawareness of the basis and this generates delusion out of illusion. This separation is followed by grasping. The baby comes out of the mother's body and then the umbilical cord is cut, establishing the baby as other than the mother. Now it is an individual somebody and we give the baby a name and with this it takes on its individual identity. It was part of mum and now it comes out of her and into its own 'existence'.

The prajnaparamita literature states that emptiness is the great mother, the mother of all the buddhas, yet each buddha is not born **out of** the great mother. Each buddha is living **inside** the great mother. She has a very very big belly; she has hundreds of thousands of buddhas inside because her womb is like the sky, never fragmenting, always non-dual. There is buddha, yes, but buddha inseparable from the great mother. They are not two, they are not one, they are non-dual.

When you have two, you have grasping. I grasp this. But with the clarity of non-duality there is nothing to grasp. How can you take the wave from the ocean? Can you take a cloud out of the sky? Can you take a thought out of your mind? I might think, *"Oh, this is a very important thought."* I think this about that thought. Both the initial thought and the thought that comments on it are unborn illusions that never leave the mind. The thought is always non-dual with the mind.

So first comes cutting and separating, and then comes grasping. The basis of cutting is the 'not seeing non-duality', and with this, consciousness arises as the manager of subject/object interactions.

Question: Is it possible to have grasping without comprehending when acting within our dualistic frame of reference?

Yes. People from many countries live in London. I might be sitting in the bus and two people are in front of me talking in their language. I don't know what they're saying but I do know that these are people talking. The activity is grasped by me as something yet I have no comprehension of the content they experience in the activity. I gain a little bit of a holiday from my busy mental activity due to my not understanding the content of their words but I still have a subtle grasping at the sense that something is occurring. I know that they are speaking a language. I can see that they understand each other. I don't understand what they are saying but I can tell that they understand – and I grasp at my understanding that this is the case.

In dzogchen we attend to two basic aspects of experience: 1) *kadag,* primordial purity, like the open sky, and 2) *lhundrub,* effortlessly arising non-dual experience, the instant spontaneous manifestation of primordial purity.

When we are having a conversation, we're just talking. Neither of us knows what we're going to say. We listen and respond. The content flows out freshly even if we use words we have used before. This particular pattern will never be repeated with this same emotion and quality of connection. If we see that our experience is always fresh, then we see that it is self-arising and self-liberating. It occurs by itself. No one is doing it. I am not doing it. By observing this we see that the concept of self is an unnecessary complication. I am speaking – yes, that is undeniable. Yet to whom does 'I' refer? When we look for the speaker, the seer, the doer, we cannot find any enduring entity. Pattern after pattern arises – yet they establish no thing. They are patterns of illusion like rainbows in the sky or like waves in the ocean. The wave arises and comes up and then it goes down and vanishes. Did it ever truly exist?

The wave arises and vanishes but if I grasp at it as if it were some-thing then my grasping makes it, for me, something solid. The grasper grasps its own idea of what it is grasping. From the very beginning there has never been even one real existent entity. The only thing we ever actually grasp is our concept of the object and there is no real existent grasper. So the grasper is a transient concept, the grasped at object is a transient concept, and the activity of grasping is just another sentence in the narrative of self, in the evolving story through which I think and talk myself into pseudo-existence.

Our essence is empty; it is spacious and open and has never become a thing. It is not a dead space for its nature is ceaselessly generous, offering diverse patternings of light and sound. Within these dynamic patternings, the patterning of selfing arises. These are the patternings of aware participation, self-arising and self-liberating in non-duality with the field of occurrence.

All of this richness is freely available and yet because the egoic sense of self is so limited and limiting it attends to the few aspects of the whole which seem relevant to it and ignores the rest. The ego fragment of the unfragmented whole makes collages of pseudo-entities from the items it selects.

This is the process of composition which is the fourth of the five skandhas. We build up pictures which we take to stand for real entities. This is an activity; this is a verb. All that is composed and seems to exist as something is in fact activity. Nouns are redundant – they are the delusions that hide the actual ungraspable dynamism of the display. Moment by moment there is appearance, appearance arising with other equally empty and unborn appearances. There are no independent entities. The naming of appearances as if they were real enduring entities is a delusional activity. It is the second level or aspect of ignorance in action. All appearance is self-arising and self-vanishing whatever our egoic narratives might say. We name and attribute fixed qualities and value to 'what' we name. Yet we are only naming concepts without referents.

Everything is connectivity and this connectivity is creative. When you grasp, you make it solid and fixed, and this prevents easy enjoyment of the process. In the actual process there is no product and so it is light and easy and free of judgement.

Solidification turns free play into a game focused on winning and losing. When we relax into our playful spontaneity we are free to experience everything as the interplay of unborn appearances.

Question: In dzogchen, are we trying to break free of the first level of ignorance, where an emergent phenomenon is made into something?

Well, we are not trying to break free. We simply relax. What binds us is not solid or real. We do the Guru Yoga of the White A. The A symbolises emptiness, the great mother, the sky, the ocean. The rainbow light around the A indicates the potential of emptiness arising as the energetic display of the five elements and so on. We make the sound of A. Everything arises from A. In the Sanskrit alphabet, as in the Tibetan, all the consonants have A as their inherent vowel. It is the sound from which all the formulations of language arise and dissolve. When we make this sound of A we gather all the differentiation in the world that arises with language and we bring it back to its basis, which is A. This is the ceaseless pulsation: simplicity to complexity, complexity to simplicity. The mind itself is like the mother and now all the children, our thoughts, feelings and experiences, go back into the mother, which they have never actually left.

We make the sound of A three times and as the last sound finishes and vanishes into silence, we relax. Then whatever is arising is accepted as it is. Instead of seeing thoughts and feelings as naughty children that have to be controlled, we allow them to play because they are in the safe garden of the mother. They are in space as the movement of space. This is non-dual openness free of the judgement of good or bad, right or wrong. Polarities are always very dangerous: friend or enemy, beautiful or ugly, rich or poor... They are the slippery slope leading us back to the ego.

Question: How can this 'allowing' happen without grasping?

Grasping is reassuring for the ego, both are forms of activity which generate disconnectedness from the openness of the world. For example, if I hide my face with my hands and say, *"Ha ha. I'm safe in here, you can't see me."* Then you might think that I have gone a little crazy because you can see me even though I can't see you. You are in the more powerful position but I do not see that. The ego is a liar, a deceiver, a cheat. I want to win and I'm willing to tell myself that I have won even when I have not. With such a positioning I am incapable of allowing whatever comes to come. I want control. Therefore, the first task is to unmask the ego and see that this phoney pretender is offering an unreliable identity. 'I', as the marker for open empty awareness, has no need of the mask of identity.

If you can stop grasping at the factors with which your identity is constituted then you will see that they are self-liberating. If you don't catch them they will not be able to catch you. To 'allow' them, to let them come and go without interference, is to aid your own insight into both your own intrinsic freedom from lack and excess, and their inability to actually add or detract.

When you grasp at something, you are hiding inside your concept of self and this is comforting, like pulling the blanket over your head. Life is still there, it's just that you've cut yourself off. However in Guru Yoga, although it can feel a little bit scary, we relax. We take the blanket off and we open to how life is occurring. Thoughts come, thoughts go. There is actually nothing to cling to.

In Britain when people come to a pain clinic with a chronic back pain the surgeon sometimes says, *"We can't operate because it's too dangerous; you could be paralysed."* The person then asks, *"So do I have to live with the pain?"* Nowadays they are told, *"Yes, you have to live with the pain, so you should get to know your pain."*

The pain clinics have started to teach basic meditation, so that the person learns to sit with the pain and what they see is that sometimes it's hot, sometimes it's sharp, sometimes it's sawing... They see that they have many different kinds of pain. It's never just one thing.

So when the mind says, *"I hate this pain"*, what is being referred to? The referent is a mental construct. The phenomenon of pain is always changing and many patients find this insight very helpful because now they can be with each moment because it's just this. With this, even if you contract away from the pain, you will relax after the surge. But if you have already tensed up on the basis of predictive concepts – *"I can't bear it, it's terrible"* – then you're making it much worse for yourself. You have become very solid, so the pain is hitting you hard. Whereas if you just say, *"Ooooh! aaahhhh!"* then it's like a wave; it's like a pulse. If you open to whatever comes and let it come and go, then you start to realise that all good things are impermanent and all bad things are impermanent. With this we relax from grasping onto something we deem to be good or bad.

The mind is like the sky. The sky is clear, and so it shows in each moment, this pattern... this pattern... this pattern. Our awareness is inseparable from this ceaseless patterning, the patternings of potential moving in the field of revelation.

If we see this then we can give ourselves to life as it comes, whether it's doing exams if you're studying, or doing your income tax return if you're employed. There are many things we don't necessarily want to do. However, we have a choice. If we sit in the ego we will become reactive, whereas if we stay connected with the world we simply do what we have to do without conceptualising or judging what is occurring. Then the free flow of non-dual display allows our life to proceed without grasping and we start to trust relaxation rather than tensing.

Question: Where does apprehension and comprehension fit into eight consciousnesses?

The sixth consciousness, mental consciousness, processes what is coming through the individual consciousnesses of the five senses. The seventh consciousness then flavours this with the five root afflictions – mental dullness, aversion and so on. This brings an emotional quality to what we're seeing.

The eighth consciousness is like a store of associations and reified patterns. We're never quite sure what is going to be evoked from the potential of what is latent in this ground consciousness. Sometimes we have dreams or daydreams, or some funny thought arises in our mind and we wonder, *"Why am I thinking this? Where did this come from?"* Because the mind itself, in being open like the sky, is ceaselessly welcoming everything moment by moment – happy/ sad, good/ bad – all kind of associations can suddenly be mobilised. As long as there is duality, our activity leaves a subtle trace just as a snail crawling across a rock leaves a little track. We carry these traces within us. Someone might grow up and become a generous person yet when they were a child, they had a big brother or big sister who was always teasing them or stealing their sweets. From these events the person carries a certain vulnerability which manifests when they feel that people are being unfair and so they react strongly even if the provocation was mild. For someone else that intense reaction would not be there. Thus in this life an echo of how it was twenty years ago can be very impactful.

Moreover, from previous lives we have our karmic echoes. The eighth consciousness is the site of many different kinds of echoes. And these echoes, empty as they are, can cause much suffering if they are mistaken for real entities. This is the basis for racism, sexism, ultra-nationalism and all the extreme positions which take prejudice to be a path to truth. Inequality, conflict war and exploitation are all grounded in the delusion that real entities with real fixed qualities exist.

Question: Do apprehension and comprehension both arise from the eighth level of consciousness? Can we pinpoint one level of consciousness for them both?

Each of the eight consciousnesses functions through some degree of apprehension and comprehension. For example, a sound is apprehended as an impact on the organ of hearing – something has occurred. The auditory consciousness is activated by that apprehension and generates a basic comprehension such as *'a dog is barking'*. This is fed into mental consciousness which seeks to refine its apprehension of what has occurred – *"Ah, it is the neighbour's dog."* With this comes a comprehension that the dog has a habit of barking at the next-door neighbour's cat. This is apprehended by the seventh consciousness which feeds in one or more of the five poisons which, for example, might give rise to the apprehension that *"It is that horrible cat again disturbing that sweet dog."* With this comes the comprehension that, *"It's time I spoke with the neighbours about their cat."* This intention, which is clearly in the form of the three wheels, gives a further emphasis to the belief in duality which is the organising principle of apprehension and comprehension in all eight consciousnesses.

With regard to all these progressions it is vital to remember that the concept of the eight consciousness is a Mahayana development of the six consciousnesses highlighted in the Theravada tradition as the five sense consciousnesses with mental consciousness as their organiser. Moreover in the Theravada and basic Mahayana views, consciousness is the fifth of the five *skandha* heaps and the third of the twelve nidana links. The first link is ignorance, the second is associations. In this schema ignorance means ignorance of the three marks of conditional existence: impermanence, suffering and the absence of inherent existence. With this view the basic cause of suffering is seen as being ignorance of dependent origination and the consequent arising of clinging and craving. This is a different approach from that of the levels of ignorance set out in the tantric and dzogchen texts.

In general how an event is apprehended will involve the interaction of karmic and cultural factors. For example in some cultures noisy eating is taken to be a sign of enjoyment, and hence a compliment to the cook, while in other cultures it is taken to be a sign of rudeness and an insult to the cook and the other diners. When people are acting on the basis of cultural assumptions their reactions seem to them to be correct, for they have no insight into the conventional nature of their beliefs. So instead of having an open field of diversity where there are many different ways of behaving, each family is establishing an oppositional structure indicating what, for them, is right and what is wrong. Due to this our minds become very cloudy because now we think we've got the truth, that we've apprehended the truth. So, if someone hears you slurping your soup, they may now comprehend that you are a very badly educated person. They are fitting what you are doing into their frame of reference which tells them 'the truth'. This is very different from thinking that this is a big world in which different people do different things in different ways.

Ego identity and intolerance go together. That's why in our practice of tantra we visualise ourselves as Arya Tara or as Chenrezi, and this divine form is revealed to be our true identity. We step free of our particular cultural formation with all its rights and wrongs and judgments; we abide in our illusory identity which allows us to be open hearted. May all beings be happy! May the silent soup-eaters be happy! May the noisy soup-eaters be happy!

Namkhai Norbu often advised us not to enter into judgment. Coming to a conclusion about occurrences is very dangerous because occurrences keep moving and changing. The farmer might look at their fields and think that they can expect a wonderful harvest. But then comes an early hailstorm and the whole field is flattened. At any moment unpredicted events emerge.

Question: Where do apprehension and comprehension fit in the four levels of ignorance?

Apprehension occurs in the first level, with the idea that there is something autonomous here. At this point subject and object have not manifested, there's simply a focus on this 'something'. The idea of grasping is an idea and the idea of something to grasp is an idea. This is an unborn illusion yet the delusion that the grasper and the graspable have real existence is starting to be present as our basic assumption. With this there is thickening and opacity, a density which prepares the way into the second level of ignorance which is the separating subject and object. With this there is comprehension because now I have an enduring reference point which is me. I am becoming conscious of myself and of others. This I is actually clear and without its own content yet in unawareness of its open basis it identifies with what it takes to be 'myself'. As 'I' faces the other items in the field, feelings of liking and not liking arise. With this as our guide we comprehend that this is good and that is bad. There is increasing comprehension of how it is to be a self and how this self relates to every other appearance.

This duality manifests as the third level of ignorance which identifies different types of appearance and experience and names them. This in turn reinforces the sense that the names refer to enduring entities. This enables another spiral of apprehension and comprehension.

The subject's encounter with myriad diverse others provides the basis for karmic accumulation. Fully committed to a dualistic view, the subject develops intentions towards an object and these direct its actions. This movement unites apprehension and comprehension. One is doing something to or for someone and reviewing the outcome. This consolidates the karmic impact of the action even when, as in most cases, there is no understanding of the process and consequences of karma. Very often we don't know why we take the world to be the way we think it is, or why we like some things and don't like some other things. Some people are very interested in wild flowers, others not. Some people are interested in birds, others not. For some reason this pattern on the object side finds or doesn't find a corresponding pattern on the subject side.

The reason proposed in dharma is that of karma, the ripening of the consequences of actions performed in earlier lives we no longer remember. Our karma is not something stored inside our body; it is not something which belongs to us. Rather it is a key factor influencing how we are with other – it is the flavour of duality that we experience in this life. Our karma is our luck: it's our parents; whether we have a big family or a small family; whether we're wealthy or poor; what kind of school we went to; whether there was war or peace as we were growing up... All of this is our karma. This influences whether we are trustful or mistrustful and that affects the kind of choices we make. The expectations in a culture about what a girl is allowed to do and what a boy is allowed to do is also an aspect of karma. Karma arises from our belief in duality and it manifests as the kind of world that we encounter. Our thoughts feelings and sensations arise in relation to the kind of events that occur for us. We impact the world and the world impacts us.

Question: Do 'making it something' and 'grasping it as something' happen simultaneously?

Yes, these happen simultaneously. As soon as we see that there is something there, then we apprehend it, we take hold of it. If you say, *"James, I want you to catch me some air"*, I will do my best but it's quite difficult. But if you had said, *"James, give me the pen"*, then it's easy, *"Here's the pen."* So you can apprehend something, to apprehend means to take hold of, so I can take hold of the pen but I can't take hold of the air and I can't take hold of space and I can't take hold of the ocean.

What you do with the ocean is to open to it. You open to the sunset, you open to the snow on the Himalaya, you open to the sky. And the openness of the object and the openness of the subject arise together and this is the basis of meditation. But as soon as you come into grasping at things, then the world becomes small. For example, I have a pen. How lucky I am to have a pen. But the pen has my hand, so who is winning? My hand is the prisoner of the pen. *"Would you like to drink your tea, James?"* Yes, but I can't take hold of the cup because I have a pen in my hand. It is important to see that when I hold the pen there is situational advantage in that I can write, but there is also situational limitation. Precision in the formation of intention is empowering because it allows me to do something but it's also cutting me off from doing other things. The exit from this constraint is to maintain the Three Wheels of subject, object and their connection within non-duality. Merge your mind with the great mother and enjoy all your unborn children.

If you wish to find your non-duality with the all-inclusive dharmakaya it is vital to release yourself from reification and open to this ongoing ungraspable revelation. Every appearance is movement, and shapes are always changing, therefore don't make permanent conclusions about anyone, and don't put them in a box. Situational definition and existential definition are very different. In order to be with others we have to make situational definitions. *"Is your tea hot?"* That's a reasonable question. I'm not putting you in a prison with that one. But if I say, *"Oh Jane doesn't like hot tea..."* that's different. Maybe today she doesn't like it so hot and tomorrow she wants it very very hot. It depends.

So the guiding principle is: let's see. Don't imagine. Don't assume. Don't predict. Just see and respond.

When does direct perception, the first moment of seeing something, occur? Does it occur before the moment of 'making it something'?

The first fresh moment is simply seeing, seeing patterns of light. It is not seeing 'something'. The sense of the something-ness of the appearance is an impactful arising, as is our judgement about it. The arising is not the problem. The difficulty lies in our grasping at it as a vehicle of truth. We reify the arising, ignoring how it actually is, and then construct its reality on the basis of what we take it to be. Whereas the effortless vanishing of each experience is the completeness of each moment beyond comparing and contrasting. This will show us that there are no real existents 'out there 'or 'in here'. All that arises is inseparable from emptiness. What we grasp at is in fact the non-duality of appearance and emptiness. Yet through this act of grasping, of apprehension and comprehension, we ignore the emptiness of what is grasped. We grasp at our idea of what is there and not what is actually there – which is emptiness. Moreover our own idea of what is there is also empty, as is our idea of who we are.

Because ideas seem to be graspable whereas the actual is not, the ego focuses on ideas, concepts, memories, plans. The ego grasps the abstract and takes it to be real. Awareness does not grasp but stays relaxed and open whatever occurs. Truly the past is gone. Our ideas about it are mere echoes.

We need to be careful not to set up two categories: the actual and the conceptual as if they were oppositional alternatives. Both are empty although the actual is manifestly empty whereas the conceptual seems to refer to real substances. The conceptual is how the actual seems when it is not opened to as it is.

A concept is only functioning in the moment of its occurrence. Every time a concept arises it constellates a particular pattern for a moment. Why is it a delusion? Because it seems to indicate something that is really there. The occurrence is an illusion, just as on a hot day you see water on the road in front of you although there is actually no water. In the same way, if I say *"Old Delhi"* I seem to be talking about something that exists out there. Yet if I actually go to Old Delhi, I find it is changing moment by moment. Old Delhi is not other than my ungraspable experience of 'it'. Thus as I walk about there, Old Delhi does not agree with my memories of it. Phenomena are always changing. Concepts are like a very bad musician; they're never on the beat; they're either ahead of the beat or behind the beat but they're not on the beat. The beat is self-vanishing.

The only way to truly understand this is to look at your own life, to observe yourself. When you think about friends or family or what's going on in the area where you live, see whether your concepts are illuminating how it actually is or are they illuminating your idea of what it is? Are your concepts telling the story of seemingly substantial entities which you assume are present in the world? Or are they only referring to the patterning of your mental world?

Question: Can we have direct perception of a concept since it is also a phenomenon?

Yes, the concept arises in the mind. It shows and goes. If we stay with that, there is no elaboration and our perception is direct and unmediated. However we often do not observe its passing and so we are taken in by the idea and believe that it is a medium of truth. Concepts are phenomena, very subtle phenomena. The only way we can grasp them is by making them substantial for us through reification, apprehension and comprehension. We ourselves hide the nature of concepts from ourselves. The concept comes and goes. It is just this specific vanishing moment of lived experience yet it appears to have an enduring existence for the ego.

The concept is like false teeth for an old person; they are needed for chewing up the world. But actually the world shows itself all at once. If you're going walking and you come around a corner and see the sunlight on a big tree, what a tree! Your companion asks, *"What kind of tree is that?"* Now, is this naming going to add value or not? Does calling it a tree add value? What you see is light shimmering which you take to be leaves, but that's already concepts. You have this amazing aesthetic experience in front of you but it's not enough for the ego. It is not what the ego is looking for. The ego loves the power of naming and knowing – and indeed prefers this to simply being with the appearance as it is. All kinds of stories can be added onto the reified tree and this hides the actual unreified tree of simple perception. When we are living in the world of conceptualisation it is as if our concepts are taking us closer to the tree whereas they are actually taking us away from the tree-ness of the tree.

We do need to speak in order to connect and offer kindness yet if we do speak we can hold our speaking very lightly. Then when we speak our words are like little gestures, like the movements of a massage that can soften the hard conceptual surface of duality so that we are more available and responsive. This is very different from using language to gain power and knowledge in order to control things.

If you just see the tree and receive the tree like a blessing and your heart opens and your eyes open, *"Oh!"*, you get everything and you get nothing. When you come home somebody may ask, *"What did you see?"* *"Oh, it's amazing."* *"Yes, but what was it like?"* *" I don't know. Just that it's beautiful."* There's nothing much to say. Your heart is full. Someone else might have two hours of story to tell about what they saw, yet their heart might be empty.

Each basic simple self-vanishing concept is not the enemy; the problem is when you start to build a wall with concepts and you lose the freshness of the situation. In dzogchen, the mind itself is said to be naked, fresh, raw. It's naked for it's not covered in concepts. Concepts are part of the display of the mind yet they cannot define it. The mind is fresh and each concept is fresh because it's just this. So don't compare and contrast this transient arising with other concepts or link it to the past or the future. It's raw; it's not cooked. Nothing has been added, no spices, no garam masala, nothing... just this... taste this... If we practise simply staying with the freshness of the moment then we become very relaxed and soft inside.

We have to remember that the term awareness, *rigpa*, doesn't always have the same meaning. It depends on the context. The term *Vijnana* consciousness doesn't always have the same meaning. Avoid solidifying, coming to conclusions and the ego-inflation of being right. We should be collaborating with language as a musical ungraspable presencing. We explore how to move with this music of life rather than chopping it up and solidifying our world and ourselves.

Question: Please suggest the kind of practice that should be done?

In brief, focus on impermanence. It is how everything is so enjoy your playful impermanence within the play of impermanence.

Stay with your senses. The senses are the doorway that dissolves the delusion of inside and outside. If you identify with concepts you will be sealed in a private mental world.

Pray to Padmasambhava and do his Guru Yoga practice. Do the dzogchen Guru Yoga of the White A.

No need for striving. Trust the intrinsic. Relax, release all identifications and fixations. Relax and enjoy the play of the mind manifesting as you!

Teachings based on a Zoom discussion, 21st November 2021.
Substantially extended and revised by James Low in July 2023.

Why emptiness is liberating

"Awakening to the fact of there being nothing frees us from the endless quest for something. Our problem is the seeming 'thing-ness' of the thing, our sense that we exist as some-thing in a world of many different things. The reification which imputes a real and enduring substance to phenomena is a deluding mental process. When this process is not relied on as a means of generating meaning, the actuality of phenomena is seen to be unfolding revelation. This revelation is the flow of experience, concrete and precise, each moment with its own unique specificity yet with no-thingness to grasp on to. Thus the anxious self can cease attempting to take refuge in illusory things and relax into the space of unfolding."

The topic for this evening is emptiness as the basis for liberation. Emptiness is an insight which we find in all the levels and dimensions of Buddhism, in all the different schools. It gets packaged slightly differently, but the basic principle is the same. The term 'emptiness' points to the insight which eliminates the habitual delusion of grasping at the world and finding things to hold on to.

This delusion has two aspects: a tendency to grasp, and the fantasy that there is something that you can grasp hold of. This is the basic structure of dualism or duality. What is it that is grasped? The erroneous assumption of inherent existence. Who is the one who does the grasping? The erroneous belief in a self-entity. Both are empty of substantial reality.

These two deluded beliefs are part and parcel of everyday experience. They are so familiar that we take them for granted yet they are actually constructs arising from our fusing of concepts with appearances. The applied concept seems to fix the transient appearance and impart to it a sense of inherent existence. But when we see that all the aspects involved are transient and insubstantial, then their intrinsic emptiness becomes clear. Insight into emptiness is like a screwdriver; it unscrews the hinge points which keep the edifice of samsara in place. It is also like a lubricant because it allows the fricative movements of subject and object to be less conflicted, less generating of unnecessary energy and so life moves more smoothly.

WE USE NARRATIVES TO CREATE SOMETHING-NESS

The Buddha's early teachings repeatedly draw our attention to the fact that all phenomena are impermanent. Impermanent means they are changing. You can read this in two ways: that there are things which change, or that there is ceaseless change in the endless patterning of experience which our mind conceptualises as the appearance of things. When we take the first reading you get an increased sense of motility and possibility, but there is still the basic assumption that there are entities which exist. What are these entities? They are often referred to as *'dharmas'*, things, phenomena, individual existents.

The Buddha also pointed out that all compounded things are impermanent. Usually we see phenomena as existing as something in themselves. For example, beside me there is a table. On the table there is a cup and a watch and it would appear that they are just there, simply being what they inherently are. We look around the room and see people. When you see somebody's face it seems self-evident that somebody is there. We are able to function in the world on the basis of our confidence that we look out on a world which is pre-formed. We believe that it is there before we encounter it. We feel that we exist apart from the world although we are always in contact with it. The world exists apart from me and I encounter aspects of it as I engage with it. Moreover, I am confident that I can accurately describe my experience of it.

In fact this world, my world, the world of my experience, is inseparable from my narrative about it. The concepts of self and other are the fundamental building blocks of our constructed world. I am defined in and by the stories that I and others tell about me. Through our definitions we call into 'existence' our experience of self and other, and then we elaborate their qualities through commenting on them.

We make commentaries *about* the world. We generate meaning *in* the world through the kind of narrative that we can generate *about* the world. This narrative becomes a kind of thread. We take the entities of the world as if they were loose beads and we string them onto the thread of our narrative and make the necklaces of meaning with which we adorn ourselves. With this we also disguise the fact that we 'exist' as characters within our own narratives.

For example when you see a picture of the Hindu goddess *Kāli* she wears a necklace with fifty skulls. These fifty skulls represent the *āli-kāli,* the vowels and consonants of the Sanskrit alphabet. When these basic building blocks are put together as words you can start to manifest your narrative. You can start to make a story. The sounds of the vowels and consonants have little meaning in themselves but when they are combined in patterns it is as if their combinations carry inherent meaning. They become signs pointing to referents that seem to have inherent existence. Generally, we think that there are trees and because they exist the word 'tree' can be applied to them. In fact, it is the word and concept of 'tree' that gives separate identity to the shape to which we apply the term 'tree'. The something-ness of the tree is not in the object 'out there'; rather it is an experience generated by the concept.

What we think of as reality is based on ideas. Moreover as long as the mind commences its operation on the basis of the seeming given-ness of stuff, what we have is the elaboration of *interpretations* of stuff. Our commentaries both arise from and reinforce our belief that we live in a world of existents, of inherently existing entities about which we have our own opinions. Because we are very good at beguiling ourselves with our own creativity refracted through reification there is always more to say. We ourselves and our worlds are the interplay of the identifications and evaluations arising in the infinite conversation of *samsara*. Subject and object provoke and inspire each other into endless mutation. This is the flow of signifiers and signifieds dancing and creating the patterns we believe in and by which we live our lives. This points to the second meaning of the Buddha's statement that I referred to earlier, *"All phenomena are impermanent."* There is only change. The seeming stability of phenomena is an illusion generated by our conceptual interpretation.

You can go to therapy for five years, ten years, fifteen years, twenty years but you will never get to the bottom of yourself, because the self is an unfolding process which is fed by the very action of talking about it. We our world is also fed by and elaborated through the ways in which we think and talk about it. Once there is something, there is something about which something can be said.

With dharma we have learned that everything is impermanent and compounded. We also have our own sense that we were once small children; we went to school, we went through lots of changes and have developed all sorts of personality characteristics, memories, tendencies and so on. Yet although we know all of this about ourselves, there still seems to be a core sense that we exist as an unchanging self-entity, *'I am myself.'*

This belief is strong and powerful. All the evidence of change, the fact that we have moods, we have feelings, we have hopes and fears which arise in interaction with the world, indicates clearly that there is there is no isolating sealant around us. We may feel that we are an individual, that we are a separate monad entire unto ourselves, and yet our physical presence is in ceaseless communication with our environment. We look out and light comes into our eyes; we hear, we speak, we drink, we piss – this interaction is ongoing. The interplay of our hopes and fears and all the feelings that we have, arise in relationship, and yet, here I am as me. You are you. The 'someone-ness' that I experience in you and in myself is not foundational. It is not real or enduring as a fixed entity. All the components of myself are in flux, fluctuating in the forcefield of dependant origination. The 'I', the personal self that I have taken to be my root, my core, is in fact a flow of becoming whose actual root cannot be found. It is empty of substantial existence and yet here we are – undeniably present, but not as we think we are.

Ignoring the actual openness of our ground we cling to identities formed through a variety of narratives. Narratives link concepts together in patterns which are wrongly taken to indicate the existence of entities. Some narratives are given to us in our childhood, through our parents and through going to school. We learned how to elaborate particular kinds of interpretation. We learn not only to make commentaries on direct experience, but that we can make commentaries on indirect experience, and then further commentaries on indirect experience of indirect experience of indirect experience. At school you might have had to write an essay on a classic play like *King Lear.* To do that you read some commentaries on *King Lear.* Then you looked up a critique of these commentaries on *King Lear.* Building castles in the air. And yet the teacher reads it and tells you, *"Oh, that's good! I think you are really starting to understand what's going on here."* The more ideas you have, the more others think that you are able to make sense of what is going on.

WORDS CAN NEVER PUT A HANDLE ON ACTUAL PHENOMENA

Buddhism, however, goes in the other direction indicating that the less you elaborate ideas and the less you rely on them the more you are likely to directly see what is going on. The function of meditation is to release our addiction to ideas as being the vehicle of truth. Conceptual elaboration is a very powerful force. It's the way in which one thing leads to another in an endless chain of signifiers confirming the real existence of what is occurring. Because of the very nature of language there is always more to say. Each word has little meaning in itself. Meanings unfold within the semiotic web of interaction and linking. There is no single perfect word that can voice the truth and end all commentary.

Yet in our yearning for simplicity we believe that the signifier and the signified exist in a very simple correlation. If there is a cup, the cup is something which is signified through the use of the idea of 'cup'. I say *"It's a cup"*, and when you look at it you say, *"Yes, James knows what a cup is."* On the basis of your own belief in the true existence of the cup you believe that I am able to accurately identify what I am holding in his hand. This is not a frog or a dog, it's a cup. That makes sense. This is how we tend to proceed.

But, of course, someone else might say, *"Well, it's not actually a cup; it's a mug."* So now we can get into some fine distinctions for it is not just a mug but it is a particular kind of mug. Moreover, should you so wish, you could use it as a weapon. You could bang someone very hard on the head with it. You could break the edge of it and gouge out their eyes. You could use it to bail water out of a boat. There are many, many functions which are potential in the object yet are hidden from us by our desire to know precisely and definitively what it is. So, in order to give myself a sense that I know what is what, I have to exclude many aspects of the potential of the object. I make the object something for me and so the actual object, which is not something as such, slips away unnoticed,

We tend to believe that we know who other people are yet everybody is multiple, eluding all fixed entities. We have many aspects to our personality, we have many moods, we have diverse potential. These aspects are not controlled by us for they are co-emergent with circumstances. We are participating in a vast shimmering of participation. We only have access to certain aspects of other people and yet we feel we know who they are. It is self-confirming to be able to say, *"Oh, I know what they are like."* This desire to apprehend appearances as objects which we take to be existing in and of themselves - as a 'mug', as a person, as a man, a woman, whatever – maintains our ego sense of competence and confidence. We have worked hard to enable ourselves to move through the world applying the right identificatory categories so that we gain some purchase on what is going on. Just as this mug in my hand has a handle that lets me hold it easily, so all the objects in the world seem to have a handle. We grasp them with a conceptual handle that we ourselves have fixed on to them.

Dzogchen texts refer to the nakedness of the mind. Naked means no clothing, no handles. The mind is compared to a round ball. A ball has no edges or corners, no top, no bottom. There is nothing to grasp and hold onto, and yet in our everyday existence our ease of being in the world with others is entirely facilitated by our capacity to find the handle and then use it correctly.

This is a mental activity, one which is self-deceiving because it only works if you imagine that the handle that you grasp belongs to the object. This means that my power as an ego-self requires me to live in a dead world of fixed objects. It is the fixed reliable knowability of the object that allows me to feel safe in my dependence on it. This sometimes comforting delusion is inherently unstable since, as the Buddha pointed out, all things are impermanent, dynamic and ungraspable.

The pre-Socratic philosopher Heraclitus is famous for saying, *"You can never step in the same river twice"*. A very simple thing to say, but it is profound. If you regularly go to the River Thames for a swim, you might say, *"Every day I swim in the River Thames."* However every day when you plunge into the Thames, you are swimming in different water. Different water, but the same name. The phenomenal actuality of what you are encountering is fresh and new, but you reassure yourself about what you are doing by adhering to the name, 'I am swimming in the river Thames'. The stability is not in the water. The stability lies in your capacity to convince yourself that your concepts are giving you an accurate account of something being there. The river, the ceaseless flow of water, is wrongly taken to be a stable entity. This is delusion.

EMPTINESS: ABSENCE OF INHERENT SELF-NATURE

The names we use to define appearances do not reach the actual appearances. They do reach our concepts, our imaginings, and this co-mingling of name and imagining generates an opacity, an impenetrability which we take to be the substance of the thing. In fact the actual appearance has no thing-ness. It is pure or mere appearance, an appearance whose ground and essence and manifesting is empty of existence. All appearances are, in themselves, unborn. This is intrinsic, simply how it is. Yet it is hidden from us by our own relentless determination to trust our concepts and our narratives as the vehicle for truth.

If we simply stay open and present before what we take to be a flower and desist from adorning it with our concepts we will find that all our projected words and identifications slip away. There is an immediate actuality, but what is it? It is here, it is this. It is so clear. Yet we cannot see what it is. It is not a what, not a thing. It is luminous appearance empty of self-substance. As such, in not being anything in particular, we find ourselves present with an ever-revealing potential. This emptiness or absence of defining substance is the ungraspable gift of all appearances. It is due to this that any object or any person can sustain multiple usages, multiple definitions, multiple identities, without ever being reduced to any one of them as its defining truth. The essence of all appearance is emptiness and with the absence of definitive individual essences there is the space of possibility within which the creative potential of the mind moves in its now playful vehicle of language.

When we take ourselves to be 'real' and existent, we also take the world to be 'real' and existent. The duality of self and other is the basic polarity that supports the delusion of individual identity. When we see that this delusion is merely an illusion that has been thickened by belief, we start to awaken to the emptiness of the categories of 'self' and 'other'. They have no true referent and are merely conventional terms sucked into the limiting project of maintaining our erroneous perception of real entities.

Despite ceaselessly creating the many aspects of the world which we encounter we do not recognise what we are up to. It is only when we release ourselves from the dualistic confusion of unawareness that we can start to be aware of our own open empty ground and start to taste our own intrinsic freedom.

As long as this is not awakened to we tend to deny our part in the moment by moment emergence of our world. With this we place ourselves at the margin as small people who are at the mercy of the many factors of the big world. *'There is always stuff out there and I don't quite know what it is. And I don't quite know who I am. However there are some big people somewhere who know what's what and so I should rely on them...'*

This is the fear of the ego, a fear that the ego gives to itself by frightening itself through imagining that the world exists as something knowable and that we lack the knowledge we need to function well. We imagine that the wise are able to avail themselves of knowledge produced through conceptualisation. We seek to copy them in this through relying on our dualistic consciousness, our capacity to know things by apprehending their true shapes through our reliance on concepts about them. Consciousness knows about shapes; it deals with knowledge of apprehendables. It consolidates knowledge that can be apprehended through the five sense consciousnesses. Mental consciousness formulates data in a way that gives you a handle on them. What you are grasping at is your own projected fantasy. There is actually nothing substantial there but this nothing is very rich. It is the glimmering, shimmering radiance of the mind which is never exhausted. It has infinite potential yet this is not seen directly. Instead we grasp at our own projected shadows and take them to be substantial and real. When you are committed to the duality of subject and object as being the truth of experience, the unreal unborn unestablished openness of radiant presence is not opened to as it is but is experienced as overwhelming and destabilising.

Concepts themselves are not inherently harmful or limiting. It is our sense of ourselves as a self, as an ego different from all other egos, that distorts concepts. Instead of being used as tools for thinking, tools that support conventional clarity, concepts are recruited to support the delusion that we exist as individuals independent of our environment. For the ego-self, freedom from reliance on concepts would generate uncertainty and anxiety. Our adult concepts support us in attending to the many tasks that are required in order to maintain our habitual sense of identity. Aligning with what we take to be necessary can easily keep us from taking responsibility for how we live our lives. Necessity becomes the organising principle which hides from us our basic openness, the uncompromised sphere of our creative potential.

The world is actually open. Each moment is fresh. When we release ourselves from our preoccupations, we find that rather than being a thinker solving problems we are in fact an open presence. We are open because we have no fixed content. We are not a construct. We are not reliant on or produced by the transient content of our mind. Our mind itself is a simple unreified awareness. It is this openness which illuminates the open freshness of the world. Everything that occurs is experience.

In his earliest teachings the Buddha pointed out that there is an absence of inherent existence in people. People are composites of the five heaps or skandhas: form, feeling, sensation, composition and consciousness. He is pointing to the self as a fabrication, as an illusion generated by the functioning together of these five factors. Our mistaken belief that this composite is in fact a single entity with inherent existence is a veil of delusion which comforts and confirms the illusory self whilst hiding the door to liberating awareness. In his *mahayana* analysis of these factors, Buddha Sakyamuni points out that all constituent factors and all phenomena also have an absence of inherent existence. The more you look into any entity and try to find what is its core essence, the more you find that there is nothing underlying appearance. Everything rests on nothing, inseparable from nothing, and is without the least separate defining unique individual essence.

INTERDEPENDENCE

All seemingly separate entities arise in dependent co-origination, in interdependence. Each form is inseparable from the dynamic relationships from which it emerges, and which sustain it and which will bring about its vanishing. For example, who we are has been influenced by our parents, by the mood and culture of the times of our early youth, by our gender, our state of health and so on. We emerge moment by moment as the patterning of myriad constitutive factors, some seemingly outside us and some seemingly inside us. The movement of the trajectory of patterning of our transient becoming is propelled by the alternating pulsation of proactive and reactive mobilisations.

Our sense that we are simply 'ourselves' is naive yet useful since it allows us to avoid the dynamic complexity within which we appear as momentary expressions of the ever-shifting patterning of that complexity. We are an inalienable part of the field of emergence. Our sense of apartness, of singularity as this specific isolate, is a delusion arising from unawareness of the indestructible integrity of the whole.

This whole is not a bland homogenisation. It is rich in diversity. Each and every appearance is an appearance of the whole and shares the empty essence of the whole. Due to this there are no truly separate phenomenon each with their own self-guaranteeing essence. Each appearance is within the field of appearance as an aspect of it. Each 'thing' that we are accustomed to seeing as an existent, as an entity, is in fact inseparable from the seeming otherness which surrounds it.

For example, this mug in my hands appears to be self-existing as something which is here just by itself. Yet even the mug is interactive. It appears to be self-existing if you ignore the fact that I am holding it. If I remove my hands from it, we will have a mess on the floor. So, what will I do with the mug? I better put it somewhere. Every something is somewhere. You can't take the somewhere out of something. Each 'this' is co-emergent with 'that' which is all around it. When we start perceiving self- existing entities, the essence that we perceive in the entity is an essence projected by our mind. It is our mind which attempts to stabilise that which is inherently unstable.

SAMSARA

The endless attempt to stabilise the unstable fuels the continuity of the illusion of *samsara*. The effort to freeze the world, to turn the unpredictable interactive flow of experience into something fixed and reliable, is wasted effort. The only glue we have with which to effect the stabilising is our own deluding belief that the world is composed of inherently existing entities. Dissatisfaction is part of our experience because although we are good at deluding ourselves as to the reliable existence of phenomena, their actual instability keeps challenging our assumptions. Our commentary, which serves to construct the world as we take it to be, binds us to the endless task of creating the uncreated. We enter into judgement; we imagine the world to be other than it is and so frustration arises as we try to make events conform to our ideas. If you decide that that form is better than this form and work to get from this form to that form, you are likely to find that there is something wrong with that form too. Life goes on in this way until you come to your death. This is what *samsara* is, the endless, endless adjustments of forms.

For example, look at what has happened in England to our education system in the last thirty years, or to our universities or to the National Health Service. There has been endless tinkering, endless changing. All this effort yet nothing definitive has been established. Each person has their own idea and is not comfortable when the arena they inhabit does not conform to their idea. *"My way is best; things have to change."* Well, the river is flowing. You don't actually have to push the river since it will change anyway. The reason people want change is because they have convinced themselves that there is stability and that they are stuck with something they do not like. But the stability exists only in their own mind. However, instead of looking at their own mind and thinking, *"I could just change my thoughts about this since the object is going to change anyway"*, they say, *"I'll change the object. Then my mind will feel some relief because I don't like how the object is at the moment."* Due to this, rest, peace and simple ease is displaced into the future and kept out of reach.

When we look at our own mind in meditation, we see thoughts, feelings, sensations and experiences. They arise and then vanish – this, then this, then this... They offer nothing to grasp hold of for they are appearance free of inherent existence. They are there for a moment; they each have an impact by which the current topology of our experience reshapes itself. To see this directly is to see that the constituents of our identity have no real existence. Nothing which occurs for you, whether in the world or in your mind has inherent existence. There is neither fixed reality nor nothing at all. Whatever occurs is occurrence inseparable from emptiness. It is not the occurrence of something but the occurrence of nothing. Each 'it' is how nothing appears without itself appearing. It is our own mistaken belief in the true existence of appearances that persecutes us, not the arisings themselves, for they are like appearances in a dream.

If bad thoughts come, you might get terrified and retreat from them and feel that you need to change them and push them away. Yet, they will go by themselves. You might have good thoughts, you might want to hang onto them and build on them and develop them, yet they vanish by themselves. All mental phenomena are impermanent. All outer phenomena are impermanent. The illusion of permanence is generated by the reliance on abstractions, on concepts which form a second order discourse, a kind of miasma. Immersed in this fog it appears that when we are thinking about something, we are actually in touch with the thing itself and thereby are gaining true knowledge of the world.

However thoughts grasp thoughts and that is all they grasp. Furthermore, thoughts are always dissolving. Although thoughts are innately, intrinsically, empty they generate the illusion of reliable existents. They arise as illusion and vanish as illusion and yet we are deluded by these illusions into imagining the real. This is similar to being in the cinema. You are taken into a narrative that seems to be true and to be going somewhere. It endures for a short period of time and then it's gone. What was that all about? We believed in the movie, we got taken in by the characters and some meaning, some value, seemed to be there. Yet it was an illusion. You might tell someone, *"It was quite a good movie, you should go and see it."* What would they get? Well, they get what you got: sand pouring through their fingers.

On a nice hot day sitting on a beach somewhere in the Mediterranean picking up soft warm sand and letting it dribble through your fingers would be quite pleasant. But if you realise that the whole of your life is dribbling through your fingers, that's another matter. There is nothing to hold on to so what is it all about? What is it all for? It is the absence of inherent meaning that allows the creativity of meaning making. We are not fixed entities in a fixed world. Each moment unfolds with our participation. The potential of the world meets our potential and this gives rise to the patterning of this moment. Meaning is a construct. It is constructed by mental activity devoid of inherent existence. It is the play of emptiness.

But why on earth would I be interested in a buddhist view that says everything is devoid of the meaning that I think it has? What am I left with if all fixed meanings dissolve? Well, these fixed meanings have never actually existed. The absence of fixed inherent meanings feels like a loss to the ego-self which seeks to cling on to something, anything. Yet this ego-self is itself ceaselessly dissolving. Meaning is emergent. Moment by moment 'self' and 'other' emerge as specific interactive patterns which then dissolve giving space for the next moment of emerging. If the objects of the world were intrinsically meaningful, we would be merely the audience observing the drama. It is because the appearances of the world exist as potential that they can endlessly display new meanings. Co-emergent experience is the ceaseless display of the potential of our unborn mind.

Our mind is not a fixed thing. Thoughts, feeling and sensations are not things. The appearances of the world are not fixed things. Devoid of fixed existence, the interplay of myriad empty patterns is our ceaseless display. This is intrinsically satisfying and integral. Being complete, it requires no added-on concepts to complete it. Its intrinsic meaning illuminates the meaninglessness of trying to make meaning.

EMPTY YET FULL OF RICH POTENTIAL

The *dzogchen* tradition points out that all phenomena have the same ground, the open empty availability within which all possible forms arise. If you awaken to the empty ground then everything which arises is like a rainbow. We have all seen a rainbow in the sky and yet nobody has managed to catch a rainbow or touch it or put it in their pocket. We experience a rainbow; in fact we're often touched and moved by seeing a rainbow. This magical ungraspable appearance offers us a taste of the actuality of all appearance. The truth of our life is the fullness, the richness, of momentary experience which never becomes an appropriate-able entity. What we appropriate is the sloughed-off skin of the moment. Just as a snake sloughs off its dead skin, when we grasp something life itself has slithered away. Life is fresh and always changing. To devote the years of our lives to the accumulation of snake skins is a good way to become bored and sad and uncertain about ourselves.

In order to turn towards the ever-fresh we need to examine who is the one who appropriates.

"I am. In order for me to be me – to continue being the one whom I know I am – certain factors around me have to remain the same because if there is too much change I don't like it. I become anxious. I don't know what's going to happen." This is the voice of the ego, of our belief that we have and are an enduring personal identity. It feels true yet it is an illusion which continues because it is believed in rather than examined.

Our ego arises from our unawareness of the fecund space we manifest in, from and as. Having lost integrity with our own ground we are off balance, and habituated to using what we take to be object formations to prop ourselves up. The objects we are attached to, our possessions, music, friends and so on, become like a series of flying buttresses that are holding up the shaky edifice of our notion of who we are. We don't want to fall apart.

But who would fall apart? When you observe yourself in the morning you have a sense of the content of your experience, certain sensations in the body, certain feeling tones, certain thoughts. This is the current inventory of yourself. By the time you get to the afternoon, and you take the inventory once again, the sensations are different, the feelings are different, the thoughts are different. Your morning self has vanished. Your afternoon self has arrived. Effectively, your morning self has fallen apart. And it wasn't so painful! In fact we are not a fixed entity nor even a ceaseless flow of fixed identities. Rather we manifest as part of the ceaseless unfolding of the basic space of presence. Dissolving and arising are inseparable as the display of the unborn.

Emptiness is not a hellish void, it's not oblivion, a chasm of despair and existential lostness. Emptiness is the plenum void, the full void which ceaselessly shows its rich potential. This potential shows itself as ungraspable appearance. It is neither something that really exists nor nothing at all. It is the middle way free of all extremes and polarities.

In the buddhist traditions of the higher *tantras* and *dzogchen*, this open potential when awakened to, is referred to as the *dharmakaya*, the aspect of the mind which is empty and full at the same time. It's empty because you will never find it as a substance or an entity. And yet it's always full of the unfolding of experience, which is its own shining clarity. That clarity, that bright luminosity, is called the *sambhogakaya* which means the aspect of enjoyment. Enjoyment points to the vitality of all the flavours of experience of the richness of the world, the immediacy of presence. Within this non- dual presence there is the apparitional movement called the *nirmanakaya*. Our apparitional forms arise with our environment. Our potential of posture, gesture and expression is unlimited and is called forth in our non-dual presence. Thus our body, voice and mind are not properties we have, rather they are the illusory constituents of ungraspable participation in the ungraspable luminosity of the ground. This is the lightness of being, a being which is pure presence free of reification. When we relax out of our anxious habit of holding on to our egoic false identity, we find ourselves as part of the undivided whole.

Self and other are not mutually exclusive entities but co-participants in the patterning of the field of luminosity. When it is clear to us that every arising has the same source, the open empty ground, then the burden of reification and selectivity falls from our shoulders. No longer having to organise what we experience into hierarchies of value, we are available to receive the vibrant immediacy of each occurrence. Our connectivity is intrinsic and not based on selective correspondence. All is the radiance of the source – including the thoughts which deny this. We are grounded in the ground and so have no need to set one thought against another. All are welcomed with all pervading kindness.

The stage on which our life is unfolding is referred to as the *dharmadhatu*, the space of all *dharmas*, of all phenomena, of all experience. It is both an infinite source and an infinite hospitality. It is called the source because there is no other base or ground for appearances. It is also the site of hospitality in that it is spacious enough for every appearance to get exactly the right room to be as it is.

NON-DUALITY OF THE MIRROR

The traditional example often used to show the non-duality of space and appearance is that of a mirror and its reflections. The reflections are in the mirror. You can't take a reflection out of a mirror. The reflection is **in** the mirror and it both is and is not the mirror. Without a mirror you wouldn't have reflections. When you look in the mirror, you see reflections; you don't see the mirror. The mirror is the infinite invisible host which generously shows itself in the form of its transient situational content.

We go to the mirror for the reflection and take the image to be the thing itself. Yet without the mirror, you wouldn't have the reflection. When we ignore the mirror and focus solely on the image it is as if image is there by itself. It is the emptiness of the mirror which allows it to show endless reflections. The reflections are in the mirror without touching or marking it.

Similarly, it is the emptiness of the mind which gives rise to ceaseless experience. The emptiness of the mind is the unimpeded expanse of awareness. This clarity is the illumination of both experience and experiencer. Neither aspect of co-emergent experience has inherent existence or enduring identity. They are always fresh and never repeated. They are not representations and do not stray from simple presence. They are manifest illusion – precise, unique, mutually impactful and ungraspable.

In *tantra* ignorance is to be transformed into wisdom so that it ceases to be an obstacle. By containing every occurrence within the mandala of the deity these appearances are transmuted from existent entities into the illusory display of wisdom. This requires great concentration and commitment since the temptation to reify still lingers.

In contrast the view of *dzogchen* points to the clarity of intrinsic wholeness. Everything that occurs is an apparition in the mind and so the view of *dzogchen* indicates that there is no need to try to correct ignorance and the problems that arise from it. Ignorance is an illusion within the mirror of the mind. The source base has never been lost for it gives rise to all of *samsara* and all of *nirvana*. Whatever occurs is always within the infinity of the non-duality of awareness and spaciousness. There isn't a subject on the one side and an object on the other. There isn't an 'inside' on the one side and an 'external arena' on the other.

Although we experience subject and object, inside and outside, these are merely empty concepts in play with empty appearance. They have no power to establish even one atom as a separate entity with inherent existence. Seeing the empty nature of appearances paradoxically makes them more bright and distinct. We discern the variations of shape and colour within the whole. This discernment is enlightening whereas differentiation, the act of distinguishing this entity from that, is a dulling reinforcement of the delusion that separate entities exist in themselves. Seeing the self-arising and self-vanishing of all phenomena – including all the mental phenomena of thoughts, feelings, sensations, memories and plans – shows us that there is no basis for the construction of dense dulling entities. Everything is the play of luminosity, the unborn generosity of the source. To see this is to relax and release oneself from the effort to maintain duality.

The dissolving of the delusion of real entities frees us from appropriation so that our clarity gives rise to appreciation of the aesthetic richness of the variegated display. The one taste of emptiness and the variegated tastes of appearance are inseparable. Form is emptiness: emptiness is form

When we see the diversity of colour, shape, taste and so on arising for our senses, we feel internal responses of enthusiasm and eagerness or shyness and moving away. This rich pulsatory movement is illusory. All of this is happening and yet nothing is happening. This is the great mystery of emptiness.

Our minds develop dualistic categories such as 'only one thing or many different things'. Our mind works by setting up oppositional categories, each of which defines itself in terms of exclusion. If something is hot, it's not cold. If someone is tall, they are not short. But, of course, they are only tall in relation to some people. Someone else who is seven foot tall could arrive and suddenly the tall person starts to look small. Something that is hot to the touch is not hot at all in terms of molten steel.

All of these categorisations are relative and yet our mind structures our experience as if mutual exclusion, 'this' is not 'that', is based on internal essences. Yet it is the very dynamic of exclusion that creates the seemingly separate singularity of 'this'. 'This' is 'this' because it's not 'that'. So, the this- ness of 'this' is inseparable from 'that'. 'This' and 'that' are born together and it is the dynamic of seeming exclusion which allows us to take 'this' to be 'this'. In this way 'this' is linked to 'that', and 'here' is linked to 'there'. The absence of inherent existence in any phenomenon is the relativity of all that is encountered since all the phenomena in the world are mutually arising.

DEALING WITH LIFE'S UNCERTAINTIES

Here we are in this room together. We look around, we see different people. Some people we know a bit, other people we don't know. Bits of history we've had with people arise in our minds, different possibilities of stories... What is all this? This is the creativity of the mind. What is established by it? The potential for patterns generated from the arising and vanishing of appearances. We see someone we haven't seen for a while and we go towards them to say hello. We are assuming that they are knowable. We have condensed our past experiences of 'them' into predictive knowledge that is valid across time. For us they are our interpretation of them. If we meet someone whom we don't remember having met before, we are a little more hesitant because it seems there is no real bridge that allows us immediate access to that person. But if we smile at them and they respond, then some tentative bridge of connectivity develops as we build up a narrative picture together.

Our actual encounters are not between myself and yourself as existents. Rather, the current patterning I take to be me encounters the current patterning I take to be you. We are so skilled at imagining existents that it seems obvious that both you and I exist as separate people. In fact what we are experiencing is the excessive activity of the mind, a congealing of idea and appearance which thickens the appearance so that it can be conceptually seized as an entity. This is self delusion generated by residual excitation. We are rarely relaxed and at ease. We tend to be anxious as our thoughts scan past and future, judging and solidifying the vanished and the not-yet-come. The light of the mind is the lived vibrancy of direct experience. What blocks this is not the hard, self-existing nature of things out there in the world. What blocks our appreciation of this is the gravitational pull of the solidifying orientation of our own conceptualisation.

The ego, our felt sense of self, our sense that we exist, that we know who we are, is not reliable. We are not a fixed thing. We are patterns arising and vanishing. Yet in our egoic belief that we do exist we avoid opening to our intrinsic unborn openness and turn towards enclosure, separating self and other, past and future.

We install concepts as the vehicles of truth but then we suffer because we do not actively think most of our thoughts – they arise for us, suffusing us, taking us over. We are the site of the arising of the results of previous actions. We are our karma, and unless we are able to recognise the fusion as it occurs, we will be swept into reactivity and impulsivity. Being certain that we are someone, we rely on something other to resource us. We are not complete in ourselves. We need something else yet each something is impermanent and leaves us still needy.

It is impossible to hold on to the always-already-vanishing. If we see the vanishing as vanishing we can work with the circumstances of dynamic phenomena. But if we deny the vanishing we are condemned to strive to maintain the continuity of our mistaken idea of the reality of the 'things' on which we rely. This effort is the energy driving samsara since it is the root of karmic accumulation in its linking of deluded dualistic conceptualisation to intention, to enactment, to validating conclusion.

CHOOSING HABITUAL FORMATIONS OVER THE INFINITY OF SPACE

Due to concept-based striving, the relationship that we have with the world is no longer direct. It is refracted through a cloudy crystal which casts an opaque light that appears to reveal substantial forms. This is very different from refraction through a beautiful crystal which increases the potential for experience.

If you feel depressed, hopeless and worried, this mood can permeate any situation. Then, perversely, hope can be upsetting whereas hopelessness can be very reassuring. *"My life is shit. It has always been shit. It will never get better. At least I know who I am. What about you? You look chirpy and cheerful. Ha, you'll be sorry!"* In that way the stasis of fixed belief can wrap itself around us as if it is giving us definitive knowledge. The accumulation of knowledge is, as it were, the internal paralleling of the external accumulation of things. As these linked structures are built up it can appear that we are creating an edifice that will protect us against the vagaries of existence. However when we observe what is actually occurring the attrition of structure is constant. People lose their faith, their jobs, their health. Whatever we have ebbs away. So what will I rely on? What will I take refuge in?

We can take refuge in the Buddha. That's fantastic. Take refuge in the Buddha. We don't know where he lives – nobody has seen him for quite a while – but take refuge in the Buddha. Take refuge in the *dharma*. We've got a library of dharma books here, buy more *dharma* books, take them home, read them, think about them, put them on the shelf, bow to them every day, take refuge in the *dharma. "I – take refuge – in the dharma."* Subject – verb – object. I – am made secure – by what I have, if I possess these *dharma* objects. If I have a shrine, I can clean it every day, offer a lamp every day, fill the bowls every day. This will give me a sense of security based on object constancy. Object constancy is very important for small children who need to know when they are going to be fed, where their toys are and where they are going to sleep for the night. It helps them settle.

However, for us as adults this kind of security is unreliable since we are the ones who are making it happen. Rather than reassuring myself by stabilising the patterns of my life, perhaps

I can find who it is who is doing what I am doing. What is the true source of this activity which I claim to be mine? Our ground, which is emptiness free of the division of subject and object, of self and other, gives rise moment by moment to the variety of empty appearance. All the dualistic activities of daily life are not actually different from the unborn source and if we see this then they have no power to limit us for we truly see non-duality. You don't have to change what you do or what you wear or what you eat or how you talk. You don't have to try to be a better person. You simply have to observe in each moment of arising that this is the display of the source. Unborn, it is always fresh, self-arising and self-vanishing.

However, if this is not clear for you in the moment of its occurrence – if you are not clear that you, with all your thoughts, feelings and so on are a part of this display – then you will mediate occurrences through the dichotomising of grasper and grasped. Projecting graspable existence onto what you take to be the object, you will find that you, the subject, are grasping at one thing after another. We imagine the handle on the 'object' and then we grasp that handle. This is the consolidating function of conceptual elaboration. We are lost in the forest of our own concepts, unable to see that this forest is also the radiance of the ground. The source gives rise to all the appearances of *samsara* and *nirvana*. If we see this non-dual emergence, there is clarity regardless of whatever concepts and assumptions arise and pass. But if the non-dual is not seen, then some arisings are taken to be self and others are taken to be not-self and the exit from *samsara* is hidden in plain sight.

There is too much going on, too many details to sort out. Analysis, planning and thoughtful intention will not bring us to the end of duality. Only the integration of the ego complex within the field of non-dual appearance brings true freedom. The seemingly born and existent is actually unborn. Opening to this openness shows the immediacy of self-arising self-vanishing appearance within which all dualities are self-liberating.

Who am I in the moment when I am my unpleasant ego-formation? When I am in my anger, or my jealousy, or my selfishness, or my pride? I am thought catching thought. One thought acts as the subject. The other thought is labelled as the object and these two tumble together, on and on and on, going round like a perpetual motion machine. The subject experiencer seems to be bright with its own intelligence and knowledge yet it is not stable, being reformulated through its interaction with the object. The actual illuminator of both experiencer and experienced is the mind itself which never changes, never moves. The constructed ego self is always changing and always moving for in fact it is the fresh energy of the mind itself unborn, ungraspable, arising as a specific transient pattern.

EVERYTHING IS THE IMAGINATION

These transient patterns are empty of existence. They are illusions which the deluded ego imagines to be real. Imagining is a mental activity, the formation of sequences of ideas. They are vehicles for emotion and it is this emotional intensity which generates the sense of something real existing.

In *tantra* we use intentional imagining to deconstruct the seemingly inherent validity of our habitual karmic imaginings. The ritual texts give us a script by which we enrol as Padmasambhava, Tara or any one of the vast pantheon of deities. The more we fuse into the presence of the deity the more we dissolve the false ground of existence and open to the actual ground of unborn space. By fully entering identification with diverse deities, the seeming 'reality' of habitual identity is revealed as just another empty imagining, an illusory apparition.

The imaginal is not imagined **by** someone. It is the instant presence of the potential of the ground. If we believe that we really exist as our opaque karmic imagining, then it is quite a process to become the deity. But if we relax and open to our unborn ground, we find that diverse imaginings are instantly present without effort, without the duality of subject and object.

Every appearance is the unborn display of the vitality of the mind.

The mind has no definitive, restrictive, essential self-substance. It is open and empty and simultaneously the infinite potential of the imaginal. The imaginal is all that ever occurs. It is the sky, the earth, the ocean, the birds, the fish, the human beings. We are all moving in the imaginal, the patternings of light, sound and all the other ungraspables.

When we are aware of our ground and potential as present yet not personal or possessable, we have the freedom to be part of apparitional connectivity. With this clarity our forms are neither defined nor defining fixations but relational aspects of the unborn field. Freed of the notion that our form is an entity, we are present in the co-emergence of formations as we arise in specificity with friends, children, colleagues, and so on. We never arrive at our 'true self' since our selfless selfing is the truth of all selves. This is non-dual kindness as the many kinds of manifestation display as moments of relation. Kindness illuminates the intrinsic inclusivity of the ground source.

Our apparitional forms emerge within the apparitional field. They are aspects of it, and no matter how great their diversity, they do not separate from it. The circumstances of the current patterning of the field are the circumstances with which 'my' apparition emerges. The field is an integrated communicative field and the contact between field patternings and 'my' patterning is vibrant as the presence of awareness.

The empty unborn mind displays the non-dual field within which all movement is the kindness of responsivity. The variety of responses is the ongoing co-emergence of patternings. For example, if you step on a pavement, on a wobbly stone or on mud, the field will respond to the pressure of your foot and your apparitional form will respond to that response. Thus potential is in play with potential and this frees us from the limitation of subject-verb-object. Unreified potential has no limit.

We're not setting out to correct other people or to impose our ideas on them. Non-dual relating is the emergence of formation in the moment of formation of the experiential field. We are all participating in the non-dual unfolding of the apparitional world.

In this way the empty integrity of *dharmakaya* awareness reveals the clarity of instant presence, the all-at-once-ness of appearance. Within this we arise as responsive patterning. We are neither pre-choreographed nor leaves in the wind, blown hither and thither by circumstances. Co- emergence is the subtle interfacing within which you are neither the controlled slave nor the controlling master.

PARTICIPATION

The undivided whole is often described in terms of three inseparable aspects. The first aspect is **essence**. This is the face we had before we were born, the face we will never see. This face is awareness inseparable from the infinity of the space of all phenomena. Our essence is aware space. Like the mirror, it shows all without ever being seen itself. It is always empty even as it shows its fullness.

The second aspect is **nature**, the complexion of the face. Our face shows our life. Our energy, our health or our sickness shines through as our complexion. The luminosity of the mind itself is the display of this shimmering potential, as when the dawn light reveals the outlines of the world before the bustle of the day begins. The potential is the clarity of unborn-ness. The absence of thingness is the potential revealed in instant presence. Each moment is fresh, open. It is the opacity of conceptual identification that promotes the delusion of over-determined entities.

The third aspect is **kindness**, the movement of energy within this field. Kindness is our participation as one-of-a-kind. We are kin. We have the same source. There is no real difference between us. We are light moving in the field of light and even our darkest thoughts cannot separate us, or anyone else, from this field. With the dissolving of the delusion of duality, intrinsic connectivity replaces personal identity as our site of presence.

Participation is not subjectivity and is neither intentional nor effortful. It is the energy of the ground source responding with flexibility and sensitivity to other illusory phenomena in the field. The dissolving of the ego-nexus allows the whole to heal itself from its imagined wounds. With this we are no longer seeking others to validate that we really exist. We are free to respond, unreified and free of the tendency to reify. The reactivity of the self-referential ego is gone and clarity responds fittingly.

BEING RESPONSIVE WITH MINIMAL INTERVENTION

We are not trying to enlighten the ego. The ego is itself delusion. Enlightenment occurs when we awaken to our intrinsic unborn awareness. The tradition of transmission is the means by which we are enabled to look for the light where the light **is**. The ego wandering in *samsara* exhausts itself by looking for light where it cannot find light, and then cheats itself by imagining that obscurity is light. We're not trying to turn darkness into light. We are finding light where light is.

The traditional example for this is the fact that if wash and wash a piece of coal it will never become chalk. Coal is coal is coal. If you don't have buddha nature, you can't be a buddha. Because, as with all beings, you do have buddha nature, you simply have to open to it. You do not have to improve it, or earn it, or be given it. What obscures the light intrinsic to your awareness is the habitual attempt to make light by rubbing concepts together. All such dualistic activity of seeking merely hides the intrinsic.

The aim is not to rescue people from *samsara* but to let the light of presence awaken others to their light. Rocking between the polarities we pass over the ever-open middle way – success to failure and back again, high to low and back again – caught up in the momentum generated by being always off-balance. If we can but rest in the midpoint where there is equalness then the light is relieved of its veils of projection and prejudice. We settle, we open, we receive, and then a response may or may not arise – it depends on circumstances. Emptiness is wisdom, connectivity is method. There is no need for technique. Rather than seeking how to do it we attend to how it is.

When we relax and receive, we see that the field of movement is not dependent on us. We are already within it and it is not what we think it is. However life is, do not reify it since that cuts you off from the source. As the texts say: *"If you go up to heaven, go to heaven. If you go down to hell, go to hell."* Some people have easy, happy lives, some people have a lot of sickness, some people have loneliness, depression, sorrow... however it is, that's how it is. If you take it seriously, you enter into judgement about it and say, *"I shouldn't have this kind of a life. Things should be different for me. I don't deserve this."* Taking this position vis-à-vis yourself is part of the endless fragmentation that the ego-self endures. With this there is not only me in my sorrow but also me with thoughts about myself in my sorrow: endless elaboration, endless commentary. Of course this fragmentation hasn't actually fragmented anything, yet if you believe your thoughts to be true they will fragment you!

The emptiness of the mind is the basis for its hospitality, for the rich diversity of experiences, of how we are in the night, in the day, in happiness, in sorrow. Being with how this moment is, is actually the only site of our presence. When we go into memories of the past or anxious expectations about the future, we find that we have entered into a place which is nowhere. And that nowhere-ness is very, very dangerous for us because there is no end to trying to transform 'nowhere' into 'somewhere', 'no-thing' into 'some-thing'. Yet the paradox is, if we settle into the nothing, the empty, the open, we find that everything is immediately present.

Now we come to the empty ending of the empty evening. It has been a pleasure meeting you all and I wish you well in your practice.

Public talk given at Shang Shung Institute, London on 25th February 2016. Revised by James Low in April 2022.

Mindfulness, contact and healing in psychotherapy

The key focus of this short piece is an initial exploration of the synergy between mindfulness and contact in the practice of psychotherapy. Here the term mindfulness is used to indicate a state of conscious attention: one intentionally attends to what is occurring. This requires that one finds the middle way between identification with what is occurring, either by sensory fusion or by conceptual appropriation, and distraction and non-attention, by preoccupation, dullness or agitation. The term 'contact' refers to the middle way between the polarities of merged confluence and separative isolation. Contact implies 'being with'. This avoids both falling into and pulling away from. For example, if one looks at a painting one might be drawn into it and become immersed in the colours and shapes. Or one might be disinterested or disparaging and thereby hold oneself apart from whatever the painting might offer. In the sense of contact used here, to be in contact with the painting is to be available to it so that one can avail oneself of its potential without abandoning one's own presence.

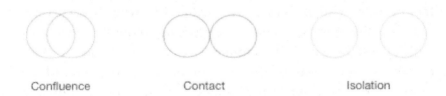

Confluence   Contact   Isolation

Firstly, a general overview of current practice is offered followed by a brief exploration of some of the different aspects of contact. In the simplest terms and with specific reference to the arena of psychotherapy, the key difference between dualistic and non-dualistic approaches is as follows. In the former, the self, the individual identity, is believed to be an autonomous or quasi- autonomous entity existing in connection with, yet essentially apart from, its environment. In the latter the self is held to be a dynamic participant in the ever-changing field it is part of. When this non-duality is lived the self arises as the ever-changing display of the effulgence of the invisible ground of presence.

At this time many approaches to psychotherapy concern themselves specifically with cognitions, memories, feelings, and behaviours, which may be identified as conscious or unconscious. Due to this they privilege certain aspects of the individual over others. Although this selectivity is affirmative of the therapist's professional identity, functionally it is merely another mode of the biased patterns of interest and non-interest that have generated the majority of psychological problems brought by the patients.

When the therapist starts from within an explanatory model their gaze is already prefigured: they are looking for the aspects that their model indicates to be significant. They are looking for something and with that attitude there will always be something that can be found.

When mindfulness is used as a support for such limited and limiting approaches its use helps to gather attention towards the areas of already established interest. When mindfulness is taught to the patient they learn to attend to what is occurring. The identification of what is occurring requires categories which could be culturally familiar, such as feeling sad, or other categories which may be the less familiar such as the Buddhist 'four foundations of mindfulness' which offer a detailed analysis of experience through a sequential focus on body, feelings, consciousness and phenomena of. Such categories and the clarity they offer can bring a fresh sense of personal aliveness and of the potential present in embodied inhabitation of an ever-changing environment. With this, patients can become more conscious of what they are encountering moment by moment in the interplay of subject and object. This helps to release identification with habitual associations permitting a fresh experience of self and world.

For example, with the intentional practice of mindfulness of the breath, attention, once it is securely focussed on the breath, is no longer available to reinforce habitual memories such as those of neglect in childhood. Moreover any affect resultant from that neglect is deprived of reinforcing attention. The withdrawal of attention from these emergent phenomena causes them to gradually lose their seductive power. In this way the seeming givenness, density, and validity of habitual configurations of subject and object, self and other, are gradually lessened allowing more access to the as yet unawakened potential of aliveness. This conjunction of mindfulness techniques and psychotherapy methods of assessment, diagnosis and treatment can bring concrete benefits to both therapist and patient.

We should not forget that Sigmund Freud had, over 100 years ago, established key principles to avoid confirming the patient's neurotic assumptions. Firstly, the rule of abstinence, a radical minimalisation of the everyday dialogic that maintains the sense of oneself as one takes it to be. No social chat or formalities, the use of a couch and the avoidance of face-to-face encounter all help to create an unpredictable setting that does not support familiar knowledge. Secondly, the therapist/analyst is required to maintain a free- floating attention free of bias – everything that occurs is of value. This attention is on the present moment and must be guarded from tendencies to look back over what has occurred or leap forward in expectation of what might occur. Thirdly, the patient is encouraged to free associate, to say what ever comes to mind without editing. As the habit of socially aligning repression is relaxed more aspects of experience come into consciousness. Learning not to anxiously edit one's own life into an acceptable narrative opens one to the happenstance of the moment. This happenstance is free of imposed order yet it is not chaotic; it is an example of autopoiesis. The patient's struggle to allow this is aided by Bion's encouragement to the analyst to be without memory or desire.

Attention is the sustaining lifeblood of both subject and object. Our attention flows to them because we believe them to be real and important and they are reinforced in their seeming reality and importance by the intensity and quality of the attention we pay them. When this fact becomes clear for us we can start to ease ourselves out of the restriction of reification and investment and begin to explore direct experience rather than experience mediated through concept-based entities. By attending to attention itself it is freed from being a servant of habit formations and their underpinning assumptions and so there is the chance to open to experience with a fresh view or ethos. Experience is no longer merely a means to an end, taking us somewhere else, but is a vibrant end in itself as the ongoing appreciation of how this moment actually is. This is the deep potential of mindfulness which can take both therapist and patient beyond the aims of improving social adjustment and/or the achievement of increased personal authenticity.

Thus on a general level Buddhist dharma or teaching and psychotherapy are both concerned with deconstructing misleading identities by examining the constituents of such imagined entities and how they are taken to be real. The Nyingmapa school of Tibetan Buddhism organises the teachings into nine vehicles or pathways, each with their own distinct patterns of view, meditation, conduct and result. According to the view of the first vehicle, analysis of a person in terms of how they are constituted reveals our sense of the person to be an epiphenomenon generated by the collaboration of five dynamic constitutional factors, each lacking inherent existence and unable to create anything possessing inherent existence. These constitutional factors are known as the *skandhas* or heaps, and they are form, feeling, perception, composition and consciousness. This demonstration of the absence of inherent existence in persons is taken further in the Mahayana tradition constituting the third and subsequent vehicles. This analysis shows the absence of inherent existence in phenomena. Instead of encountering separate people and things, we find ourselves participating in and as the dynamic matrix of dependent co- origination. Attentive investigation followed by non-conceptual meditation reveals our presence as radiant openness. Repeated immersion in this openness reveals that at every level of experience individual essences and substances are in fact empty illusion, ghostly projections in the theatre of emptiness.

In our practice of psychotherapy we similarly find that the patient's sense of 'always' being depressed or anxious can be investigated in terms of causal events in the past and predisposing factors operating in the present. This shows the long-held limiting beliefs about one's state and identity to be false and misleading constructs, constructs based on a filtering and organising idea rather than on the actuality of phenomena. Attending to both the processional history of these factors and to their current pattern of their dynamic presenting permits the falling away of fixed sites of identification, such as, *'I am depressed, that's how I am.'* As long as the new conceptual restriction of a diagnosis is not rigidly adhered to, there is a chance of participating in the unfolding of the as yet latent potential.

Neuroses of all kinds can be usefully considered as ghost forms. The past moments which were their genesis are gone, dead, never to return. And yet these strange wraiths haunt us so that illusion thickens into dull dark delusion. Resistance to awakening to the unreality of the thoughts, feelings, sensations, memories and so on that restrict us seems, paradoxically, to be life affirming. One exists through one's attachments: I have a body, a mind, a voice, clothes, work, home, food and so on. Identity is generated and maintained by the items we identify as really existing and then select or reject. Subject and object are born together. Subject, this undeniable sense of I, me, myself, is inseparable from object. Self is not self-existing but is the ever-changing result of ever-changing causes. Awakening to this free flow of co-emergence allows one to live in and as the particularity, the unique specificity, the ungraspable strangeness and complexity of each moment. To take oneself to be a knowable person inevitably dulls the freshness of presence into its shadow, the insistence upon being an inherently existing self-entity.

However in psychotherapy the very structuring of the work confirms the validity of self and other as separate real domains and this is likely to remain as the basic organisational polarity of experience since therapist and patient engage as two separate people. In a therapy session two people are physically present in a room together. Whether they are fully available to each other is another matter. The setting installs these two people in different roles with different tasks. These roles are invested with different degrees of authority and they also allow differentiated displays of power and levels of accessibility. Conventionally it is the therapist who has the greater power and who is in charge of the frame and structure of the session. Moments of genuine contact are subversive of this choreography of power.

As is well known, the term 'therapist' has its origins in the Asklepian tradition of minimising technical intervention in order to allow healing to occur. The therapist is one who attends to and is attendant on the psyche of the patient. Psyche can most generously be taken as both soul and spirit and as encompassing all aspects of an individual from the most ethereal to the most substantial. This requires the therapist to be present and not to be preoccupied or distracted. In order to help the 'work' go well both therapist and patient wait patiently in undemanding availability for the epiphany which initiates the upwelling of profound healing.

The discipline of learning to be available for the other in this way involves becoming attentive to the many factors which can diminish one's availability. Availability is both a receptive openness to the many aspects, nuanced and gross, of the patient's way of being in the room, and a capacity to see the other 'as they are'.

Receptive openness requires a non-judgemental welcoming equanimity. Any bias towards or away from aspects of the other or of self that emerge in the interaction will obscure the patterning of the patient's experience. Since the patient's attitude to the therapist is often inflected by their desire to be the object of desire of the therapist, any indication of likes and dislikes by the therapist will tend to encourage the patient to present themselves in the way that most fits their image of the therapist's object of desire.

When practised in this way without agenda, the therapy functions through quiet presence allowing the non-assertion of personality to open a space in which healing can occur. Mastery and leadership of the process, no matter how skilful, are obstacles to this wider and deeper healing. The presence of the therapist is like a wave pulsing between visible and invisible, impactful and non-impactful. The visibility of the therapist supports the working alliance, the sense of 'being in it together', but then they have to relax to become merely an aspect of the space which facilitates the awakening of the patient to their own spacious being.

The capacity to see the other 'as they are' is crucial and yet exquisitely difficult to 'achieve' since it is a matter of non-activity. Simply to see the other as one takes them to be without distraction or elaboration is difficult enough; to see the phenomenal actuality free of obscuring interpretation is well nigh impossible if one has only intellectual rigour or mental acuity as one's support. To come to see that what one takes to be seeing is actually perception inflected and infected with imagining can be quite shocking. If I largely imagine what I see, then what I describe, what I say in order to live 'truthfully' with others, is not a true objective account of what is there. For me my 'what is there' is truly mine, mine alone and the play of signifiers which seems to establish shared values, facts and experiences is just another imagined 'reality'.

The modern European project of phenomenology initiated by Husserl and taken up by Merleau-Ponty ran aground on the difficulty of using thought to bracket off thought. Thoughts are sticky and, like words, lose their impact and value when presented in isolation. Since thinking is linking, the mental effort not to link is too exhausting to be sustained. This being the case, mindfulness, as the privileging of simple attention over informed interpretation, can be beneficial in the ripening of psychotherapists.

Seeing phenomena 'as they are' can be considered from the point of view of the Mahayana concept of the two truths. Relative or fictional truth refers to the truth of phenomena as they appear when duality is our frame of reference. In this frame, experience is taken up as a means to an end orchestrated by intention and effort. Relative truth rests in the belief in real entities. I exist as me, you exist as you. Our existence as sentient beings and the existence of all the things we imagine and encounter are based on our experience of separate totalised entities. Each of these individual phenomenon stands for itself by itself, and our experience of it, which includes our linguistic definition of it, is taken to be the truth of this thing itself.

Absolute or simple truth is the truth of phenomena as they are when non-duality is our frame of reference. In this frameless frame, experience is an ungraspable end in itself, freely arising and freely vanishing while offering the satisfaction of aesthetic enjoyment of the ephemeral. With absolute truth all entities are effortlessly released from their imprisonment as isolates and are revealed as seemingly finite moments inseparable from the infinite.

Relative truth has two levels, impure and pure. With impure relative truth we experience the inseparability of our identification of something and our feelings about that something. Thus I might experience spinach as being horrible. My feeling about spinach is 'for me' located in the spinach: I am truthful, spinach is horrible. When such fusions of identity and feeling are applied to people we have, for example, the idealisation of certain musicians as universally wonderful and, on the other hand the denigration of people who seem to be intrinsically inferior or threatening. I exist as a finite entity suffused with shifting patterns of affect while fluctuating between distress and excitement. In this state the world is as I take it to be and my assumptions and beliefs remain unexamined in their function as my vehicles of truth. Fiction is taken to be fact and therefore assertion rather than curiosity becomes the dominant approach.

Much Ado About Nothing

Thanks to Dan Fletcher of www.cartoonbox.co.uk

Awakening from this delusion, according to the Buddhist tradition, is aided by encountering and being mindful of 'the three marks of conditioned existence': dissatisfaction, impermanence, and the absence of inherent existence in persons.

Dissatisfaction, suffering and disturbance have two main causes: not getting what we want and getting what we do not want. Moreover change brings suffering as new situations often bring a sense of being de-skilled and loss of confidence often feeds into loss of confidence. Although these disjunctions between what actually occurs and what I would like to occur are everyday occurrences we are still shocked and disheartened when they arise. Learning from experience is not so easy when we inhabit our paradigms and remain attached to our axioms and expectations.

Impermanence is everywhere, always. The movement of the planets, of the seasons, of the clock, of the life of the body, the voice, the mind – nothing is stable. When we look and look and look we come to see that not one really existing enduring entity can be found. We have tried to build our existence from the fleeting moments of time. Events arise and vanish. This is how they are and no one can alter this. We know this yet act as if it were not so.

The absence of inherent existence in persons is indicated by the five *skandha* heaps mentioned above. Form presents itself as shape and colour – my form and the form of all 'things'. Shape and colour impact my capacity for experience, generating feelings which can be classed as positive, negative and neutral. These feeling tones influence my perception, the way in which I apprehend and give value to certain aspects of the field whilst discounting others. This selection I make is activated by my opinions, interpretations and through this interaction a moment of consciousness is generated: 'that is a red pen'. I comprehend what is occurring. The seeming clarity of this moment validates the three wheels whose turning generates the world for me: the subject, the object and the relation between them.

Reflection on these three marks of conditioned existence awakens us to the way false beliefs, habits and instincts regarding self and environment lead sentient beings to endless suffering. Not being discrete entities with finite beginnings, middles and ends, sentient beings are revealed as transient forms manifesting out of their misapprehension of the actual status of their existences. The absence of inherent existence is also the interdependent arising of all appearances. Interconnectivity, when directly perceived, gives rise to an inclusive kindness or openheartedness (Tib: *Thugs rJe*) towards all sentient beings. This warmth of welcome deconstructs the beliefs which secure biased identifications of autonomous beings. The seeming truth that because you are 'this' you cannot be 'that', for example that an enemy cannot be a friend, is exposed as mere conceptual confusion. Suffering arises from delusion and so lifting that obscuring veil becomes our ethical orientation.

With pure relative truth we are able to distinguish between the object identified and our own feelings about it: *'Spinach is very popular but for myself, I just don't like it.'*

Appearances are still taken to be 'real' to have their own existence and to be expressive of their own essence. The separation of subject and object is cleaner and therefore the subject, in recognising their feelings to be theirs, can see the object as something more neutral, more open to diverse interpretations. This also allows the subject more opportunity to observe and consider other people's relations with the object and to notice that they see things in it and about it, which the subject does not. Free of the foreclosure of projected feelings being taken as true and reliable, both the object and the subject arise as potentials rather than as defined entities. This brings a curiosity about the lived present, about what is actually occurring, and with this, a sense that meaning is created by engagement. The subject still seems to exist as a finite entity yet with a mood of calmness and non-reactivity. The world and its occupants are not fixed entities 'out there' but are potentials that manifest situationally in tandem with the manifesting of my potential as currently revealed.

Awakening from this belief in the illusion of real entities is aided by encountering and being mindful of 'the three doors to liberation': untouched by signs, undirected by hope and intention, and emptiness of all phenomena.

Untouched by signs indicates that language floats above actual phenomena, talking to itself. Our ceaseless commentary on ourselves and our world talks them into their (seeming) existence. Our making sense of 'things' is dependent on concepts. All concepts in their actuality are fleeting, arising and passing in seconds. Yet they are taken up as the validators of the true existence of all that occurs. By analysis and meditation one can come to see that actuality is not what we think it is, for it is forever untouched by signs.

Undirected by hope indicates that one is at peace in presence. Hope has us leaping into the future, imagining different scenarios and how we might operate within them. But these are mere mental fantasies. They exist nowhere but in the mind just as clouds exist only in the sky. When mental energy is no longer projected into an imagined future we are released from hopes and fears and can settle into the infinity of the ever-vanishing present moment.

Emptiness of all phenomena indicates that everything that appears is not the appearance of something else: there is no inner essence or substance supporting the presenting appearance. Appearance is the display of both our open potential and momentary capacity for experience. The basis of this potential is the intrinsic brightness of our all-revealing awareness while our momentary capacity arises from the interplay of self and other as field factors. When we relax from our fixation on dualistic looking we find that we see much more, we receive the whole emergent field all at once. With this the non- duality of fullness and emptiness is apparent. There is nothing to be emptied out in order to 'achieve' emptiness – all experience, both what is experienced and the experiencer, are intrinsically empty.

Reflection on these three doors to liberation widens our attention to encompass all aspects of experience inanimate as well as animate. All that arises for us and as us is unestablished as existents. Appearances are not the appearances of 'something' but are simply appearance with nothing behind them or in them. They are the inseparability of appearance and emptiness. Everything is my experience including 'myself'. With everything included within experience this directly reveals that neither the experienced nor the experiencer is a finite entity. Free of conceptual division all experience evokes inclusive kindness on the basis of phenomena being not-other and not-self. Now non-duality becomes concrete with the deconstruction of the deluded conceptualisation of discrete entities.

This shift from immersion in impure relative truth to the increased clarity of pure relative truth often arises in breakthrough moments in psychotherapy. The hated mother, so self-absorbed and selfish, is revealed to have other aspects. For example, we suddenly recall that she had close friends who loved her. These aspects were always there yet invisible due to the intensity of our own affect-ridden conclusions about her. Rather than being an apprehendable two-dimensional figure the other is revealed in their unapprehendable sculptural complexity. Now we encounter a subject revealed (yet always only partially) in co-emergent experience rather than as a mere knowable object. Life becomes dialogic emergence rather than monologic definition.

As the over-determined other is being freed from the prison of one's projections one is simultaneously freed to think and feel and not merely be the bearer of thoughts and feelings. The frame is still the dualism of subject and object where self and other can each arise as subject or as object. Even with this relaxation of anxious determinism, free deep open inter-subjectivity tends to be a rare occurrence rather than the normality we might wish it to be. This is because we are fabulists intoxicated by our own tales, whether emotion-driven or rational. Moreover our fables are the very substance of what we take to be self and other. What we call 'reality' is a story. Belief in this story is required if we are to be taken as 'normal' by others. The pull of group delusion is intense. To maintain even a limited sense of the illusory nature of phenomena while participating with others and experiencing the power of their assumptions can be a very lonely experience. The dharmic antidote to this is to increase kindness which, while personally heart-warming, can in turn increase one's troubling sense of the desolation that envelops so many sentient beings. It is not surprising that the word 'disillusioned' carries such negative connotations.

Absolute or simple truth is what is revealed when the veil of separation thins offering less and less opacity of screen for projections of identity. What we see is light, what we hear is sound – both are dynamic, instant, ungraspable. Our grasping grasps concepts and nothing else. Self and other, me and you, are ideas, ideas arising in the mind as the mind. They are fictions, inventions, signifiers without actually existing signifieds. They are 'real' merely because they are believed to be real. Their basis is the self-deception of make- believe, of let's pretend. The play of the ever-fecund mind is inseparable from its emptiness, its ungraspability. So much occurrence, so much happenstance, and yet all phenomena are simply the unborn radiant display of non-dual experience. When the habitual and unrecognised effort of self-creation is no longer fed by belief and investment, 'I' as simple presence is non-referential and non-indicative. 'I': open empty infinite presence.

Awakening from the belief in separation and autonomy manifests as effortless mindfulness of the integrity of our three-fold presence: essence, clarity, and connectivity.

Essence indicates the essence of all, and this is emptiness. This is not a nihilistic vacuum. The emptiness of all is inseparable from the awareness which reveals all. Empty awareness is like the sun in the sky illuminating equally in all directions.

Clarity is the ever-unfolding field of experience, the inseparability of subject and object. Clarity is the brightness of display revealed by the light of awareness. However things appear to us, they are themselves the clarity or bright display of the essence, our essence. Separate entities are merely the shadow of the imagined and imagining self.

Connectivity is our ceaseless participation in the field of disclosure. Moment by moment posture, gesture, facial and verbal expression are arising in interplay with other field factors. We and all beings are always already within the field. This is our home, our belonging. It is actually inalienable. Yet due to relying on concepts as vehicles of truth we have wandered into the labyrinth of our own imaginings. We have hidden that which cannot be hidden for it is also the hider. This is the play of illusion – see it and there is awakening. But if it is not seen there is endless delusion.

The open empty ground of this presence is not, of course, mine alone for it shines forth as the other, as everything. When the interpersonal effort of mutual confirmation subsides we see that: I am not who I think I am, I am not who you think I am, you are not who you think you are, you are not who I think you are. The subsiding of effort occurs with the dissolving or self-vanishing of the familiar sites of identity. Entities show themselves as they have always truly been, appearances full of sensuous vitality yet devoid of self- existence.

Reflection on this followed by direct revelation of the non-duality of open empty awareness and open empty phenomena brings a final deconstruction and dissolution of all reifications. Inclusive kindness is all-pervading and unimpeded as the wisdom of emptiness.

Mindfulness or recollection is usually taken to be inseparable from duality: someone is being mindful of something. This certainty applies in both impure and pure relative truth where mindfulness can bring a clarity of attention which allows the de-reification of projections both affective and cognitive.

However when we approach mindfulness (Tib: *Dran Pa*) with the view of the ninth vehicle known as Dzogchen, the great completion, we enter the domain revealed by absolute truth which is radically different from what we have encountered within our habitual terms of reference. In Dzogchen the term 'mindfulness' is applied to the non-dual recollection of the actual ground and field of being, the original openness of awareness. This unchanging intrinsic openness is not apparent while experience is mediated through the two aspects of relative truth. The actual, the as-it-is, has been obscured by absorption in fictitious imaginings. The creativity of the mind obscures itself by itself. Because this is the case actual direct recollection of the mind itself is not an activity performed by a subject. Rather it is the effortless simultaneous showing to the show-er of how it is when recollection of arisings identified as entities is allowed its own inherent demise.

This points to the possibility of therapy becoming a mode of awakening, of liberation, rather than simply a means of development and adaptation. Few therapies are able to avail themselves of this deeper potential as they lack the sense of co-presencing, of the contact of presences rather than of the meeting of entities. What is required is a view and a preparatory practice which supports the therapist in offering naked availability unclad in theories, accumulated experience and so on.

The Gestalt approach to therapy offers an orientation which could offer a starting point from which to effect a shift from dualistic to non-dual contact. Such a shift requires the therapist to abide in relaxed open presence always available for contact. It is this accepting availability itself that facilitates profound meeting with the truth of the other and for this truth to be experienced beyond conceptualisation.

When the therapist is present as the patterning of their self-formation then that invisible furniture exerts a subtle influence on the interaction. The presence of the therapist as a person with specific qualities may help to induce a sense of trust and containment but it also is likely to elicit familiar patterns of adaptation in the client, for example adaptive idealising child to strong caring father. Preoccupation with habitual contents of the mind defends against ontological insecurity by diverting attention from being/presence itself towards unanswerable questions of identity which can feed existential anxiety. However as the therapist gains more sense that their aware presence is not some stable 'thing' or self- essence to be maintained, but is the medium through which their potential for creative connectivity manifests, they can start to release identification with the current content of their body-voice-mind continuum. With this the therapist can relax into their foundational openness which is self-proving, requiring no confirmation or validation. In turn this friendly presence offers neither a confirmation of nor a destructive abandoning of the patient's habitual reiteration of their own identity patterning. This non-confirmation offered within welcoming presence allows the patient to shed the clothing wrapping their sense of individual self. Unclothed, the naked self is naked presence and with this the patient can awaken to who, what and how they have truly always been.

When the therapist expresses interest in the symptom, in the truth of the patient's story, and the patient's sense of self, they are colluding in the hiding of the as-yet unactivated potential of the patient. The patient is not who they think they are nor are they who the therapist thinks they are. Identity is constructed out of concepts, out of the editing of experience, whereas presence is not composed of thoughts, memories, sensations or any of the other manifold contents of personal experience. The relaxed presence of the therapist provides a holding environment within which the non-confirmation of the patient's habitual identity may lead the patient to a new and surprising sense of being fully here.

However the deconstructive potential of non-confirmation could also be experienced as destructive abandoning by a patient with a less than secure attachment.

Therefore the guiding principle is to avoid separating contact with the patient's profound potential from simultaneous contact with their growing edge.

Meeting the other where they are without demand offers an ambiance of acceptance facilitating both the release of identification with self-sabotaging patterns and the awakening of the potential to awaken. This unites the wisdom of relaxed openness with the compassion of contactful presence. This brings a wider and deeper meaning to the commonly held idea that the therapist employs an intentional use of self. Here 'self' is used to deconstruct reified self.

Simple presence is not the presence of someone or something. This is different from the general usage of the term 'presence' where it indicates either the presence of something other, for example beauty, God, pain or the presence of myself as myself, for example, *I love being with you all, I feel so present in your company.*' Here someone or something is presenting and this announces their 'presence' whereas non-dual presence is instant and is not a personal quality. In fact it has three inseparable aspects: the presence of the unimaginable, inexpressible ground /base /source; the presence of the indivisible field; and the presence of our ungraspable participation. These three aspects were referred to above as 'essence, clarity and connectivity'. Since we are exploring experience that is outwith accurate description in language many different terms have been employed within the Buddhist tradition to say the unsayable.

The aim of Gestalt is the integration of the seemingly disparate parts of the person. From the dualistic point of view this requires active intervention such as contact-increasing experiments. From the non-dual point of view the invitation to be present with, in, and as the presence of awareness that is always already present is itself healing in wholeness by releasing identification with parts taken as entities. There is no need to integrate self-states into a coherent self since all self-states and environmental states are already integral in the infinite hospitality *(dharmadhatu)* inseparable from awareness.

For as long as one is not able to be present in awareness then ego-self will continue to be caught up in its pulsation between identification and dis-identification with the transient contents of the mind. The patterning of these contents can be classified in various ways including for example the diagnostic categories of the DSM5. The paradox is that a strong flexible resilient ego can take some interest in its own dissolution whereas a fragile sense of self is unlikely to see the invitation to relax as anything other than a path to terrifying collapse. Hence patients with psychotic disorders, dissociative disorders, borderline structures and so on should be facilitated only towards ego-syntonic contact until stability is gained.

Gestalt points to contact as the middle way between confluence and isolation. With confluence subject merges with object or with the other's subjectivity. For example, if you watch a film and are absorbed by it you are no longer monitoring what is going on. This fusion can be experienced as a blessed relief from the burden of self. Yet the relief is momentary for the sense of self lingers on and in its inherent limitation easily feels overwhelmed and withdraws to a self-protective isolation. While the fragile ego is shuttling between these polarities it is unable to avail itself of the midpoint of contact, the door of presence which is always already open.

Mindfulness as non-distraction, non-merger, non-dispersal is a useful practice as a support for maintaining clarity of attention towards the object of attention. If attention cannot rest on the presence of the object it is likely to follow speculation about the object, inventing a substance for it which it does not possess, or it may lose contact with the object and follow after other more interesting phenomena. Mindfulness in this mode not only strengthens the capacity to gather one's attention back to its intended object but also to gather that intended object back to the simplicity of its actual presenting appearance.

The Gestalt cycle outlines a simple description of how a person can move towards contact with the factors in the environment required to alleviate a felt need. The quality of this contact is determined by the relative degrees of clarity and obscuration present in the moment. Firstly we can look at contact in its dualistic mode.

As with the Buddhist wheel of life, the momentum of the Gestalt cycle of interdependent moments means that there is no actual beginning. Conventionally however, sensation is often taken to be the starting point. Here we will look at the stages of the cycle as described from a dualistic point of view.

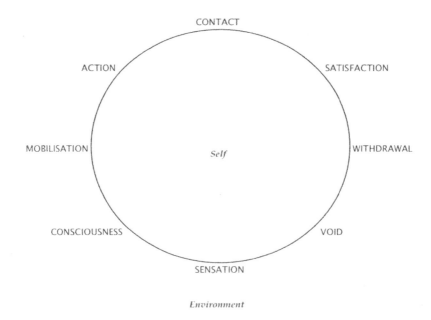

The Gestalt cycle

To give an example of how this process unfolds, a *sensation* arises in my mouth and throat. When this enters *consciousness* I notice the sensation which I identify as indicating thirst leading to my sense that *'I'm thirsty'*. Now the subject, I, has a specific colouration, thirst, and this leads to *mobilisation,* a gathering of embodied capacity and sense of the current environment. If no liquid is available I may be able to release the sensation into the background so that it is non-intrusive. However if liquid is available I start to formulate a sense of what I want and how I can mobilise to get it. This leads to *action* in which I am purposefully going to the kitchen and performing all the activities necessary to make a cup of tea. If I can sit with this cup of tea, feeling its warmth in my hands, savouring its aroma and bringing it to my mouth so that its refreshing flavour is in *contact* with my taste buds, I can find myself fully in contact with the tea. I am not thinking of anything else – the tea is worthy of my undivided attention. The fullness of this moment brings *satisfaction* followed by *withdrawal* from both the presence of thirst and the focus on the tea. Now there is a *void,* a relaxed open non-preoccupation and this availability to the field allows new *sensations* of impingement to arise.

In this example the potential of the moment of contact is more or less availed of, according to whether one is available for contact or not. Gestalt is concerned with the ever- varying interface of self and environment. Self and environment are mutually influencing and the many permutations of availability which this generates means that there is no limit to the specific interruptions to contact which arise.

However, some common interruptions are outlined here according to the stages of the cycle. This is shown in the second diagram. With **desensitisation** there is anaesthetisation so that many of the factors which impinge on a person make no discernible impact. Even when there is an impact attention maybe **deflected** from it due to distraction and preoccupation. In the next stage limiting and prohibitive **introjects** such as *'you are worthless'* or *'what's the point?'* are activated in the person blocking mobilisation and confining them within the beliefs they have internalised. Action is often blocked or limited by *projection* whereby one is sure that one knows how the other person is going to respond or that the task is too difficult. At the point of contact there can be a **retroflection** or avoidant turning away from the object so that the energy of arousal is turned in on the self, manifesting as thoughts and feelings, for example as blame or self-recrimination. The satisfaction arising from full contact can be diminished or avoided by self-referential *egotism* which holds one's self apart from the experience. The contented withdrawal resultant on satisfaction can be interrupted by a **confluence** with satisfaction and an unwillingness to let it go. Such immersive identification diminishes the very satisfaction it clings to. Full withdrawal leads to a healthy void rich in the potential of new interactions with the field of experience. This openness to the happenstance of life is obscured by holding on to a fixed sense of one's own *existence* for then the cycle ends in a return to oneself rather than to an availability for fresh experience.

When life is understood in terms of existence and nonexistence then nonexistence as death, as oblivion, as nihilistic nothingness, as boredom, as *ennuie* and so on is something to be feared. This fear often drives a foreshortened engagement with the cycle where one goes from a mental event arising in consciousness to mobilisation and activity, with one's endless busyness employed as the exhausting maintainer of the ego's sense of agency. It is not surprising that the most difficult of all yoga *asanas* is the corpse posture, *shavasana*, where one is simply doing nothing at all.

At each of these points the discipline of mindfulness is likely to be efficacious in limiting the impact of habitual interruptions. The quality of contact is limited by the constraints of duality. The sense of subject and object provides plenty of fuel for the subtle ongoing commentary that clouds the space of awareness. This subtle narrative flow reifies self-reflexive proprioception which in turn confirms that, '*I am doing this; this is happening to*

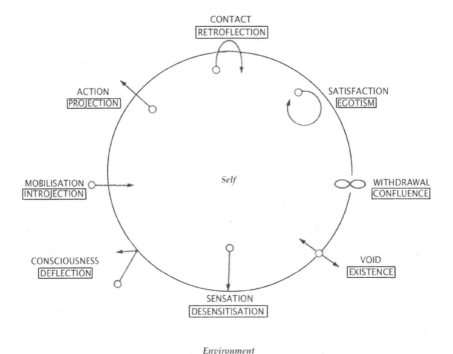

CONTACT
RETROFLECTION

ACTION
PROJECTION

SATISFACTION
EGOTISM

MOBILISATION
INTROJECTION

Self

WITHDRAWAL
CONFLUENCE

CONSCIOUSNESS
DEFLECTION

VOID
EXISTENCE

SENSATION
DESENSITISATION

Environment

Interruptions to the Gestalt cycle

me'. Unexamined assumptions are employed as the guarantor of this deceptive normalcy.

Yet self and other are merely conventional terms and do not point to truly separate entities. Our environment exists for us as experience. Our self arises for us as experience. The field of experience is not actually divided. The ongoing communication between these two aspects of the field is our life. Life is connectivity, random and intricate. Self and environment are neither just one nor are they two – they are non-dual and manifest in dependent origination. When reification is recognised as the deluded and deluding consequence of not attending to non-duality, the reliance on the contrived function of consciousness ceases and the integrity of the field is revealed as awareness of co-emergent diversity. Now each moment is self-arising and self-liberating and the causal chain of the

Gestalt cycle self-resolves into the completeness of each moment. Freed from the endless trajectory of the arrow of time, past present and future are clearly always within the deep and infinite present moment.

Our basic choice is between freedom and restriction, between awakening to infinity or one damned thing after another. When we choose the familiar we have the seemingly comforting staleness of the known. We are in a world that we can take for granted. Then contact is merely contact with the idea of the object. This is similar to the meditation techniques and paths that seek improvement and development such as more concern for others, lucid dreaming, or ability to observe one's thoughts, feelings and sensations.

To choose freedom is to let go of the supports of self-identity, to let go of knowledge and interpretation based on science. This is similar to meditation as simply being present with whatever is occurring, neither adopting nor rejecting but allowing the freefall of experience as it arises and passes without commentary.

When mindfulness is not mediated by concepts, subtle or gross, it is the inherent integrity of the mind as the sphere or space of experience. Now there is no object to be recollected and no mindful person to do the recollecting. The intrinsic clarity of the mind reveals itself to itself in the inseparability of infinite stillness and uninterrupted movement. Open awareness needs no recollection, no mindfulness, since it is self-present from the very beginning (Tib: *Ye Shes*).

For open awareness there are no interruptions to non-dual contact since contact is immediate as the infinite variety of radiance. For the individual ego there are endless interruptions to contact. No matter how hard the ego-self tries to improve or purify itself, its own self-reflexivity binds it to duality. The issue is not about trying harder – since the intrinsic is here, always. Release tension, relax effort, open to the ever-present presence. Open presence is intrinsic and infinite whereas distraction and fusion are contingent and finite. Whatever effort the Gestalt therapist makes to remain present at the contact boundary will itself lock them in a dualistic encounter no matter how fine and unbounded their contact seems.

When we awaken to non-duality we see that presence and distraction are not mutually excluding polarities. Within the mirror of presence, focus and distraction, clarity and obscuration, arise and pass as empty reflections. It is unhelpful to conflate relative dualistic presence with open infinite presence. Presence as open awareness is undeniable and ungraspable – it is not a thing among things. With this, therapy moves beyond problems to be solved and becomes an invitation to live in the shining heart of the mystery of the self-healing whole.

Limited contact is the fullness of the moment when I am in contact with someone or some particular thing. This is deepened when contact arises between us as intimate inter-subjectivity – neither of us is doing 'it'. In fact we do not know how to make 'it' happen – all we can do is to put ourselves in the way of it by not succumbing to our habits of conceptual interpretation. This negative capability, this capacity to not know, is actually the profound door to the openness which is the ground of presence. With open non-dual presence we are present as sky to sky – the ungraspable de-selfed self and the ungraspable de-othered other are vast, deep, unveiled and undivided.

With this, therapy as self-development on a path of struggle falls away, revealing therapy as self-liberation, as the fact of intrinsic freedom. Since the other is not other and self is not the primary site of identity, the play of co-emergence manifests the inseparability of wisdom and compassion, and healing is effortless and continuous.

POSTSCRIPT

The pure unadulterated tradition of Dzogchen maintained in Tibet has now been generously made easily available in the wider world. This pure tradition is the basis of my teaching and practice and I endeavour to uphold its integrity. However in writings such as the above I seek to offer some bridges whereby at least some of the enlightening tradition may be encountered by those with interest. The pure form will be of greater value – yet for those who cannot or will not avail themselves of this unbroken flow – to put old wine in new bottles may be an ethical gesture of connection and inclusion.

Many new crises erupt as the consequence of past and present selfish beliefs and activities, and if the views expressed in the short piece can aid the development of kindly connectivity then its purpose will be fulfilled.

If traditional or adapted presentations are worked with respectfully and with a kind wish to help others then all should be well. But if the motive is self-serving and engendered by a desire for status, power, wealth and so on then this egocentric orientation is likely to cause problems for oneself and others. In Tibet the hierarchical structure of society made it easier to protect the teachings from those with merely worldly intent. Now in our more unstructured social formations with easy media access to all levels of teaching and practice it behoves each student to maintain the humility and integrity which will keep them close to the whole.

An article written by James Low in May 2019.

Depth and light

REFUGE

Since we got up this morning, we've all been taking in many things, in our toothbrush, in our cup of coffee... We rely on many different things. Dzogchen is not about finding new things in which to take refuge but about learning how *not* to take refuge. Samsara is created out of grasping, holding on to things, holding on to our status in the world, our occupation, our health and so on. Once we understand this, we see the relation between subject and object and that the ego is an identity formation, which is to say that it is creating meaning. Samsara is effort. Nirvana, however, is peaceful and the term means 'no effort'. We, poor lost slaves, are so used to making effort that it is normal for us. When we make effort, we create ourselves, and this further commits us to the maintenance of our sense of who we are.

In dzogchen we take refuge in the mind itself. I can take refuge in my watch if I want to know the time. This is a dualistic refuge. *I* stand in relation to my watch and use the watch for a function, which is meaningful to me. We do this also in how we present ourselves to other people. That is to say, we take refuge in the image we have of ourselves. We hope that other people will hold in their mind some positive image of us, because we live in this eternal feedback looping.

From the point of view of dharma, subject and object are born together. They are inseparable. That is why there can be no stability in samsara since things happen, and when they happen, they get to us. As things happen, we happen; and as we happen, things happen. Hence no stability.

We are like a small pond; at first when it starts to rain there is a still surface but then when the drops start to hit the surface of the pond from each point of contact, a little rippling circle spreads out. Then each ripple meets other ripples, and you have increasing complexity, because when the ripples come together they interact and energise each other. We are like these ripples. We look at other people as if they are clearly defined entities. I am me and you are you whereas in fact we are labile, moving, changing, touched and influenced.

This morning as I came out of the front door, I was feeling quite expansive. The door opened, I stepped out, and then I realised, *"Fuck! It's raining."* So then, like a tortoise, my head drew down a little bit. It's like that. A feeling was rising in me, and then it meets the rain. This is our existence, moment by moment, endlessly tumbling on, like the ripples on the pond.

It's all complex and we can't be present with everything, so we simplify. We do this by editing. There are many things that we ignore and this gives us the chance of stabilising our sense of what is going on. To pull some things into the foreground and push other things into the background is normal. We do this according to the necessity of situations and our own tendencies and predilections. In that way, the world is like an umbrella. The umbrella will protect you but only if you hold it up. Yes, you can have the simplicity of knowing what is going on, but only if you actively edit the world. In fact, this activity is so normal for us that we're not even aware that we're doing it.

In order to practise dzogchen, however, we have to be aware of all this effort, aware that we live in a state of arousal, ready to mobilise. Why mobilise? For protection. The fact that other people also want to protect themselves is a danger to us. When it's raining and people put up their umbrellas, each individual's umbrella is for their own protection however the structure of the umbrella is to have spokes with sharp spikes at the end. So the fact that you are protecting yourself from the rain means that I am now worried lest you poke me in the eye.

Mrs Merkel says, *"Let's welcome in the refugees."* Other people say, *"Why? What's in it for me?"* Can we transcend this self-interest? Often not. The ego is like a rubber band. We can stretch it so far but then, *Tak!* [hands snap together] *"Hey, what about me?"*

This is why in buddhism compassion is inseparable from emptiness – because from the point of view of our self-referential nexus, our ego, to be generous is effortful, and effort costs us. If a cafe starts to offer free coffee to everyone it will need a sponsor otherwise it will go bankrupt. When we do buddhist practice, we ask, *"Buddha, dharma, sangha, be my sponsor. With your blessing, may I become bigger and more generous than I feel just now."* The danger with this is that if you later forget your refuge, you may retract this request and just think, *"What about me?"* The false refuge normally functioning is the sense that we are a fixed, knowable self.

In dzogchen, we take refuge in our own mind and so we have to be clear about the difference between the mind and the contents of the mind. When the mind is offering hospitality to a thought or a feeling, it feels as if that thought or feeling *is* us. I am holding a glass of water and 'glass of water' becomes a kind of compounded noun for what I'm holding. Clearly, there is glass and there is water, but when we say 'glass of water' the whole thing comes together. Not only is the water in the glass, but the water seems to define the glass. The glass retains the potential, however, to be free of water and filled with orange juice. When it's 'a glass of water', it's 'a glass of water'. When we are angry, we're angry; when we're jealous, we're jealous. This is very important to see.

WHY ATTACHMENT AND RENUNCIATION ARE IMPORTANT IN BUDDHISM

There is self and there is other. That's very straightforward. The other is there: I am here. I have a choice; I can let go of the other. When the feeling or the thought arises, however, it doesn't arise as an object; it arises as me. I remember a long time ago in India knowing an American guy, a very sweet man, who became a monk. He did it in a very nice traditional way, giving away all his possessions. But then the next day I remember him going into a café in Boudhanath – we were in Nepal – and asking if someone could buy him a coffee! He offered to exchange his watch for the cup of coffee and indeed these two things may be easy to identify and exchange. The desire for a good cup of coffee, however, is more difficult to locate. It's doesn't come from the outside, knocking on the door. It pervades us, the way grey thin clouds are pervading the sky today.

Non-attachment is only slightly diminished by renunciation. This is because there are only so many things that you can renounce: you can't renounce the contents of your own mind. You may, with very diligent shamatha practice, be able to calm the mind but then you become unable to function in the world. To be in the world means to be available, and to be available for others is to be available to be inhabited by the thought formations, the feeling formations, that promote connectivity.

Dzogchen speaks of integration. It is a term, which is easily misunderstood. We are not integrating – we are being integrated. For as long as the ego is doing the integration, it's a case of the tail wagging the dog. Integration happens to us.

Tibetan buddhism is a very complex arena, being a melange of the simple purity of the dharma and the complex sociology of Tibetan culture. In this room today we can choose to sit wherever we find a comfortable place. In Tibet, however, people would be very careful to sit according to their status. Status and power go together. In Tibetan buddhism, dharma has power, but it also has dharma protectors since there are bad forces that will attack the dharma. The more power you have the more you are aware that others can usurp your power. This is a structure. C.R. Lama was very opposed to the idea of using a structure of power. He used to say, *"If ordinary people have sex*

216

in the bushes, everybody looks. Whenever a yogi has sex in the middle of the road, nobody sees." What he meant was that our job is to be invisible.

Once I was with him in a cafe in Calcutta. This was at a time when he liked to drink coffee. *"Two coffees"*, he said to the waiter who replied in Tibetan, *"Special coffee?"* Rinpoche then started shouting at the waiter *"I say coffee!! Coffee!! Nothing is special! Just give me a coffee!"*

It's very much like that. Nothing is special. If you read the **Heart Sutra**, everything is empty. What is the most important thing about anything? It's emptiness. Emptiness is the definition of all things.

The qualities that things have are like flowers in the sky, like rainbows. If you take these ornamentations to be the essence of the thing, then on the basis of interpretation, the world is fragmented into millions of different separate objects.

When we take refuge, we relax the effort of the mind; we allow the energy of the mind – rigpa itself, the energy, which creates all the phenomena of the world – to relax. Central to this is the question: *'Why do I do what I do? What is the basis for my manifestation into the world?'* Well, a lot of what we do is simply habitual, and the function is to reassure us about the continuity of our definable ego-self. If we didn't do these things, who would we be?

This is the basis of renunciation: I am not who you think I am, and I am not who I think I am. 'I am' is prior to thought.

'Being' is a difficult concept in western philosophy and also in madhyamika philosophy where being is often identified with existence itself. You then get a critique not to take things as truly existing. But we have the sense that we are here, and in that sense being is how we refer to presence: we are here. What are we here as? That will depend. It may depend on your bladder, on your knees, on whatever else you think you should be doing, if you need to put more money in the parking meter...

This is very important. The space of being fills itself with particular contents.

What status do these thoughts have? It's impossible to practise *thogal* unless you understand the status of the thoughts through which we create the seeming solidity of the world.

When we believe in something, it becomes very true for us. The fact that it may not be true for other people doesn't necessarily interfere with our felt sense. A person with obsessive-compulsive disorder may check many times that their door is locked. Somebody else might tell them, *"Listen, of course the door is closed,"* but they still have to check for themselves. My 'not-sureness' is closer to me than your confirmation that the door is closed.

This is why it's very difficult to help other people, because ignorance and confusion is a vital ingredient to ourselves. Releasing that identification, that merging, that fusion, is very important. Falsity is always possible and getting lost is very easy. In this urge of falsity is the longing for identity. To have a sense that all phenomena are empty and that I also am empty is a little bit too abstract for most of us.

That is why we have created the methods of tantra. Tantra gives us a new identity. We start with a sense that our identity is real, but problematic. So we go to the holy lama and say, *"Oh Rinpoche, I have heard you are a master of illusion. I have heard that you are the great forger."* A forger is someone who makes false documents. *"Rinpoche, please give me a false passport. I want to be Tara. Can you change my photo a little bit?"* Then, because you know you are going to have to pass through the Great Customs in the Sky, you need to practise being Tara, because Great Customs have a big torch and they shine it in your eyes, *"Are you really who you say you are? Are you really Tara?!"* [Frantically:] *"OM TARE TUTTARE TURE..."* After a while, are you Tara or are you who you were before?

Tara and your ordinary self work together to introduce you to the ground of your being, which is emptiness.

Going from something to nothing directly is quite difficult because these little tendrils coming out of us, wanting to grasp on, will grasp anything. Tantra has a great focus on faith. If you don't believe in the practice, it's not going to work. You fake it to make it. *"Through this practice, I will become somebody else."* Like an actor getting in a role, you remember your lines again and again and again. You go from the point of being this ordinary self, to being this special being, to being nothing, to being in the mandala. As Padmasambhava said in four famous verses in the **Leudunma**, *"Everything which appears is the form of the guru's body: appearance and emptiness."*

When we imagine Tara or Padmasambhava or whatever other deity, we are imagining a form that is made of light. We, in taking the four initiations, have the light coming into our body, purifying it, so that our body too is light. Then the light of the guru's body, or the deity's body, and our body merge together and shrink down to a small point, a *tigle*, which then dissolves into emptiness. Then from that, everything arises as appearance and emptiness. When we see form, it is emptiness, but we don't see emptiness. What we see is the reflection of our own cognition. We look around a room and we think, *'This is a woman, this is a man, this is the ceiling, this is the floor.'* We do this to reassure ourselves that we know what they are. This is very dangerous.

HUMAN KNOWLEDGE NOT REQUIRED

Recently we brought out this little book, COLLECTED WORKS OF C.R. LAMA. The first two chapters are about the history of dharma and the essential point of dzogchen teaching and in them he writes several times, *"This requires no human knowledge."*

Remember when you were at school and learning to write with a pencil, doing spelling and little sums, was your best friend then not your rubber? It could make bad things go away.

However we now have a problem because the very thing that we should be rubbing away we think is good. Every time teacher says, *"Oh, very good! Now you understand."* the Buddha is weeping. There is a lot of human knowledge and what does this human knowledge do? It generates the false sense of being able to identify phenomena by applying names and concepts.

Here is a watch. When we were young, we had to learn how to tell the time. That is a convention. For whatever reason, historically, in our culture, we decided to divide a day into twenty-four hours. The daytime has twelve hours and so has the night. We learn as children that when the big hand is at the top and the small hand is at the top, it means twelve o'clock. You can even get special clocks for small children, so that if they wake early in the morning, they are told that they can't get out of bed until the big hand is pointing there and the small hand is there. Mama doesn't want to wake up too early. On the basis of Mama wanting to have a bit more sleep, the child is being told a story.

So human knowledge is the elaboration of interpretation. A favourite short verse of CR Lama begins, *"MA CHOE TROE TRAL LA MA CHO KYI KU..."* 'Ma Choe' means 'not artificial'. 'Choe' means a creation, as in *'I am making something; I am adding something'*. Art involves artifice, that is to say, it is made. Generally, when we say 'artificial', it doesn't sound too good, but art is also very nice and we value the skill of artists and artisans. From the point of view of dzogchen, however, all of this human intelligence is not necessary, which doesn't mean it's wrong or bad, but that it has been highjacked.

A scalpel is designed so that a surgeon can make a clean incision and do something helpful. A serial killer who uses a knife has learned what a knife can do. Both may even start to enjoy using them because in fact, it's like being a composer. The composer knows what the violins do, what the drums do, what the clarinet does. The conductor has a little stick; the killer has a knife. We would normally consider this to be perverse. Most of us find the arms industry perverse in finding new ways to kill people. There is good thinking and bad thinking on the relative level, but each is still an evaluation within the dualistic system of signs.

The difference in dzogchen is we're looking at the *ground* of thought. When we relax into the open ground of the mind, all thoughts, feelings and sensations are the energy of the mind. On that level, they are all intrinsically ethical.

ETHICS OF EXPERIENCE

The founding buddha of the lineage is Kuntuzangpo, Samantabhadra, whose name means 'everything is good, all is good'. 'Good' because it is the display of emptiness within the field of emptiness. Straying from that, we become perverse, taking this light – this flowing energy which is also ourselves – and turning it into a means of self-empowerment. Seeking control over our environment, we go in search of mastery. In samsara we can be busy with so many activities. It is not the activity, which is wrong but rather that the field of interpretation, which gives rise to our sense of the meaning of the activity, is delusional.

When we do shamatha meditation here we are not doing it to quieten the mind and have fewer thoughts. Thoughts, feelings and sensations are not a problem in dzogchen, even though some forms of dharma see them as obstacles.

Some prayers say, *"May we be free of obstacles"* but others, with a so-called 'higher' view, say, *"May the obstacles be the path."* So what kind of path is this? This is the path that goes nowhere. Going somewhere is very important.

—Come, let us go on a journey together!

—Okay, that's nice. Will we get ice cream?

—Come, let us sit and not do anything, ever.

—But I'll get bored. I want something to happen. Other people get to go out and play.

"I want to. I want to. If I had that, I would be happy. I need that to make me happy."

When you hear this inner whining child, then you know you're lost. Your need for more indicates that your activity is in the service for the ego. All that is involved in any of these activities could be in the service of the other. It's not the service of the other over the service of yourself, since that would be another form of duality; it's the benefit of the field. We will look at this in more detail later but for now, the key thing is to start to recognise that, *'I am lost. I don't know actually what is going on. I don't know what to do with my life. I don't even know why I do what I do.'* But that kind of thought is very scary, so I pretend that it's okay. Better to not know, *'Who am I?'*

So dzogchen is about questions, not answers. And many of the questions don't have an answer, or rather, not an answer that can be spoken.

STUDYING IGNORANCE

The thing about our education and our cultural formations is that we are all good talkers. We can explain what is going on. We can justify, but *'Who am I?'* we can't say.

Kadag practices, the vital ground in dzogchen, are about questions and the enemy of the question is the quick answer. We have so very many answers to give to each and every dharma question. These answers of ours pull the freedom-oriented potential of the question back into the mire of samsara. *"I follow Tibetan buddhism. I follow the Nyingmapa school of Tibetan buddhism. I follow Lama Dingdong. Lama Dingdong is the hundredth incarnation of Guru Chungchung. Here is a picture of Guru Chungchung. If you pray to him, you will get many benefits."* Now we know where we are! A lot of dharma is like this, and it's very attractive however dharma then becomes just a simulacrum, a doppelgänger, for ordinary samsaric ideas. What should be the door of freedom becomes a mirror in which you just see more of your own reflection.

Buddhism says that samsara is grounded in ignorance. Beneath all this elaboration of our knowledge, our appreciation of Mozart and so on, is ignorance. We're in a room, and there is one door. The way we got into this room is through ignorance. That's what it says over the door: *"Do you want to be ignorant?"* I feel a bit insulted by this because of course what I want is knowledge! So I go around the room, tapping the walls – where is the door of knowledge? By now I have got more and more knowledge, but somehow this knowledge doesn't open any door. Every now and then I come to the door *"Do you want to be ignorant?"* but where is the door *"Do you want to have knowledge?"*

The door of knowledge is through ignorance, through not knowing, through becoming a bit stupid.

If you look in buddhist magazines or websites and see publicity about buddhist teachers, they don't say, *"This is the Great Kartoffel"*[1] Dorje Dummkopf Chenpo[2], a smiling radiant man who has mastered this and that and who will give you this and that initiation. Once you get this, then what do you do with it? What does it open?

We are the students of ignorance. If we understand how we are ignorant then we understand the ongoing state of ignoring. When we walk around in the town, we are paying attention to lots of different things, we are having thoughts about things, about how people drive, or the rain, or when will the shops close and so on. What are we ignoring when we do that? Who is the thinker of the thought? Where does the thought come

---

[1] Great Potato

[2] Great Vajra Fool

from? We study a little mahamudra or dzogchen, and we come across these questions. We might think they are very important and write them down in a special notebook, which we keep safe on the shelf. Finding out how you ignore what is already here, involves *being here,* not going anywhere else, not adding anything else. We have to take our normally divergent, free-associating, multi-tasking, distracted consciousness and gather it in to focus on the question.

If we are going to take refuge in our own mind, then that means finding out what the mind is – not *telling* the mind what it is. When we are telling our mind what it is, when we are developing our story of personal identity, we are further denying the ignorance out of which speak in elaborating these illusory formations. So it is very important to start to look at the key concepts through which we define ourselves and see how much supportive power they actually have.

If we say, *"I am a woman"* or *"I am a man"*, what does this indicate? Does it give us some clear definition of identity? Well, it does tell us which toilet to go into, but it is also the beginning of a whole series of options, of endless choice-points. As we observe this we can become aware of how we are constructing myself! In a simple activity like shopping for clothes we can see how we construct ourselves: *"I couldn't wear that. Other people wear it, but I couldn't wear it. I wouldn't be me if I were wearing that."* This questioning, this inquiring is available everywhere, all the time.

The Buddha said on many occasions that all compounded things are impermanent. This is why we are always busy; what we create starts to collapse, and as it is collapsing, the space opens for something else. You do some cooking, and then the next day you look in the fridge. *"Oh! Nothing there. I'll have to go to the shops. What will I eat?"* How will I decide what to eat? You might think, *"I will only eat German food because I have to support the German economy."* You might think, *"I won't eat dates from Saudi Arabia because I don't support the Wahhabi branch of Islam."*

Then you can see how you are creating or constructing yourself. Why are you doing it? Why is it important? Does it matter? It matters to me because I am located within the semiotic web. 'Semiotic' means the web of signifiers, of interpretation. Inside this web, the meaning of one thing is related to everything else. So due to dependent co-origination, due to the network of causes and circumstances in which I am located due to my age, gender, nationality, education and so on, the world is revealed.

The key point here is to try to shift from reliance on the signifier – *'I am this shade of lipstick; this is the shade that suits me best'* – to seeing whatever we engage with as being a gesture of connectivity.

LHUNDRUB: THE FIELD

The reason we have to make these choices in the field of options again and again is because we are energy; we are not fixed entities. We are forming, deforming and reforming, on and on and on. This field of experience is called, in Tibetan, *lhundrub*; 'Lhun' means the radiance, the *rangzhin*, the showing of the radiant energy of the mind itself. This is everything; it's me and it's you. When we say 'me' and 'you' we're already in arithmetic – one and one are two – but the more we relax the interpretation, we see that the field arises undivided.

By attending to the field, our energy is evoked, sometimes restricted, sometimes invited forward. Then we have the harmonisation or, if you like, the integration of active and passive. This is what is indicated in images of deities in *yabyum*, in male and female forms conjoined.

Due to the particularities of iconography in buddhist statues and paintings, the male is usually bigger than the female, and very often in this world, men's bodies are bigger than women's. In terms of the symbolism, the female is much bigger than the male, because wisdom, as space, is passive-receptive. Passive-receptive doesn't mean powerless. A mirror is passive-receptive, but it's also active because it is showing reflection, but without effort. The mind itself is showing all the time, but it's not having to squeeze its resources out, like we squeeze toothpaste from a tube. Mind doesn't have a limited capacity and there is no end to the showing.

So you can start to observe, moment by moment, as you interact with other people, how you come into formation and how the free pulsation of your energy is restricted by particular thoughts. These thoughts are self-referential; they interrupt the flow of relatedness. When you observe this, you observe the beginning of samsara. When duality arises in the mind, subject and object split, and subject goes into itself to try to work out what to do. What it needs to do, as part of the field, is *be* part of the field; then you're part of it.

Self-consciousness, anxiety, and desire to be in control – we have many such methods of retraction and condensation through which we go into ourselves, into our memories, off into the future – and we're just not here.

Maybe you think that you don't know what to say or what to do but it is not about knowing. Of course you will get it wrong sometime. This is the International Realm of Fuck-up where nobody gets it right. 'Right' and 'wrong' are unhelpful frames of interpretation. Guilt and worry are highly self-referential, indicating a fantasy of omniscience and omnipotence that *'I shouldn't get it wrong.'* Statues of wrathful tantric deities often stand atop a prostrate Shiva Mahadev. He represents the big ego, the one sitting on top of Mount Kailash in charge of everything, the one who will destroy the world just because he's in a bad mood. Buddha says, *"Ah, ah, ah. Sweetie, don't take it all so seriously."* That is all very important since *we* are the big ego, and in that spiral of self-reference, we become lost. Nobody can save us from the fact that we are here, and that it's our life. Moment by moment: *Where are we? Who are we? How are we?* This is grown-up time – no mama, no papa. We stand where we are.

We will now look at *kadag* and *lhundrub.*

DZOGPA, FINISHED, ENDED

Dzogchen means 'the great completion' or in some sense, 'the great ending'. When something is completed and ended, there's nothing more to be done. It is what it is and needs no alteration or improvement.

C.R. Lama used to explain dzogchen as like when a person gets divorced, next they lose their house, then they lose their money, then they become very sick, and next they are lying in the gutter, dying. This is 'dzogpa', finished, kaput. Nothing more is going to happen.

This is a very nice example because it indicates that the enemy is hope. Hope is the imagination. We imagine something other than what is here, and then our intention is mobilised towards realising our hope, making our dreams come true. That tilting forward busies you into interaction of subject and object.

So really dzogchen is saying whatever you have or whatever occurs for you is enough; don't try to change this into something else. Of course this is a meditation instruction for those relaxing into the open presence of awareness. With awareness, activity arises in the manner of a dream and the consequences of actions also arise in the manner of a dream. Whereas when we identify with our self-referential ego-position the choices that we make are invested with hopes and fears and we are not indifferent to outcome.

What is natural and what is artificial? One person might feel that they need botox to continue being who they naturally are but another person might consider using botox to be artificial. That is to say, 'natural' can a very misleading term since we all are creatures of culture. In fact what looks natural may be artificial. 'Nature' comes from the Latin root, 'having been born', which means having a beginning, coming into existence. In dzogchen we refer to the natural state of the mind, but actually mind has no beginning, so it's not 'natural' in the sense of 'having been born'. This shows the difficulty of finding the right terms to translate the dzogchen meanings.

What is natural is the world, is the display of manifestation, which is arising and passing all the time. Everything that you can describe, everything you can hold, everything you experience through your senses is arising and passing.

Garab Dorje, the first human teacher of dzogchen famously taught that the essential thing is to see how it is; then to be clear that this is how it is; and thirdly, not to imagine that it's something else.

This first is called *ngotro* in Tibetan and means 'pointing out'. This pointing out is not very complicated; all that's required is that you see what is pointed to. If you go for a walk in the park with a child who's three and a half, four years of age, they're likely to stop: *"Oh! Look at this!"*

Then the parent says, *"Oh, it's a caterpillar."* Essentially, they're saying to the child, *"If we name it, we don't have to keep on looking at it, because I'm in a hurry."* *"No, but Mommy look! Because look how it's doing, oo oo. If we lie on the grass, then we can move like the caterpillar."*

There the child is the perfect guru. The child is desperately trying to say, *"If you look, it's amazing!"* – and it will stop you in this busyness of your life. But once you say, *"It's a caterpillar,"* life moves on and instead of walking in this amazing place, you're walking in the labyrinth of your own mind.

Being able to see our mind is *kadag,* primordial purity. This purity is beyond pure and impure. This is very different from Nietzsche's 'beyond good and evil'. It's not a transcendence of a dialectical form, but understanding the impossibility of the truth of any dialogic formation.

The purity of the mind indicates that there is nothing present except the clarity that there is nothing present. This clarity is the natural luminosity of the empty space of the mind – the non- duality of the dharmadhatu (Tib. *chöying*) and vidya (Tib. *rigpa*). There are not two things, merely the presence of the mystery that our presence is a groundless presence, and yet here we are!

For example, sitting here, we each have some sensation in our body. We both are our body – the manifestation of our subjectivity – and our body can also seem to us to be an object. In vipassana meditation, as we develop focused attention and mindfulness, we can scan our attention through our body and identify the transient moments of sensation which are occurring. We can also conceptualise these moments and construct a seemingly stable edifice that we take to be our body, the basis of our enduring sense of self.

We are used to the sense that we can know certain things about ourselves. We can know things about our body, about how we speak and about the contents and qualities of our mind. This is our normal way of knowing. However with this approach to knowing, we will never know our mind directly because the mind itself is a subject that can never be an object. When we grasp at our mind or know something about it we are always referring to the contents of the mind and not to the mind as awareness.

The immediacy of experience, the felt quality of our subjectivity, is undeniable in its presence yet is also never itself an object. When we turn the mind into an object, that is to say, when we think or say for example, *"My mind is very heavy with despair"* or *"I can't think straight today"* we are talking about an image or representation of what we take our mind to be. These patterning of representations are always impermanent, arising and passing as moments in the stream of thoughts and feelings. Our mind is full of representations yet itself is unrepresentable. It is the very openness of the mind that allows it to display so many ideas, images and representations. When we take the pattern of representations with which we construct our self-identity to be who we truly are then we hide the mind with a screen of its own manifestations.

Primordial purity of the mind means that it has never been contaminated. It is not contaminated now and it will never be contaminated. What is contamination? We know in many parts of the world people don't have good drinking water, due to a variety of causes. The water, which was once pure, has now become impure, because something got mixed with it. One thing stands in relation to another. You need at least two things for there to be contamination. One thing cannot contaminate itself.

This purity of the mind is often represented by a small ball, called *'tigle'* in Tibetan. This *tigle* has no fixed size; it's the smallest possible form and it's the largest possible form. It encompasses everything, and yet you can't find it anywhere as some-thing. Because the mind is empty of substance, it can't be defined.

Space itself has no limitation nor does it belong to anybody. In modern times we understand that the sky, the lower form of space, is said to belong. Countries have 'air-space'. Recently Turkey shot down a Russian plane and said this was because, *"It came into our air-space and we warned you not to do it."* When you look up in the sky you don't see any national divisions. This is an abstract categorisation that's fixed into maps and the basis of that, at a certain point an aeroplane crosses an invisible line and it is likely to blown up.

The great anarchist slogan is 'Property is theft'. This is because the world doesn't belong to anyone in particular, but due to the blessing of the arising of lawyers, everything has become own-able. When something can be owned, it can be set apart from the thing just next to it. If you have a garden, and you have a fence around your garden, the fencepost goes down maybe half a metre. One metre down, the earth is completely the same under all the gardens, but if the tree growing on your side of the garden stretches over into my garden, I can cut off the branch. The branch belongs to you though and I may be asked to return it to you. This is in English law, anyway. In that way, the definition of something as mine gives me a sense as to whether there is intrusion or not, whether something is being defiled or spoiled. Because of lawyers I am entitled to say how this is going to be.

This is the narcissistic 'will to power'. As the Rolling Stones sang, *"I am going to say how it's going to be; you are going to give your love to me."* My terms. My garden. My shoes. My life. My wife. You don't look at other men. I am going to put a veil over you, because you are a very precious commodity. This is how contamination works. Once something is separated off and owned it has a boundary around it and boundaries have to be protected.

"Greece and Italy are failing to keep out immigrants! These people shouldn't be in Europe; we should be here. We belong here, but they don't. Let's build a long wall right across Macedonia to keep them out. If the Greeks or the Italians want them, they can have them but we don't want them. If we let them in here, what will become of us? Germany won't be German anymore; Britain will be changed too and we don't want change. We believe in permanence." You can see the fear that arises: 'we will be contaminated'. Blood and soil, it's an old story, something to defend.

KADAG: PURITY OF THE MIND UNCONTAMINATED BY CONCEPTUALISING

Kadag, however, is pointing in a very different direction; it points towards the mind itself.

That is to say, our mind, our awareness, our being here, is both empty and full. Full because we have thoughts, feelings and sensations. When we take these contents of the mind to be central and definitive of who we are, then this particular patterning of ourselves as we encounter the environment gives

231

rise to sensations and feelings such as *'we like'*, and *'we don't like'*. We feel a lack, a vulnerability. We feel anxious about being overwhelmed, and so we become aggressive; we push the other away.

Thinking about the three root poisons, the first is mental darkness and refers to reification, to making things strongly real. It is predicated on the splitting of subject and object. Once I have my own individual territory, however, there is a vulnerability. Having got it, I could lose it so now I have to hang on to it. And who will take it away? Ah, now I have an enemy too. I don't really feel complete though and I feel that I need more. There are two reasons for this. One is impermanence; experience cannot be held. You drink a nice coffee, it's a wonderful flavour, and then it's gone! The residual flavour in the mouth is not the same as that initial hot intensity, and gradually the trace flavour also dissolves. Experience is beyond appropriation.

Appropriation means getting a handle on something, so when we get something, what are we getting? We get cognitions. We get mental constructions. We get ideas. *"Mmm, that was such a good coffee!"* What is that? That was a sentence. You can't pour a sentence or a thought into a cup and drink it. It is as if it's present with me, but it's cheating. On a cold night, when you don't have a scarf, you can visualise a scarf: *"Oh, this scarf is so warm; I feel so warm,"* and you feel warmer for a while. You're warm because you're imagining warm, you're making warm by imagining warm.

The key point here is to see that in the world we normally inhabit, everything is contaminate-able. The ordinary, dualistic, interactive present is contaminated by duality. What we grasp is an abstraction. If you say to someone, *"I love you,"* the 'you' that you love is an idea, because actually we don't know very much about the other person. Even if you live with someone, you don't see them all the time. You don't know what they're thinking; you don't know the sensations in their body. They go out and they come back, and they tell you a story about what they did. A story is a story, even if it's an honest story. Even if it's an honest story, it's not what actually happened. That's what we hold on to. *"Listen: last year, you told me da da da da da. I haven't forgotten."* That's what we hold on to; we hold on to a concept, an idea, an abstraction; the moment is gone.

It is very important to understand this because this is what is meant by *'kadag'*: the natural purity of the mind is pure because of the self-liberation of all phenomena. Tibetans say, *'Chi shar rang drol,'* *'whatever arises, goes away by itself'*. It goes away by itself; you don't have to push it out. The coffee went. If you had kept the coffee in the cup, it would be cold by now. It was an espresso coffee so why would you want to drink it cold? You can't keep it. You participate with the coffee at the time of participation. By participating with the coffee, you get the coffee – but you don't get anything. The coffee itself vanishes. There is a time for coffee to come and a time for coffee to go.

This is how it is; this is our experience. Experience is transitory. Reliance on concepts merely creates the illusion of permanence.

This links us with the pre-Socratic philosopher Heraclitus. He says you can never step into the same river twice. For buddhists this is a very profound saying. If you stay attached to believing in the name of the river, you can *say, "I've bathed in this river before,"* which is to say, *"I have bathed in the name of this river many times before."* That's possible because names as abstractions seem to have this pseudo-eternity. The actual water in the river is flowing; each second you're in it, the water is changing.

Phenomena, the presenting actuality, is primary; interpretation is secondary. *Kadag* means the purity of the mind which is uncontaminated by conceptualisation. Concepts cannot catch the nature of the mind. You can listen to many instructions on dzogchen, but they cannot say how the mind is. Hopefully however the words operate as a kind of massage, so that by relaxing the tense restrictions which maintain the seemingly seamless flow of thought-construction, you start to just be open. We have always been open.

This is a glass of water. This is a glass that happens to have water in it. Two different ways to describe the same thing. When our conceptualisation is *'this is a glass of water'* then the water- glass combination seems to be one thing. When our conceptualisation is, *'this is a glass which happens to have water in it'*, the glass is not inherently or intrinsically a glass of water. The fact that water is in the glass gives an added definition to what is in my hand. When we bind the concept of water into the glass, it becomes a water-glass. The infinite potential of this object in my hand is reduced. We could use the top part of the glass to cut out biscuits. If you were in a leaky boat you could use the glass to bail out. There's no limit to the potential of the glass; the limit is the restriction of our imagination. Even to call it a 'glass' is to draw attention to a certain feature of it. We don't need to think of it as glass, but once you think of glass you start to think, what can you do with glass?

This is form. In the buddhist way of thinking, form means shape or colour. When you see the glass in terms of its form, you start to imagine all kind of possibilities. That is to say, when we recognise *this is a glass,* this appears to be the recognition of a meaning that is inherent in the object. *A glass is a glass is a glass* – if you believe. If you don't believe, it is maybe something else. If you give this glass to a child of ten months, it will bang it on the table, and that will be a cause of pleasure for the child and anxiety for the parent because the adult is holding the idea of the glass whereas the child is not. What is the glass-ness of the glass? Maybe it's a projection? Everything in the world can be redefined, and it frequently is.

Okay. So now the mind has been constructed – in our mind – as being a thing like every other thing, but the mind itself – *rigpa,* awareness, the mind which is *kadag* or primordial purity – is not a thing. You can't find it in order to stick some label onto it. It is everywhere; it's always present, otherwise we wouldn't have any experience because the mind, like the mirror, shows what is there. What we experience is always the revelation of the mind. When we look for the mind, we get the reflection. When you look for your mind, you get the ideas, the memories, sensations, hopes, fears and so on.

IS IT A BIRD? IS IT A PLANE?

What is the mind itself? It's not a statement. It's not a definition. It's not a thing.

In many religious traditions, one is careful about saying the name of God, because God likes to be anonymous. Yes, God created the world, but then at the finale, he nipped off somewhere else and said, *"No, I wasn't there; it's nothing to do with me."* Nowadays we pray to God in Heaven, where he sits on a throne with Jesus Christ at his right side and Mary at his left side. He also has a special dove hovering above his head. You can learn a lot of things about Heaven, who all is there, where they are and what it is like. It's the same with Guru Rinpoche's heaven, Zangdopalri and Amitabha Buddha's heaven, Dewachen. All ideal real estate. *"Yes, sir. We have some very nice properties there. Can I interest you in them? For a mere one hundred thousand repetitions, you will be ensured a small enclosure with its own garden."*

These are projections, responses to our anxiety, to our wanting to know what will happen. The more you observe yourself, the more you see the anxiety of the ego. Like a drowning swimmer, we catch on to whatever floats by. When I travel in the London Underground, I have to struggle not to read the adverts. Words! Oh, what do they say? I don't want to go to the cinema. I don't want to buy anything. I don't need anything, but I do need words.

The words are not giving me a way to something else; the words are giving me my self. The wheels of my mind are turning, moving in this world of constructed meaning. Letting go of that is how we open ourselves to *kadag*.

As it says in many of the texts, you can't lose your mind, you can't gain your mind; you can't buy it, you can't sell it. It's not a commodity. It's not a thing among things. What we need is already here, and it's hidden from us by our own activity. Effort doesn't help, because effort is about lack and about construction; it's about the agency of the ego. Letting go. It is what it is.

It's very difficult to accept how it is when you're already judging how it is. For example, when you were a child perhaps an aunt sent you a present, but when you opened it up you didn't like it. Then your mother said, *"Oh, now you have to write her a little note now, thanking her."* and you are thinking, *"Why do I need to thank her for a present I don't want?!"* How to receive a gift? *Kadag* is the given. It is there from the very beginning. It's always there, always already there. Emptiness is the gift of how it is. *"But it's not what I thought it would be!"* Who am I - the ego - to be judging the buddha-nature? Why should I think that my thoughts are reliable?

Perhaps in the course of our lives we have made some mistakes. Perhaps we have got lost and confused. Afterwards we might think, *"Wow, I didn't... I, I didn't see that coming."* Hmm, maybe I'm not so smart. When I say, *"But my mind should be something else,"* and you merge with that thought, then you separate from what is arising, and you enter into judgment about it, trying to push away the thoughts you don't like, trying to hang on to the thoughts you do like.

Sometimes when we practise, the mind is very dull. At other times it is agitated and excited. Sometimes we go off in stories. That is what is arising. When we think *"I don't like it,"* or *"It shouldn't be this way,"* then this is a thought commenting on a thought. *Kadag*, however, means untouched by thought.

The local Berlin bus will not take you to London. You can make many journeys on the local Berlin buses and indeed they are very nice buses, but they won't take you to London. Thoughts will take you to thoughts. Jump on a thought and reliably it will take you to another thought – it will not take you to the mind itself. If you want to find the mind itself, be present at the vanishing point of thought. That is a difficult point to find. Because these thoughts are very regular. The key point is that the mind, from the very beginning, is naked; it's not covered by anything. When the ego looks for the mind, it finds many obscurations between it and its so-called 'true nature'. In Tibetan, they say this is like the farmer who goes looking for the cow on the hill when the cow is safely in the byre. If you go looking in the wrong place, you can be looking for a long, long time but you will not find it.

Who is the one having the thought? Experience is occurring. *Who is the experiencer?* This question is central, and we have to allow the question to open and become the soft quality of our attention to what is occurring. The danger is for us that a thought arises that says, '*I am the thinker.*' The space of inquiry is filled with an answer and a solution. The space of not-knowing is not allowed to be there long enough for profound knowing, or rather being to appear. It's like when you were at school you learned what you could do in the playground and that you can't do the same in the classroom. It's not that what you do in the playground is wrong; it's that it doesn't belong in the classroom.

Similarly, when we meditate, thoughts are not so very important. When we're interacting with other people, yes, thoughts are very important, but in meditation, our focus is on '*Who is the one who is here?*'

This term *the given* is not ideal, but certainly in English there's a big, big difficulty in translating technical terms of dzogchen. It means, '*it's just by itself*'. In Tibetan, they use the term '*rangjung*' – self-existing or self-validating, not created by anything else. The given doesn't need gifts. The mind in its fertility, in its creativity, is always giving gifts. All kinds of experiences arise;

237

they give themselves. We don't need to hang on to them. Gifting never stops, and the given needs no gift.

In the traditional formulation in Tibetan, they say, *'Ke wa me pa gag pa me pa.'* *'Ke wa me pa'* means unborn. *'Gag pa me pa'* means never-ceasing, not ever blocked.

Unceasing is this flow of experience – perceptions, colours, shapes, hopes and fears, desires, all kinds of stuff – ceaseless; it never ends. This is life, but the unborn, this is emptiness itself and the mind is inseparable from this. The mind is like the sky; the sky just *is*; it's the given. Many things move through the sky. Clouds offer themselves to the openness of the sky. The space of the sky receives the cloud, but the sky doesn't hang on to the cloud. When the wind blows, the cloud moves. The sky is open, not trying to hang on to the clouds.

We, however, try to hang on to particular thoughts or ideas or constructions. This is the litmus test, this is the real fulcrum point for meditation: to see, do we tilt into believing the thought, the meaning that the thought gives, the constructed thought, or do we trust the given?

RELAXING EMOTIONAL INVESTMENT

To use the language of mahayana buddhism, this is relative truth and absolute truth. Relative truth is categorised in two parts: pure and impure relative truth. Impure relative truth is where you see phenomena; you take them to be existing; and you have an affective relationship to them. There is affect, an emotional and intensified reaction to something, which is taken as existing in itself.

Linked to this we have the idea of the two obscurations. The obscuration of the afflictions, or contaminating emotions – stupidity anger, desire, jealousy, pride and so on. That is what is operating in impure truth; there is the strong, intense feeling tone reaction to what appears to be there. The second obscuration is the obscuration of the cognisables, of that which can be thought about and known. In particular, this refers to taking the thought, or the name, as equivalent to the actuality of the object. So I have a thought, such as *'this is a glass'*, and I am telling this object what it is. Having put that name into and onto the glass, I now address the glass in terms of my own projection.

    —I don't know why anyone made you! —Why were you born? Eh? Speak to me!

We have to remember this is not a philosophy; this is *us*, this is what we do. Our practice is relaxing the emotional investment, and then the glass becomes something neutral, just there. It's just there, as the glass. This is called 'pure relative truth'.

One way that we do this in mahayana is by saying that all sentient beings have been my mother in a past life. They have done very kind things for me and I have an obligation to them. This person may annoy me now, but when they were my mother, they fed me, cleaned me, clothed me and did many things for me. In relation to the kindness they have offered me in the past, any momentary irritation now is irrelevant.

We are trying to move from bias and prejudice – 'my friend', 'my enemy' and so on – to equanimity:

"May all beings be happy, and may they be happy just because they are. Not because they deserve it, not because I like them, but just because they are. They have not earned it, they may not even deserve it; it's not the fruit of their good karma. In any case, may they be happy! May all fucking arseholes be happy! May all torturers be happy! May all vicious, cruel beings be happy!"

    —But why should bad people get as much happiness as the good kind people? —That's a very good question.

    —It's not fair; I've tried really, really hard to be good. It's not fair.

    —It's like this due to causes and conditions.

—But I have studied and learned the game-plan of the world, like learning to play poker.

Beings get enlightened because of their buddha-nature. Dzogchen, mahayana and tantra each take a slightly different focus in this regard. Mahayana talks about the accumulation of merit and wisdom. Kalu Rinpoche used to say that if you want to go on a journey, you can walk, and everyone can do that. If you want to go on the train, you can do that but it will cost you some money. If you want to go on a plane, that's faster but it will cost you even more. Tantra is like the plane. If you don't have a good accumulation of merit and wisdom, you won't be able to get on the tantra plane. This is what is meant by the colophon often found on traditional texts. It reads something like, *"This text is preserved for those great beings with highest karma. Don't let it fall in the hands of the bad guys."* Unfortunately, the bad guys also have buddha-nature and no matter what bad things they do, they can't destroy their buddha-nature. The way to get enlightened is awakening to your buddha-nature. We already have the plane ticket, we just don't know where the airport is.

This is the big difference. If you see this, then you realise relative truth.

Kadag, the primordial purity, is the given, it's just here; it's present all the time, everywhere. It's not created by our virtuous deeds, it's not spoiled by our negative deeds. The content of the mind is created by other thoughts, other feelings, and so we can expand, we can contract, we have all kinds of experiences – these are interactive and relative – but the ground nature out of which they arise is unconditioned.

An example given in many dzogchen texts is a piece of coal. You can wash it every day for hours, for years, but it won't turn into chalk. It's either coal or it isn't. In the same way, our awakening arises on the possibility of the awakened, which is already within us.

Awakening is not about going from here to somewhere else; it's about being here now and really opening to what this is. Opening to what this is, is like opening to a beautiful sunset over the ocean – all that's required is that you're not distracted. You see the ball of the sun gradually sinking over the rippling horizon. You start to feel the breeze that comes as the sun comes down. The breeze comes in, onto your face. You will get the whole thing; it's given to you, but you have to be there, not distracted, not on your mobile phone, not taking a selfie of yourself in front of the sun. This is what meditation is: being open to what is.

NGOWO AND RANGZHIN: THE FACE AND ITS COMPLEXION

In terms of the practice, there are three aspects of our situation. We have the basic actuality, or the given-ness, *ngowo* in Tibetan. Some people translate '*ngowo*' as essence but the word 'essence' in English can be problematic. For example we refer to essential oils, which are a distillation, but *ngowo* is not a distillation. *Ngowo* actually is the word for 'face' and in a sense, although we can move our face around creating different expressions, our face is a kind of given, it's just the way we look.

Ngowo is our mind at rest, not doing anything, not even moving. It's like the mirror. You can never see a mirror, because the mirror is always showing something that it's not. When you look in the mirror, what you see are reflections. When you look in your mind you don't see your mind, you see thoughts, sensations, feelings, memories and so on. The fact that you can't see your mind doesn't mean it's not there; it is showing itself through the presence of these experiences.

You can't experience your mind; it's a state of being. Not being this or that, but just open being, pure being. This mind, having no top no bottom no sides, is not located anywhere, yet it shows itself ceaselessly. It shows itself as clarity. By 'clarity' is meant an illuminating power and what it illuminates is itself. Self-luminous.

In Tibetan this is called *rangzhin*, a term which refers to the complexion of the face. Through looking at somebody's face and experiencing their complexion, you read something about them. Are they healthy or sick, are they tired, or sad or happy? The potential, the richness, the display of the empty given-ness of the mind shows itself as the complexion, which is our field of experience.

The mind reveals the field. On one level, we experience ourselves living inside our skin-bag, looking out of our eyes, listening out of our ears. But if we relax a little and don't interpret, when I see you, I see me, because you are my experience. In that moment of perception, there is no separation between subject and object. As we look around this room, here we are, Saturday afternoon, alive, seeing many different things. How do I know that I'm alive? Because something is happening. Happening for me. What is happening for me? *You* are happening for me; you are my experience. My experience is you. This is what is meant by 'non-duality'.

When I was at lunch, sitting at the table talking with a few people, a kind of shaping occurred around the topics. We find ourselves called into being, or showing ourselves, by the mood of what is going on. On one level we can say that we're having a conversation with some people and words are passing between us but we're also, together, collectively, creating a mood. A mood in which things can be said, more or less. What is occurring is generated by the participation of the people conversing together. For each person, it's 'my' experience; but it's my experience, given to me by what's occurring. This subject and object movement is not two different things.

To use a traditional example, there is the ocean and there are the waves. We use two terms 'ocean' and 'waves'. What's the difference between ocean and waves? Well, the waves show themselves on the surface. When I try to look down I don't see down into the ocean. The ocean I don't see, and the waves I do see. So what are the waves made of? The ocean. The waves are made of the ocean. The ocean is the wave, and the wave is the ocean; but the wave rises up and seems to be something.

The water of the wave has no absolute separation from the water of the ocean. It is one but not the same. This also is a meaning of 'non-duality'. Non-duality means not only one thing nor many different things.

The wave and the ocean are the same and different, but the difference doesn't destroy the same. The difference is a variation on the same. It is a difference devoid of contradiction. The wave is not stealing something from the ocean. When the wave crashes back onto the ocean, the ocean is not getting angry and telling it to come back! Whether the water is in the depth or on the surface, the quality is the same.

This is the example given for *rangzhin*, the radiance of the mind, the openness of our mind without any limit. Because it has no limit, it has no inside or outside. If there is no outside, there is no other so whatever is occurring is not coming from somewhere else. The richness of the experiential field is the mind.

You may start taking photographs of the waves and comparing one wave with another. You may have a table covered with different photographs and you say, "Well, *these ones here look similar, but I don't know where that other one fits in.*" Then we could do the same in this room here and say, "Well, *there's people with black hair; now they should all go in that corner, and people with blonde hair, go in that other corner. Oh, but some people with blonde hair are tall and some are short... So tall blond people go in that corner, and small blond people go in that corner.*"

In the given-ness of the emergence of experience – here we are – there is diversity without separation.

Once you get into naming and labelling and conceptualising and making associations, then you start to have separation. If you take a handful of water from the sea and look at it for a bit and then pour it back into the ocean, the seeming separation was only situational.

In the same way, when we grasp at a thought or a feeling and make a construction around it, it is as if we have got hold of something. [Pointing at the flowers in front of him:] These are very nice flowers. Something is there, and I have a feeling-tone response. The flowers are in the vase; the vase is on the floor; the floor connects all the people sitting in the room. It is part of the room. We can appreciate the belongingness of the flowers; or we can take them up with our mind and see if we know all the botanical Latin names for them or what would be the best environment for them, and so on.

This second aspect, *rangzhin,* the showing or display, is the undivided field that is full of diversity.

When we look and we see people and we see them as individuals, this is a kind of optical illusion, because our focusing of our attention on one person involves the allowing of the rest in the room to fade back. You can observe this for yourself quite easily. If you just open your gaze to the side of your eyes, to your peripheral vision, you can really see right around the room. You see everything, but you don't see anything. It's a kind of panoramic or inclusive gaze. Then you alter these optical muscles, and you bring the focus back; then you're focusing. In that moment, something becomes more present and something else is receding.

Now, if I'm looking at one person, it is as if the room vanishes; it is 'as if'. The room hasn't actually vanished. It is less present for me, but it is still present. This is happening all the time, as we focus in on something and then expand out. Things become enriched by the quality of our attention, and then they become more ghostlike and opaque as we start to think, *"Oh yeah, lots of people."* When we start to focus on someone in particular, usually we're looking for something. *"Oh, have I met you before? What is your name?"* Some truth hidden someplace: will it come back to me?

From the point of view of the practice, clarity is what it is. What do we get by knowing someone's name? What does it add to the experience? You see someone, the angle of their head, the texture of their eyes – whether they're in soft focus or not. You get a sense of their breathing. This is the simple clarity of the mind.

THUGJE: PARTICIPATION

Now we have the third aspect, which in Tibetan is called *thugje*. Normally *thugje* means 'compassion' and in the dzogchen tradition it is sometimes translated as 'energy'. Nowadays I often translate it as 'participation'.

For example here in this field together, here in this room in the Kamalashila Institute, due to some stimulus, due to some wind blowing, we find ourselves sitting in a particular way, talking in a particular way and so on. By seeing you, I speak; my speaking is for you, but also my speaking is *from* you. That's amazing. The words come out of us from the invitation of the other. It's not all up to me; I'm not in a bubble. We are working together, albeit with different roles, at this particular time. Your receptivity is my participation. That's why I'm looking around all the time, looking at people's faces: *Where are you? How are you?*

This third aspect, the energy or the expression or the participation, is a field factor. My speaking is the field moving. Your listening is the field moving. Your attention is not some passive nothing-at-all-ness; it is an active presence-ing, a participation which generates a mood and a swirling of a being-in-it-together-ness, which is very important.

Why would we be lonely? When are we ever cut off from other people? If we are available, what shall we do with other people's availability? *"But they're not available in the way I want them to be available, so I can't participate the way I like to participate. You see, my problem is that I am a wonderful actor, but I always get the most shit audiences."* It's not like that; the audience comes first. The others dictate what can be done. Things can be said or not said according to the mood. A comedian learns to trust the room. Because if he's learned a joke and he wants to tell the joke but it's not the right place, then he has a problem. People don't laugh, and he loses the audience. What this means is we are never on the outside; we are never separate or apart or alone.

The infinite spaciousness of the mind gives rise to this field of experience within which our participation is moving. If we simply trust the openness, the display and the participation – these three are inseparable – this is awakening according to the dzogchen tradition.

SHORT SITTING PRACTICE

So now let's sit in a simple way. On one level, it doesn't matter how you sit, but if you sit with your skeleton supporting you, it makes it a little easier because you have less additional sensation. Gaze is open into the space in front of you, without staring at something. We're just here, present. Stuff happens. You may see people's bodies moving a bit. You might hear noises from outside. You're aware of the warmth of the room. Thoughts and feelings arises, sensations in the body. Each of these phenomena is perfectly entitled to be here. They are not illegal immigrants. They have a valid pass and we allow them to pass through. They're not looking for a permanent place to stay; they're not looking for citizenship. They come, and they go.

Who is the one who is sitting? From moment to moment, you find identification. You might have a sense that you are your head, or that you are some movement inside your head. Or you become aware of your shoulders and your body. Whatever kind of identification comes, don't push it away, don't merge with it, just allow it to be there. If a thought arises, *'I don't know what I'm doing. What is this for? I am bored.'*, don't merge into the thought and don't try to push it away either. Offer hospitality, and the guest will stay for a bit and go. The less engaged, the easier the guest goes. Once you start mobilising into some kind of reactivity, little hooks go into the thought-form, and you have investment and reactivity and so on.

So, without doing anything ritualistic or artificial, we just sit, gaze open, and allow existence to arise and pass, the lips slightly open and the tongue turned up on the palate.

[Period of meditation.]

Some of you are familiar with practicing this way and you can do it for longer. When you are new to it, just practise in the same way but for shorter periods.

LHUNDRUB: ARRIVING ALL AT ONCE

The practice is both still and dynamic. The more we relax our participative energy, the more the energy of the field is free to come and go. This arising is referred to as *lhundrub. Lhundrub* is not inside or outside; it's everything that's occurring, the entire field of experience. *Lhun* means a heap, and *drub* means to make or shape or bring together and so it indicates *arriving all at once.*

Are we to focus on experience or focus on interpretation?

If we focus on interpretation there are a lot of things to say about what's in this room. There are photographs, statues, people, different kinds of clothing, hairstyles and so on. When you get into that interpretation or analysis, you move towards a pseudo-stasis, the seeming presence of things that you can hold on to.

Lhundrub indicates that it's always full; there's always something happening. If you're at the seashore looking out to sea there is a seamless movement of the waves. It's not like one wave arises followed by another separate wave. Nor do the waves come to an end. It's not like 'waving' is arising out of the sea in many different forms. This is the meaning of *lhundrub*. What is appearing is experience – experience emerging from, or the showing of, the luminous emptiness of the mind.

Over the years the dzogchen tradition has been elaborated with different stages, different kinds of practice and so on. Dzogchen may be organised in different ways but basically there is *trekchod* and *thogal*.

TREKCHOD: CUTTING LOOSE FROM WHAT?

Trekchod means cutting, cutting free, cutting loose. Cutting loose from what? Cutting loose from my sense of myself and my sense of other which is composed or constructed upon a reliance on interpretive tools: *"I am attached to certain memories and ideas, and the arising of this patterning of mobilisation and volition gives me my exclusive topology. I am interested in certain things; and they become more real for me, and other things become less real."* This is what has to be cut.

Trekchod means not falling into the arising movement of grasping, not accumulating reliance.

The Bible speaks of not building your house on sand. When you come into experience, everything is sand flowing. You can't hold on to it. In fact you don't need to hold on to it, but you see also that you can't build anything on it. *"Because I feel like this today, tomorrow I am going to..."* How I feel tomorrow is not available today. I can't build on tomorrow. We might feel, *"Tomorrow I'm going to enjoy going to the theatre."* but then tomorrow comes and, *"I am so tired. I don't actually want to go to the theatre. Why on earth did I buy the ticket?"* The person who bought the ticket and the person who now has a ticket to go to the theatre are not the same person.

This is what the Buddha's first teaching about suffering means: we are not who we think we are.

Even though I may think that I have 'found myself' — perhaps through therapy — I am not a fixed thing and to be so would be terrible. We find ourselves opening and closing, responding and not responding... We are fluctuating.

LHUNDRUB: WHAT IS HAPPENING

If this is the case, then what is happening? This is the central question for *lhundrub*. *Lhundrub* is what is happening, it's the situation; it's this particular shape. It's like this, and then it's gone, and then it's something else.

What you have is the exquisite taste of this moment, which will never be repeated. You can't hold it, but you can taste it; you can be there. You don't need a memory to go with you, you don't need a selfie to remind you, but there is an energising enrichment, which is the trust.

　　—It will be fine. It's Kuntuzangpo. It's okay.

　　—Are you sure? Is this really how you want to live? —As if you have a choice!

Consumerist capitalism may provide you with mangoes in the middle of winter, but you don't have a choice between summer happiness and winter sorrow. It doesn't come in packages. Health doesn't come in a package. Some people have genetic tendencies toward a particular kind of illness; some people have astrological susceptibilities towards certain accidents and so on.

Does it matter? We are here – if we are here! If we're not here, where are we? If we're here, we're here and then we die. Then something else happens – or not; you can believe or not believe. There are the bardos, first this one and then that one...

You can buy *The Rough Guide to Tibet*. 'Rough Guide' – it's a brand name – but you can also get a ***Rough Guide to Tibetan***

Death. It's a guidebook. The guidebook is not written by people who went there and came back. If I buy my Rough Guide to Berlin, the book says, *"I hope you enjoy this book. I've never actually been to Berlin so send me a postcard and let me know if anything is not accurate."* This book is a work of the imagination.

What we have is here and now. The past is gone; the future hasn't come. Here and now is *lhundrub*.

Translators working with Namkhai Norbu Rinpoche refer to it as 'instant presence', which is, in a sense, presence in the instant. This is present and I am present. I present myself to this, and this presents itself to me. This co-presence-ing or co-emergence is *lhundrub*.

THÖGAL: DIRECT EXPERIENCE OF ENERGY

Lhundrub is the basis of *thogal*.

Thögal is working with experience, working with what is occurring. Light, sound, taste, smell. The texts write a lot about sound and light, but all the other senses are there as well. What we see here in the room is light. The eye is connected with light. What we think in the room is 'people' and 'things' – men, women, tall, short, sitting on chairs, sitting on the floor...

Thögal begins when you can see without instantly interpreting. *Thögal* is the direct revealing of the energy of the world, unmediated by our interpretation. This is why in the tradition they say first you have to be clear about *kadag*. That is to say, to experience the emptiness of the field, to see how our own thoughts elaborate the details at which we then grasp. It's seeing without elaboration, without interpretation.

Question: But how will I know what I'm seeing?

James: What you're seeing is the radiance of the mind, the light that arises out of the mind itself, out of the *dharmakaya*. Because it is light, you start to be able to work with the light, because there is appearance without internal essence or substance. Mind puts the substance and the essence into the object, into the people. We see someone and we think, *"They are nice. I like this person. I'm attracted to this person. I want to spend time with this person."* Or we see someone and we think, *"Mmm, they're a bit weird. I'm not sure I want to spend any time with them."* This is our normal way of operating in the world. We generate a charge, a valency on the object: *'Because I like you, you are nice.'* The projection appears to be imbedded in the other.

You can see here the difficulty of practising *thogal:* because we see *people.* The Buddha, right from his very earliest teachings on the five *skandhas,* the five heaps, has said there are no people. This is called *pudgala anatma drishti,* the absence of inherent self-nature in persons. *Pudgala* means 'sentient beings' or, in particular, 'persons'. The five skandhas of form, feeling, interpretive perception, associations and consciousness operate together to generate the illusion of a self-existing person.

Seeing people in terms of the five *skandhas* is a means for making an analysis which puts into question our habitual assumption. However such an analysis is that even if it's accurate, it happens after the immediacy of the moment. For example, I look at you and I see you as a person. Then I may think, *"No, this is my mind at work",* but already I have been caught by the illusion that you are the person whom I take you to be.

ONE GROUND DISPLAYING TWO PATHS

C.R. Lama very often said words to the effect that *"The buddhadharma has one taste. In Nyingmapa we have nine different vehicles, but they are not in contradiction; they all go in the same direction. If you understand the five skandhas, it is easier to understand emptiness. If you understand emptiness, it is easier to understand tantric transformation. If you understand tantric transformation, it is easier to understand kadag."* That is because they all point to the same thing, that the mind is chief. The mind creates samsara; the mind creates nirvana.

That is what is meant when dzogchen teachers say that there is one ground and two paths. The one ground is infinite spacious emptiness. Within this or out of this, but never escaping this, manifests appearance. This appearance displays itself as subject and object, like two waves in the ocean. We may call one 'subject' and call the other 'object' but both are water. It is only conventionally and situationally that one is subject and the other is object, rolling on and on and on. This is the display or the play, the *rolpa*, the *lila,* of emptiness itself.

Once you see that, then the ground and what arises from the ground are inseparable, but if you get caught up in thoughts about this and thoughts about that and *'me in here'* and *'you out there',* then the ground is forgotten, and then where are you?

Well, you are exactly where you should be – here and now! Because there's nowhere else to be. You think you're somewhere else, but you're here.

Chatral Rinpoche was very kind to me when I was younger. Several times he gave this same example to me, since I was always asking him, *"Why am I here?"* and *"What is samsara?",* and so on. He said, *"It's like two brothers, and they're lying in bed. One brother is awake, the other brother is asleep. The sleeping brother is having a nightmare. The awake brother says, 'Oh, wake up, wake up!' When the sleeping brother wakes up, where is he? He is where he's always been: in his bed, safe, with his brother."* In our nightmare, in our mental activity, in our construction, we are not here. But we are always here.

Although many methods have been developed in dzogchen, in the lineage from C.R. Lama we are not involved with technical methods and that is because when you apply a technique, you are introducing a sense of agency. [James scratches his head:] *'I am scratching my head.' 'I am the one who is scratching my head.' 'I am sitting here.'* Grammatically, they not so different, but very different. "I *can* scratch my head." "I *find myself* sitting here." How do you sit here? For the schoolteacher with the class of five-year-old children, who says, *"Now sit still!"* They look at each other and giggle, and if you giggle, you wriggle. But if this teacher starts to tell a story, the children are very peaceful and find themselves sitting still.

When you're doing things as the agent, even if they're dharma-oriented and harmonious, they are structurally a separation of subject and object. It's not that one shouldn't do these techniques – and sometime we can do some of these practices, like *rushen* and others – but when you do them, you get different kinds of experiences. And we have already had many kinds of experience. The problem is not experience; the problem is being the experiencer.

"Oh, if only I get this special initiation; if only I get this special teaching..." This is fantasyland, Disneyland.

WHO IS DOING THE DOING?

Dharma say very clearly that you can't lose your mind and you can't find your mind either. You can't buy it or sell it. It is intrinsic. We are here, having experience, so who is the experiencer? The experiencer, without effort, is the mirror. The reflection is *in* the mirror. As the reflection fills the mirror, does the mirror feel invaded? Does the mirror say, *"Watch out! Let me get to sleep. You keep moving over on my side; you get back on your own side!"*? No, the mirror is much more generous than that. The mirror says, *"Take the whole bed! Move, stretch, snore, fuck, whatever, I don't mind."*

The mirror is space; the mind is space. The experiencer is space and so it has infinite hospitality, without judgment. Its welcome is unconditional.

Tantric practice is not like that. Tantric practice is very conditional. You have to sit in the right way, make the right mudras, make the right torma, and do this, do that. It's very, very precise. It's a choreography like a ballet.

So we have to decide: *'Is this okay? How would it be better? What is lacking? What is too much? How will I know? I will have to evaluate.'*

Who then is the evaluator? The evaluator is someone you experience. The evaluator is cuckoo. The cuckoo is lazy. He doesn't have his own nest. He goes into someone else's nest and says, *"I belong here."* The nest is very big; it is the *dharmadhatu*. The cuckoo likes a lot of space. Or like a child setting out all of her dolls – *"No, you sit there, and you have to tell her to do that!"* – we try to organise everything. All of this busyness in our mind.

Who is the organiser? Who is the boss, who is the controller? In Tibetan they call it the *'che pa po'*, the one who is doing the doing, the doer. This is the energy of the mind; it is not the mind itself: *"I am the boss; there is no higher authority than me. This is how it has to be done."* It's very, very cunning. In the bad old days, if you got pulled in to the police station, they would put you in a chair in front of the desk. The investigator would be sitting on the other side, with a lamp beside them dazzling your eyes. The lamp is not illuminating their beautiful face; the lamp is directed at your eyes. They are in the dark. They are the all-seeing unseen one. They are the Stasi. This is the basis of the police: *"We see you; you don't see us." "You are accountable to me; I am not accountable to you. Would you like to make a complaint against me? You're very welcome. May I offer you ten years with us?"* Very scary. Very, very scary.

Now look at your own investigator. Like a dog pissing on a lamppost, your mind knows everything, but you never catch it, it slips away. When the wall in Berlin came down, where did all the secret police go? At the end of the war, where did all the Gestapo go? This is the special skill of the investigator. Slipping away.

This is why looking for your own mind is very difficult. When you look for your mind as if it's a quality of the ego, you are trying to catch the investigator, the judge but you never can catch the judge. The judge is always ahead of you; they have twenty passports.

Be clear, this is not a theory, a story; this is an instruction on the meditation. Because when we sit with our own mind, then we encounter the bit of us that wants to name and judge and move things around. In the dharma there are so many paths of development for changing and softening and educating this judge, but they take a very long time.

That is not what we're doing. As soon as you find yourself getting caught up in judgment and evaluation, don't investigate the judge. Relax into the presence, or relax into being present as the experiencer.

The judge is the energy of the experiencer that has gone into a self-referential loop. It is an imaginal construct but we love the creations of the mind, and when we enter in to that, you can do it, we can judge. A child of four, playing with dolls, will have one doll talking to the other the way the mother talks to them. *"Oh no! You're all dirty again! I have to clean you all day long!"* Yes, it sounds very amusing – the mother's voice, the father's voice is coming out of the child. Because we learn through mimicry what was the other becomes the self. The small child is showing that she can be many different people, and one of them is the judge. It sounds like a true voice of the child, but it's an echo-voice. In the same way when we get into evaluating the world, putting names and labels onto the world, it is a mimetic echo-voice. It doesn't speak the truth; it creates a world in which we can believe.

This is our prison-guard: the fact that we manifest two pulsating modes, like a damaru[3]. We are the cheater and the cheated. We create illusions that captivate other people, and we create illusions that captivate ourselves.

---

[3] A two-sided drum which is turned sharply so that the clapper hits alternate sides.

So, observing our mind, observing how we solidify the world and divide it up into hierarchies of value, this is our place at the centre of samsara.

ZABGYE: DEPTH AND LIGHT

Our topic *'Depth and Light'* is a reference to the Tibetan term *'zabgye'*. *'Zab'* means 'depth' and *'gye'* means 'to expand'. *Zab* refers to *kadag*; it is the depth of the infinite space of the *dharmadhatu*. Dharmadhatu means 'the space of the dharmas'. *Dhatu* in this usage is like an openness.

As we've looked already, everything has to be somewhere. When we look around this room we see the wall in front of us. The wall is in space, and beyond the wall there is another room or the space outside. Emptiness means there is no real barrier. Everything is within emptiness. All phenomena are located, because everything has something in front of it or behind it, above it, or below it and so on. This location-ing, or locate-ability of phenomena weaves them into the web of signifiers, because every dharma is in conversation or interaction with other dharmas.

The dharmadhatu is the space within which dharmas occur. 'Dharma' here means 'phenomena', phenomena inseparable from the dharmadhatu. So, the dharmadhatu is a space which is filled with that which is not different from itself and yet shows difference.

'Depth' refers the unimpeded openness of the mind, which includes whatever is occurring.

We have other very famous terms such as *'longchen'*, which also refer to great space or depth. The name of the famous 14th century Nyingma teacher, Longchen Rabjam, means exactly *'zabgye'*. *'Rabjam'* means expansive, filling everything.

Depth is the immediate inclusion of everything. It means that our mind can encompass everything and yet we cannot find the bottom of it or the top or the sides. So this depth really indicates that it is 'immeasurable', that it cannot be summed up. We can't come to any conclusion about it.

What does this mean? When we sit in the meditation practice and lots of things are occurring. In and of themselves none of these things is a limit but they do have an impact. Remember Dodge Ems? The bumper cars that you get in fairgrounds? You get in and you drive around and you whack into other cars and try to avoid them whacking into you. This is our world. We bump into each other, and bumping gives rise to new dharmas and new dharmas and new dharmas. New formations arise all the time; we never get to the end of them.

Dharmas don't displace space; they don't cause any trouble for space. When we sit in our mediation practice and we become irritated with our mind or confused or disappointed that we can't maintain clarity or whatever, this is not the hospitality of the dharmadhatu; this is the consequence of locating ourselves in a particular place: *'Because I am like this, I don't want that.'*

Whenever we find ourselves getting into judgment, getting into hopes and fears, we return to the question, *'Who is the experiencer?'* This is not a question formulated as a cognitive inquiry such as when you hear a knock at the door and you wonder who it is. When you go to the door to open it then your question is answered and you see who it is. That's not very complicated. So who is the experiencer?

'Here' is the experience. *[James indicates a place.]* The experiencer has to be somewhere nearby. The experience is like the door – knock, knock, knock. So, be present with the experience and you find yourself present *as* the experiencer.

In the tradition this is always described as like the mirror and the reflection. The mirror shows the reflection both is itself and is not itself.

When you have an experience – maybe you are sitting and a thought arises, perhaps about going back to work on Monday, or whatever – the thought catches you for a little bit. This is happening; it's showing. If it weren't showing, it wouldn't be here. It's showing. Someone sees what's showing. 'I' see what is showing. So who is the 'I' who is the experiencer?

We need to un-elaborate the 'I'. Don't tell a story describing the 'I' because if you start to tell a story about the one who is seeing it, you're just wrapped it into a narrative. We have to learn how to do this just by practising.

Again and again, we go off but wherever we get lost, that's exactly just where we are. If you are at the point of getting lost, then you are not lost; you are here. *"But I shouldn't be here; I should be there!"* That's a thought. If you're here, here is the only place to be. This is *dzogpa chenpo* – complete as this. It doesn't need anything added; it doesn't need anything corrected.

IT IS EMPTY BUT HOW IT APPEARS IS AS DIFFERENT

The reflection in the mirror can be clear or it can be hazy and there is no difference between being clear and being hazy – if you're clear!

What does that mean? It means that the potential of the mirror is the same whether the light is on or off, whether the mirror is steamed up or not. If you go in a dark room, you don't see anything in the mirror. It doesn't mean the mirror is not a mirror. If you light a small candle, the room is still gloomy and what is in the mirror is a little bit shady, hazy. Then you put on the main light and now the reflection is very bright. Has the mirror been improved? Is the bright reflection better than the hazy shady one?

It is what it is. This is so completely important. It is empty; *how it appears is as different.*

Tibetan language has lots of ways of talking about this difference. For example there are the two terms *'ji ta wa khyen pa'i yeshe'* and *'ji nye pa khyen pa'i yeshe'*. The first refers to 'the intrinsic knowing of the clear understanding of how things are'. The second refers to 'the intrinsic knowing of the clear understanding of how things appear'. It is not a case of either/ or. *'Ji nye pa'* has the sense of measurement, of evaluation. For example, I can see that the people over there are further away from me than the people sitting next to me. That's an evaluation. I'm able to have some sense of distance and relative proportions and location. You couldn't function in the world if you couldn't do that. If you drive a car, you have to work out where this car is in relation to other vehicles moving fast. In Tibetan they speak of something in terms of *'how it appears to be'*. That is to say, what you measure, what you evaluate, is *appearance*.

How it is, is empty. How it appears is whatever that particular shaping is. Neither has essence nor substance. Looking around this room we see different people's faces and bodies and postures and we get some sense of their age or their health or their lifestyle. We need to be able to interpret what we see in order to interact with people. This is a momentary permission. If somebody looks a bit sad to us, they look a bit sad, *now*. Maybe they are not sad, maybe they are sad, but if tomorrow we say to them, *"I hope you are feeling happier today. You looked so sad yesterday,"* we have imputed, projected, an essence into them.

Appearance means, 'just this appearance'. Because it has no internal definition to it, it is not telling you about something inside. Everything is showing the energy of the dharmakaya. As far as we know, the dharmakaya is not tired, it doesn't have greasy hair, it didn't forget to clean its teeth, it's not sad. People look the way they look. It's just like that – for now.

Emptiness and appearance: it doesn't presume, it doesn't assume. I give you your freedom to be you, and I give myself my freedom to be me. I am not going to diagnose you. I have big psychotherapy books at home for the diagnosis of many conditions. In order to make use of such books, we identify signs and symptoms, which has us looking at people in a particular way: '*How can I elicit from you information which will fit into the packaging of what the books say is your condition?*' None of this is necessary. The person shows themselves. What are you going to do with it? Either you respond, you engage, or you don't – and that moment has gone, and then there's another moment. You look back: "*Hey, now you're smiling. Why the fuck are you smiling? Do you want to trick me? I'm reading in my textbook about depression and now here you are smiling!*"

Waves on the ocean; they're unreliable. We are unreliable. How beautiful. What a freedom to be unreliable! We do not and cannot fit into the maps in other people's heads.

My need to understand you can be formulated as a violence towards you since to be open to you, to be truly interested in you, would take me out of me. When I make sense of you by pulling you into my template of interpretation, I am consolidating my own sense of myself as somebody who knows what's going on.

Like a fulcrum point, we are constantly rebalancing ourselves to the point of contact with the other. You change and I change. How will we make contact in the next moment? We can't know until that arrives. This is depth and light, *zabgye* in Tibetan. Depth is the emptiness, the openness, the ungraspable nature of the revealing moment. Light is how it shows itself. We are touched and moved, and we respond. That gesture, like a wave, goes back in the ocean, and something else happens, and something else happens...

Did we do the right thing? It is impossible to know, because it would depend on our vantage point and our criteria for evaluation. That doesn't mean that we are delinquent or self-indulgent or impulsive. What it means is that instead of having internal traffic lights – the prohibitions and encouragements that we internalised in our childhood – what we have is the other person; that they show us where they are in this moment.

The face of the other guides us. It doesn't require technical, specialised knowledge. It requires availability, which is the quality of emptiness.

POTATOES AND PEOPLE

There are many different kinds of potatoes. If you are boiling them, they need different amounts of boiling. If you boil some of them for twenty minutes you get soup. If you boil others for twenty minutes they are still hard. Saying, *"I know how to cook potatoes."* is an abstraction. The actual requirement is to look at the potato and every now and then stick a fork into it and see how it's doing. That is to say, you have to make a relationship with the potato even as you're boiling it.

The thing about the potato is important. If you look, it will show you how it's getting on. You don't need to look up books to learn how to cook potatoes.

It's the same with people; people will show you. If you get it wrong, they may show you a bit more. Why am I telling you this? Because it is important we have the confidence and encouragement to let go of this huge amount of knowledge that we carry around. It may give us predictions and methods of testing things, but it is all very burdensome.

Thangkas of Garab Dorje show him painted with a very lovely, young face. This is because what he is showing us is very innocent: if you want to find out how you are, look at how you are. If you are still not sure, keep looking until you are sure. Once you're sure, then don't waste your time thinking about other things. You don't need a PhD to apply this; you need a willingness to keep looking.

The experience is here; who is the experiencer? It's not being hidden by any force other than our own ability to attend without being distracted. The radiance of the mind is arising as all kind of phenomena – some seem like outside, some seem like inside. Experience is arising. We are aware of the experience. This is undeniable. Who or what or how is the one who is aware? This is who we are; so how are we?

Come back again and again and again to being present in the presence of the mind itself. Now we will carry this into doing some more meditation practice.

[Meditation practice]

A THIEF IN AN EMPTY HOUSE

To briefly recap, with that practice, we experience again and again that whatever is arising goes free by itself. Trusting this, there is less and less need for involvement. In terms of awareness, thoughts don't bring any benefit, nor do they do any harm.

In the traditional example, we relax in the state of being like an empty house. The less we identify with the content of the mind, the fewer precious possessions that we have. When new thoughts and feelings arise, they're like a thief in an empty house. So, subject has less interest in object, and object has less power to fascinate subject.

We are turning again and again to this point of being directly present in experience: observing as being with. Not observing across a distance, not looking at something else, at something, which is other than you, but being the presence that reveals and illuminates every transient arising.

The emptiness of the mind shows itself through its own clarity. Just as the mirror itself is ungraspable and unattainable and shows itself only through its reflection, similarly the mind itself is ungraspable and shows itself in the illuminating clarity of its own presence.

It's not about blocking thoughts or feelings or sensations; these are all the shimmering surface of the clarity of our mind. This clarity is not itself an appearance, it is not something which is knowable or analysable. Appearance is passing; experience is passing. Like lightning flashing in the sky, like a rainbow, there's nothing to get. When we stop trying to get, everything is given to us.

Whether the mind is peaceful or agitated, whether there are many thoughts or few thoughts, just stay present on the point of the arising of the thought. How do we do that? The actuality of our mind is presence and this presence cannot be located somewhere for in fact it is this present which illuminates everywhere by being present with it. This is not like a searchlight illuminating a distant object; the mind has no location and yet is always precisely here precisely now. If you locate your mind as being something somewhere you are identified with a thought and then another thought will arrive and you will identify with that. This is how we wander in samsara.

We were talking earlier about panoramic vision. By being present, but uncommitted, we're open to everything which is occurring, wherever it occurs. This means that again and again we release the feeling tone, although it feels very true for me – *'I am here; the thought is there. The thought is coming at me; I'm going towards the thought.'* – and is our ordinary way of conceptualising the movement of thoughts and feeling across time and space.

Awareness is everywhere; it's not inside or outside. For the purposes of some meditation practices, you may visualise it as located in the heart, but it's not 'a thing'. It doesn't have a shape or a form. It doesn't have a colour. It doesn't have any kind of dimension. Again and again, we need to return to being with our mind so our mind can show us what it is.

IF YOU WANT TO FIND THE MOTHER, WAIT WITH THE CHILD

What could be more important than this? If you forget where your keys are, you get upset. If you forget where your mind is, have you ever really been bothered?

Why should you be bothered since, if you think your mind is a thought, you've got a lot of other thoughts so just have another thought! Our mind is the basis of our existence. It is who we are. It is how we are, but we can only be it by being with it. This does not mean that thoughts and feelings and so on are bad.

If you see a small child wandering in the park, you keep an eye on it, and sooner or later the mother arrives: *"Oh my goodness! There you are. Where on earth did you wander off to?"* If you want to find the mother, all you need to do is just wait by the child.

The mother is the mind itself. Thoughts, feelings and sensations – these are the children. Don't split them into two separate things.

"But my mind's so full of stuff, I don't know what's going on."

Stay precisely present on the point of confusion. How do we do that? We just are; we are here. We are here. 'Here' is where we are; 'there' is where we go to. If we're not 'here', we've gone 'there'. No one came and dragged us there. The one who goes from 'here' to 'there' is a thought. The mind is already everywhere without ever moving. So by being 'here', you're in the right place.

Gradually you get a sense of what it means to be present. It's not an idea, it's not an experience and it's not a thought either.

The example is a mirror, open and empty. We are full of stuff. We are full of stuff because we are open and empty. There is no contradiction between the two. Whatever is in your mind, whatever you get preoccupied by, this is only possible because of the space of the mind. So don't go looking for the mind as if it were somewhere else.

If experience is arising, the mind is here and because the mind is here, more experience arises. This is the inseparability of *kadag* and *lhundrub.* Everything you see, feel or touch – all the various modes of experience – are inseparable from ground emptiness.

CONSCIOUSNESS AND AWARENESS

In our practice we address the sense that our mind is inside our body. *'I am inside, you are outside'* feels completely normal, and is reaffirmed everyday in many ways in all the different interactions we have with other people. The basis of this is thinking, *"I am a person and you also are a person."* Buddhism, however, is a critique of the notion of the person. What we see outside is our experience.

If I take myself to be an individual, separated from you, then you have your own life and I don't know what your life is so a hesitancy is built into our existence: *"How shall I behave with you?"*

Yesterday we were examining what is the nature of our own mind – that the mind is empty, in the sense that it is not based on a solid, substantial thing. The mind is open spaciousness and the self-display of that spaciousness. In its openness, it is without bias having no prejudice or tendency, inside, outside, upside or downside.

The aspect of our being which becomes aware of this is awareness. Awareness means the illuminating capacity of the mind. This is not like a torch. On a dark night, if you have a torch, you can see clearly that the light has a source from which it is spreading out. The radiance of the mind is like the first light of the dawn. Before the sun comes over the horizon, the light spreads out over the sky. There is the sense of it being everywhere.

This is a very strange idea, because when we think of our ordinary sense of our mind, we think of our consciousness and the thing about consciousness is that it has a self-referential looping inside it. For example, you might have been cooking something, and you come out of the kitchen, and then suddenly you say to the person with you, *"Oh, there's something burning. Do you smell that?"* You are both aware of a smell, and also that you are smelling it. So consciousness points in two directions at once. It makes us aware of something but also gives us the sense that we are the one who is aware of the something.

Consciousness operates as the strengthening factor to the sense of an individual self. In Tibetan, the word for consciousness is *nampar shepa. Nampar* means kind of shaping or a form, something which can be apprehended. *Shepa* means 'to know'. It gives the sense that our consciousness apprehends that which can be apprehended.

Awareness, on the other hand, shows or reveals that which can't be apprehended.

The traditional example used for this is a mirage. You can never apprehend a mirage. It's like the horizon – you never get there. You see it, but you can't get it. Since we are very good at cheating ourselves we say, *"Oh, it's a mirage."* By naming it as a mirage, it is as if you've got it, as if you have apprehended it. We give confirmation to our wonderful intelligent self through being able to apply a name, which we can then grab, as if grasping the name we would somehow grasp the object. This is the basis of our samsaric consciousness: that we grasp because we are able to create that which is graspable.

This is operating on the basis of the most primitive form of magic because the idea in magic is that once you find the idea of something, by getting the name, you get hold of it. Thus each of the deities has a seed syllable, and this seed syllable gives you access to the life of the deity. Mantra has the seed syllable inside it, and through that you have the connection with the deity and the power to evoke them. This is how we normally function in the world.

Tantra can take the dualistic samsaric model and transform it because the seed syllable arises out of emptiness. On that level, it's operating inside consciousness. *"I am making something happen."* We say some words and we imagine, for example, that there is a net of vajras all around. We are making this happen. What is happening? We are imagining something that we then believe to be true. This is what we do all the time. We imagine that we are in this building. This building reveals itself to us as images. This process has several stages: we see light; the light forms as images; the images are given names; we grab hold of the names; we manipulate it. *"I am here in the Bodhicharya Buddhist Centre in Berlin."* That's a nice conclusion. Now we know where we are because we trust the words. Words give us more security than just experiencing light.

We transform light into apprehendable substances, and then we have to reverse that by practising meditation to transform the apprehendable substances back into light! This is how our consciousness – getting hold of something – is the method by which we solidify our experience.

This is often called 'karmic vision'. That is to say, according to the particular causal forces that give us a human birth, we have access to a particular domain of construction. The very shape of our body and the capacity of our sense organs predispose us to certain kinds of experience. Most animals live with their nose first. Going on four legs, sniffing. Pigs have a very strong and sensitive nose. They are able to dig up the earth and also sniff out where something tasty is. That is to say, they occupy a world that is different from ours. It is very difficult to image what it would be like to be a bird or a pig, because our brain usually is not privileging smell very much; we privilege sight and sound much more. Animals like moles don't see very much but they have incredible sensitivity of nose.

From the buddhist point of view, we would say they also have a structure of consciousness. That is to say they become aware of something – something of danger or something of advantage. They are moving in the world, seeking advantage, trying to avoid danger, just as we are. Choices are being made according to the particular perception of the environment. By looking at animals we can see the relative nature of our perception.

On the basis of the functioning capacity of our sense organs, we participate in the world. The functioning of these sense organs, however, is very fragile.

TRANSIENT WAYS OF PARTICIPATION

For many years I have met every month or so with a few therapist friends. At the beginning we would always meet in a nice restaurant and have a good meal, but now we meet in the consulting room of one of the members of our little group. Why? Because now that he's older he doesn't hear very well and has to wear a hearing aid but if he's in a restaurant with a lot of noise coming from different directions, he gets very distracted. Without having made any conscious decision to change, he now finds the idea of eating in a restaurant, which used to be a pleasure, is now unpleasant.

As we get older, many of us need to use glasses for reading. If we forget our glasses, then we are helpless. I have my book, but I have these stupid eyes that can't read my book. All this is due to causes and conditions. What we take to be ourselves is not self-existing; it is relative, dependent on conditions.

This sort of reflection is available twenty-four hours a day. When you're walking down the street, you see small children running around, not quite in control of their body; you see babies in prams, they can't walk, they can't talk; you see old people walking along slowly and stiffly. Observing all this we can realise that *our body is very transient, is without essence, and depends on factors which we can't control.*

268

Subject to all such influences we are dynamic, we are moving, and it is important again and again to be aware that I am energy, I am movement, I am change. I try to hide this fact from myself by delusional narrative and I ignore the actuality of change in order to preserve the illusion of a stable image. The maintenance of the image, however, does take a lot of effort.

All this is relevant in terms of dzogchen. When we look around this hall we see people, statues, paintings and so on. This thing on the wall above me, it is as if it is truly a painting. We all know it's a painting. You would be stupid if you didn't know it was a painting. Of course, we are stupid because we know it's a painting. We stupefy ourselves by knowing *'it's a painting'*. That is to say, this is a dulling clarity. Having recognised this is a painting, a set of balancing assumptions arises, and these assumptions become like an invisible wall. If it's a painting, it's a painting. So then we ask what kind of painting is it? Who is in the painting? There's nobody in the painting; it's just dabs of colour. Whoever is in the painting is in your mind. You could take a stranger and show them this painting and ask, *"Who this is."* and they might say that they did not know. They might not know, but we know. When we know, we say, *"Oh, this is the Buddha."* This is not the Buddha; this is a lie, and it's a lie that makes us feel proud. The Buddha is not in the painting; the Buddha is in your mind. If the Buddha were really there, everybody would know, because it would be showing itself in an undeniable certitude.

When you look at this painting, this thangka of Shakyamuni Buddha, what you see is your mind. This is a very simple example, but if you take this and use it everywhere you go, you will see that self-existing objects are an illusion.

THE MIND AND ITS FURNITURE

This is the underlying meaning of *thogal*. *Thogal* is not merely a set of practices that you can learn and which some lamas like Namkhai Norbu teach. To see the nature of primordial purity in relation to experience, that is already *thogal*. This is your mind – I am your mind, everything is your mind. That does not mean that everything is your ego, your consciousness, your self. We are not describing some idealistic philosophy that tells us that everything is just an idea in our mind. We have discussed before how, when we refer to 'my mind', most of the time what we mean is actually 'the furniture in my mind'.

When you rent an unfurnished flat you put your own furniture inside and you make the flat comfortably 'yours'. When you have to move out, you take your furniture with you. The space was never yours; the space was just there and you had access to the space.

It is the same with the mind. The space of the mind is not 'ours'. It is ours if we inhabit it, but it's not ours as a possession. With furniture we can have some kind of possession. Our thoughts, feelings, memories and so on belong to us. They are the unique particularities of our located existence.

This is why understanding the empty nature of the mind – primordial purity, *kadag* – is the necessary basis of *thogal*.

In the meditation we sit and we look. Various things appear. These are revealed through the movement of our mind. When this movement of the mind is linked with its own depth, it is referred to in Tibetan as *rigpai tsal*. It is the energy of awareness revealing itself.

When we are not connected with the open spaciousness, the ground of our being, we locate ourselves as being 'myself', and 'myself' is constructed out of the particular aspects of experience which I draw together at any moment. When I look out at the world, I approach it through the filter of my own concerns, and this operates as the eight consciousnesses. These are the five sense consciousnesses, the organising mental consciousness, the consciousness of the emotive colourations, and the ground consciousness. The ground consciousness is the consciousness that can organise the potential of the mind in terms of appropriate-able entities. In the tantric system, these eight consciousnesses are said to be present in the heart chakra in the form of an eight-petalled lotus.

Through this mediation, we become aware of certain factors in the environment. We see that there are, if you like, two parallel worlds. One is unmediated or uncooked, and the other is mediated and cooked, through selective attention, investment of emotional identification and so on. That is what we already touched before when we talked about the dzogchen notion that there is one ground and two paths.

'Ground' means not just the basis and the source but it also refers to the sphere in which everything occurs. When the ground is connected with what arises from the ground, then there is no differentiation or separation and therefore no need for elaboration.

EXAMPLES OF VERDIGRIS AND RUST

Verdigris is given as a traditional example for this. Verdigris is the green patina that appears on aged and weathered copper. According to the Tibetan tradition, the verdigris arises out of the copper. Copper is an orangey-red colour and out of it appears this green patina. This is the copper showing itself; it is one of the modalities of copper. Tibetans also use as an example how orange rust arises out of iron.

When we see the verdigris or the rust as something separate from the iron, then we want to give it a specific name and work out what to do about it. *"How do I get rid of this? It is spoiling the copper."* We take something that is part of the life of copper and see it as the enemy of copper, because we have the pure idea of what copper actually is and how it should be. Then we go to the hardware shop and ask for some product to protect the copper from verdigris. Of course, a shopkeeper is always happy to satisfy your demand and will sell you something.

Right. We sit in meditation. The verdigris of the mind arises. Where does all this green shit come from? Surely this can't be me? You go to the holy lama. *"Can you give me a crap-remover? All this bad stuff is coming into my mind."* Of course, lamas can provide you with many removal methods: *"We have this excellent new Dorje Sempa scrubbing brush. It comes highly recommended..."*

This is how it goes when we see the showing of the mind as being in some way an attack on the mind or at least an attack on our idea of how our mind should be.

Dzogchen, however, is saying that everything is complete and perfect in itself, perfect in the sense of not needing to be changed into anything else. It just is as it is.

So if a jealous thought arises in the mind, it's there and then it's gone, one of the many kinds of thoughts that the mind can have. Then the ground and what is manifesting from the ground are not separated. But when you have mediation, when you insert 'I, me, myself' like a wedge in between the ground and the manifestation...

—I don't want this stuff in my mind. I don't want to be like this. I want to be kind and generous and helpful, and I'm not. So something's wrong with me. Can you help me be better?

—Better than what? —Better than what I am.

There, you can cheat yourself very easily, because *"better than what I am"* is a very dangerous statement. The only useful response is to ask, *"But what are you?"*

Buddhism has thousands and thousands of methods for making you better than you are and death will come before you have exhausted them all. Between now and your death, if you spend your time trying to improve yourself, you might never find out who you are.

'Better than who I am' means 'I am somebody who has jealous thoughts and I don't want to be somebody who has jealous thoughts.'

Hm... [Speaks each word slowly and distinctly:] *'I... have... jealous... thoughts.'* Now we come to a question of grammar. Is the problem in the jealousy? Because that's what it feels like? This horrible jealous thought arises so then you spend a lot of time trying to transform the jealousy. This is the problem of not understanding grammar. 'I' have 'jealous thoughts'. Mmm? [Makes grasping gesture.] Grasping at the jealous thought. The jealous thought arose... and passed. We run after it saying, *"Don't you come back here again!! If I see you again, I will call the police! My mind is private property!"*

It's gone. We are going after the thought, after the 'having' – I 'have' a jealous thought. If the mind is open, the jealous thought comes and goes. The problem then is not, as it were, in the object; it's in the subject and the verb.

When the 'I' is me as a person, me as someone who wants to define who I am, then the fact of the sense of having what I don't want is troublesome to me. Buddha Shakyamuni described two main kinds of suffering: getting what you don't want and not getting what you do want. Here we find ourselves with an idea of who were are, what we need, what we don't need, what we like, what we don't like. As a customer we think that we have a right to choose but maybe this is just stupidity because in making a choice, this is the very place where you insert yourself between the ground and the manifestation!

THE MIRROR AND ITS REFLECTIONS

The traditional example is the mirror and the reflection. The mirror is able to show many different kinds of reflections. These reflections come and go, and they don't leave a trace. No reflection can harm the mirror. We need to really understand this. Go home and play in front of the mirror, do lots of different things and see what the mirror does.

This is equanimity, a concept which appears in many buddhist texts. There are many terms for it but basically it means not entering into judgment, not saying this is good, this is bad. The reason why it is safe not to enter into judgment is because the reflection doesn't harm the mirror.

Nowadays there are police in most airports trained to do special identification of people's facial expressions and bodily movements, because they are doing *'Spot the Terrorist'*. If they spot a terrorist with a bomb, we say, *"Thank you very much."* A small bomb wrapped in a package can look like something else yet it's very different so clearly discernment is very important since no- one wants to be blown up. Yes, we are all going to die, but we don't want to die from a bomb, at least not just yet... No reflection harms the mirror, but reflections interact with each other.

For example, if you are looking at yourself in a mirror, and someone pushes in front of you, you lose half your face. You say, *"Oy, get out of the way!"* The reflection is vulnerable to other reflections. Reflections have no essence. They are contextual, situational, contingent. Life happens to us. We don't know what events are going to do to us to make us happy or sad, expansive or contracted.

In terms of the mirror, this doesn't matter. In terms of the reflection, it matters a lot. Samsara is the domain of the reflection. Liberation is the integration of the reflection in the mirror, showing the true nature of the reflection.

As it says in the texts again and again, if good things happen, let them happen; if bad things happen, let them happen. Don't be bobbling up and down like a cork on the waves. Good times pass, so why chase after them? Bad times go by themselves, so why worry about them? You can look in all the buddhist books and they say the same thing again and again.

Our awareness is tolerant. Something arises, and then it goes. It doesn't do anything to the mirror, but it can do something to us.

Who are we? We are patterns of thoughts, feelings, memories, sensations and so on. These energy constellations are themselves reflections in the mirror. None of us can stabilise our mood, because we are impacted by what happens. You only have to walk along your street to see some tragic situation. It affects you. How terrible not to be affected! That would mean compassion is impossible. At the same time, everything has the same taste. These are not opposites. Everything having the same taste is not the same as indifference.

TRANSFORMING THE FIVE POISONS

STUPIDITY

The tantric mandala, transforming of the five poisons into the five wisdoms, is an example. Generally, in the centre is the purification of stupidity or mental dullness (Tib. *gTi-Mug*). Mental dullness is composed of the habit of ignoring the ground, and it does that by preoccupation.

People walking along the street, talking on their mobile phones, are not very aware of other people. They are connected with something far away, and disconnected from what is exactly here. This is the nature of stupidity: we merge into our assumptions and the things that we prioritise, and we take our tunnel vision to be an accurate account of how things are.

This restricted, limited kind of experience is transformed, or revealed, as the 'dharmadhatu jnana' (Tib. *cho ying yeshe*) – that is to say the wisdom, the intrinsic knowing, of the space within which all dharmas arise. Yesterday we looked at the traditional example of taking a piece of coal, washing it every day for years and years but it still doesn't become chalk. You can't transform a potato into a banana, yet stupidity can be

275

transformed into dharmadhatu wisdom. This is because they have the same nature. The ground or basis or source of the energy that ignores its own ground – the formation of individual identity which I take to be my enduring self – is the open ground which is the mother of all the Buddhas. Ego fixation arises from finding oneself as an orphan, source-less, motherless and so one clings to the sense that one exists as what one believes oneself to be. Stupidity means to not see one's own true actuality by imagining that one is other than one is. This is the perverse power of the imagination.

JEALOUSY

The fifth transformation is of jealousy. Jealousy is the fear that something which I take to be mine, or something that I want, is going to be taken by someone else. It's the dynamic of triangulation. That is to say, it speaks of the vulnerability of whatever we have: that because there is no fixed ground to identity, whatever we take to be ours can be taken from us by causes and circumstances.

Five years ago, life in Syria was very different from now. Due to causes and conditions vortexes of pressure started to operate. Now thousands, millions of people are displaced and their homes destroyed.

When we reflect on impermanence and dependent origination, we see that there is no secure basis to our life, When we fall in love, however, we tell our beloved that we will love them forever. This is a lie, a reassuring lie, but a lie nevertheless. And it is the basis for jealousy because I did think that it was going to stay like that forever.

The transformation of this is the wisdom that can do everything, *ja wa drub pai yeshe*, the wisdom that fulfils or completes activity.

One of the things about jealousy is that it's quite paralysing. There are states of paranoid jealousy, toxic jealousy, where murder is the main result.

TANTRA TRANSFORMS SOMETHING INTO WHAT IT ALREADY IS

It's like a child having a temper tantrum. Children are very good at doing this in public. *"I don't have to. You can't make me! You're not my mother! Go away!"* Suddenly everybody is looking and wondering, *"What is that woman doing with the child? Maybe we should call the police."* But this is the mother. The denial of the mother doesn't stop the woman being the mother. It just shows that the child is intoxicated with a kind of rage.

In the same way, we get intoxicated with the idea of 'I, me, myself', that I exist, that I am *me*. Nobody's going to tell *me* what to do. I'm in charge of my life. I'm entitled to live the way that I want. We have a lot of this discourse now in the modern world. Where did we come from? We make our own air; we make our own food; we make our own clothes; we are entirely autonomous and independent. *"I am independent! I don't need anything from anyone."* This is a temper tantrum. Actually, we are highly dependent, highly interdependent.

Why? Because we are a dharma inside the dharmadhatu. The dharmadhatu is our mother. It's sometimes described as the womb of the great mother, and that's where we are.

'I am me': that is what stupidity is. It is the denial of how it is by pretending it's something else. That's why it can be transformed into *what it is*. To turn a potato into a banana is difficult because a potato isn't a banana, but stupidity can be transformed into wisdom because its basis is the same ground as wisdom has. When stupidity relaxes its autointoxication, and there is a space in which its own basis is revealed, that recognition of the basis shows the forms of stupidity to be the radiance of wisdom.

At the end of the temper tantrum when the child is tired and exhausted, and you ask,

—Is this really your mother?

—Yes.

—Do you want to go home with her? —Yes. [shuffle, shuffle, eyes down...]

So, this is how transformation works in tantra.

DESIRE

Likewise with desire. Desire means making something special and the transformation of desire is into the capacity to appreciate the particularities of whatever appears, so *sor tog pai yeshe* in Tibetan.

With the first wisdom, *chöying yeshe*, we open ourselves to being space and being present in space as this particular form, a dharma in the dharmadhatu, relaxed, contented, satisfied, part of the dharmadhatu.

But then, *"Oh! There are other dharmas too in the dharmadhatu!"* We look at the other dharmas and some we like, some we don't like. Why? They're all just dharmas. *"Oh, I like that one because it's going to give me something."*

But what do I need? I am contented. We can appreciate the qualities of what appears in the world without trying to get them.

Kuntuzangpo, the founding buddha of the lineage, and his consort Kuntuzangmo are both depicted naked. When you are naked, you have no pockets. It's obvious. So where are you going to put the things you get? Up your nose? In your ear? Naked means you don't need them. So in that way, you enjoy without appropriating.

You walk down the street... (Now I'm talking as a man)... you walk down the street and you see a woman in front of you. She has a gorgeous arse. Beautiful! Undoubtedly a princess. Ah, high maintenance. I admire the arse and walk on. Very wise. Getting involved, big headache.

Woman's voice: Men have also nice asses.

James: Exactly.

So this is the transformation of desire. It's not about shutting down or having anaesthesia. It's about aesthetic enjoyment, which is the meaning of sambhogakaya. Sambhoga means enjoying everything. Enjoying means being present in the moment of the revelation of the rich diversity of the world, and then – gone. Naked, we have no pocket for the future, no pocket for the past.

ANGER

Anger, or aversion, is putting aside or wanting to destroy the thing that disturbs us and is the dynamic of projection. It is transformed into mirror-like wisdom, *melong tabui yeshe*. The mirror shows things just as they are: A person behaves in whatever way they do. That is their activity. *I* choose the activity of being annoyed. In London underground, many people put their feet up on the seats. I think that they should not do that. Does my annoyance disturb them? No. Does it disturb me? Yes.

They do what they do. What happens, happens. This is the purification of anger. If I want to change it, I should see very clearly what it is because it all depends on the circumstances. Maybe sometimes I can say something to make someone change their behaviour but a lot of the time it won't. Shaming people in public is no longer likely to bring about behaviour change.

Mirror-like wisdom is seeing the whole context, and then you can work out whether there is something that can be done or not.

PRIDE

Pride is transformed as the wisdom of equality, *nyamnyid yeshe*. Pride says '*I am special*'. It's a separation from others and an inflation of one's own importance. One is no longer just a dharma in the dharmadhatu, an appearance of emptiness in the field of display. When we transform into the wisdom of equalness, we see that because everything is empty, all the qualities of everything are also empty. This is because they are attributional, that is to say, we give the qualities to whatever we see.

Some people don't like classical music; some people do like classical music. These are projections, opinions, personal preferences. Music is music; it's just sound and emptiness. What is there to like in it or not like in it? That depends on you. *"No, but you should really hear this. It's good, it's really good."* This is a description of a relationship: I like it, therefore it is good. The first part is okay; the second part is problematic.

'I' am saying that the liking is based on the quality of the object and that, if you just give it a chance, you will like it too. In secret we're thinking, *"And you'd be stupid not to."* This concretisation, this solidification of an opinion, is very dangerous; some people are killed because of the opinions other people have about them.

Equalness doesn't mean homogenisation. Everything is there in its particularity, and yet this particularity establishes nothing. Many different reflections arise in the mirror. Some we like, some others we don't like but all the reflections are equally valid, as reflections. You can't take the reflection out of the mirror. The unique particularity of each reflection is inseparable from the ground emptiness of the mirror. So when we say this is better than that, it's like saying, *"This cloud is much nicer than that one. This is the best cloud."* A cloud is ungraspable, but we still want to compare them.

—Every time we go to a party you start dancing with other people. Why? —I just like dancing.

—I've watched you and you're flirting with them too.

—Well, I'm only being friendly.

—No you're not. I don't know what you're up to. You're making me anxious. What I used to enjoy about you most was your free spirit, but not any more!

Movement asks for flexibility and for activity to be carried out, there has to be a workable situation. That is to say, there has to be a connection between the parts. Very often when people meet together, they meet together under the blessing of an idea. Because of that shared idea, it is as if the other person is the one who fits my idea, but sooner or later the contradictions start to manifest. For situations to be workable, first we have to examine: *'How are you? How am I? Is some meeting possible? Is it workable?'* To think that we can make everything workable is a huge ego fantasy. Sometimes it is just not possible.

Working with circumstances means that sometimes we have to reverse. One of the pieces of homework that I often give to patients is asking them to park their car without using the reverse gear. In the city when you only have a small space to go into, this is usually impossible. So why imagine we can have a successful relationship with someone if we can't go into reverse? We have to apologise sometimes. We have to step back. We have to let the other win. But why? Because that's how you do it.

This is what is meant by *ja wa drub pai yeshe*, flexibility of movement. It doesn't mean I'm going to turn into some powerful heruka and make everything happen. A fantasy of power is very unhelpful. It's about movement. We are, in any case, moving creatures. *Ja wa drub pai yeshe* is knowing whether your patterns and ways of movement can be harmonised with the situation. Because life works best when there is contentment.

MEDITATION TECHNIQUES

Before we do more practice, I want to say something about technique.

As I've indicated before and as many of you know, there are many different techniques in dzogchen. If you have the chance to get the transmission for these, then it's very helpful.

Not scratching the itch: that's a main part of the lineage teachings, but there are other styles of practice. The way I practise and communicate is mainly from CR Lama and from Dudjom Rinpoche with a focus on allowing the natural purity of the mind to reveal itself.

In Tibetan there is the term *rang bab*, which means "self-falling". In English we might say "free fall". It means when we sit in the meditation, the mind tumbles along however it does, and the path is non-interference. To say, *"I don't like this. It shouldn't be like this. I could make it better,"* comes easily to us but the basic proposition of dzogchen is that the mind is self-healing.

If you have a condition like eczema, it's very tempting to scratch because it itches, and we believe that if something itches, we should scratch it. If we scratch it, we irritate the nerve endings. We open up the skin, we're likely to get some light infections, and get even more irritation. So, there is an itch: what is the status of the itch? The itch says, *"Do something!"* Should we believe it? This is a question. Can we believe the content of our own mind? We have impulses and tendencies that call on us to repeat actions. Who am I when I don't act? If my frame of reference is winning-and-losing, it can feel as if not acting is losing, and when I assert myself, I feel more powerful. So I'm going to scratch, and in that moment there is a forgetfulness of the consequence of the scratch.

This is exactly the same issue with meditation technique. We sit in the practice; the mind is tumbling around lot and I think, *"I could make it better."* What is better? 'Better' means the importation of a set of criteria. Different kinds of thoughts, more 'spiritual' thoughts, might be more acceptable if I had to talk about them to other people, and that would make me feel better.

The central instruction, however, is not to change anything, that nothing needs to be changed. By not changing, we start to see the equal nature of all that occurs. By changing, we remain committed to our criteria of evaluation.

So, just look. The most important thing is emptiness. Everything is empty; there is nothing to be changed.

When we apply particular techniques, we need to be very clear about why we are applying them. The paradox is that if we do less, we get more, because the mind is self-liberating. Ideas are frequently misleading. The ground nature and the natural clarity of the mind don't require the ego's effort. Believing that, we just sit. The mind is showing. It shows us many different things. One of the things it shows is that I am my body. Just by sitting in a relaxed, open way, every nexus of tension – whether it's in the musculature, the tendons, thoughts, memories – can relax. To make effort to release something brings you into conscious activity, which already puts another little spin on what's going on.

As Patrul Rinpoche points out in two chapters in SIMPLY BEING, it's very easy for meditators to fixate on particular problems, to feel they're too depressed to meditate, or too angry, or that their meditation lacks clarity, or that it's not how it should be. He lists many, many kinds of ailments or meditation problems. For each of these, he gives the same medicine: stay present on the one who is having the experience. If you feel dull and stupid, be there present with dullness and stupidity. By simply being present without interfering, dullness disperses. Simple clarity is available. This he repeats again and again. There's also a chapter in SIMPLY BEING from Nuden Dorje who also says the same thing.

283

Perhaps sometimes we have the idea that this isn't enough, that I need a stronger better method, but then remember that the mind is pure from the very beginning and that it doesn't need a method to purify it since it's already pure.

C.R. Lama always said the main thing is to have faith. But why should we trust our own mind since we are lost souls wandering around in the world, messing up lots of things. What this means is when you sit in the meditation practice, and you feel this isn't right, you hear the echo of *'everything is pure from the very beginning'*.

When we sit and we open, all kind of things are coming. These are the forms of purity; these are the reflections in the mirror. You look in the mirror and you say, *"Yup, that's me alright."* Actually no, that's a reflection.

Similarly a thought arises in the mind, *"I can't meditate. This is stupid. I've wasted a whole fucking weekend now."* This is just something you are thinking. What does it mean? What actual status does it have? If you get on to a thought, it will take you to where the thought goes. It's like getting on a bus: if you sit on the bus long enough, it will take you to the bus station. The bus station is full of buses. You get off this bus and you get on another bus. If you get on a thought, it takes you to the thought station and you get on another thought and spend the whole time going around following these thoughts.

Thoughts are the display of the ground. If we don't awaken to the ground, then we're at the mercy of the pulsation of thoughts and events.

According to this lineage of practice, we sit and open to whatever is there, and open and open and open. Every time we get caught in something, we have the opportunity to see how we close down.

The key point to remember is that the one who is caught by the thought, is himself a thought. The ego is a thought-construction; it arises from the thought of 'I am', 'this is'.

Therefore, relying on thoughts leads only into the territory of thoughts.

It's like in Homer's Odysseus. When Odysseus is approaching the island where the sirens are, he says to his sailors, *"Stuff this wax in your ears and tie me firmly to the mast. No matter what I say, keep on rowing in a straight line."* As they get closer to the island, he begins to hear the sirens calling and under their spell he tries to break free and get his sailors to row near to the island. But they obey his original instruction, and since they can't hear the sirens' seductive calls they keep on rowing in a straight line right past the island.

This is meditation. If we close your ears to thoughts, we're not sensitive. If we follow what we hear, we get lost. So we need the regularity of just staying, just sitting. We feel the tonal quality of the different sort of thoughts that are arising and this is like the purification of desire: we have discernment, we're not stupid, but we have equanimity.

All these thoughts are the same – they look different, but there's no substance to that look; it's just an empty appearance.

If we block thoughts or we try to control them, that is manipulation. If we follow thoughts, we get lost. So we have to find this middle way whereby whatever comes, comes but it doesn't take me with it where it goes.

[Period of meditation.]

There are many styles to enter the practice so we can do the most simple form. Just sit and begin, since there is no interruption between the arising and the passing of thought. All thinking is the display of mind. One advantage of this style of practice is it doesn't make a strong switch between being in the practice and being in the rest of our lives. As we get up and move around, it's simply more appearance arising and passing.

The view is that everything which arises and passes is the self-appearance of awareness. In Tibetan this is referred to as *rigpai rang nang.* It's not as if there is a pure world which is then contaminated by foreign and artificial thoughts. Our thoughts and emotions, being critical, disappointed, frustrated, exultant, happy and so on – these are all the mind showing itself. When we seem to have a commentary on what is going on – *'I am talking to myself about this'* – it appears as if there is a subject talking to an object part of oneself. Both, however, are the spontaneous appearance or the easy movement of the energy of the mind. *'I like this'* is an energetic formulation. Every formulation is simply a formulation of transient energy. So where is any toxic obscuration?

Remember that the most important and central instruction in meditation is not to go after past thoughts and not to wait expectantly for future thoughts. Don't divide thoughts into good and bad, trying to get more of the good, less of the bad. This is where you have to really practise precisely, because judgments arise. It's not that the judgment is wrong. It's that we enter into the judgment, we merge with the judgment and we believe the judgment.

To have a sense of the wind as cold, this is a judgment. It has no implications; it has no necessary consequence. You could remain cold or decide to put on a sweater or a shawl. When we merge and say, "Oh, I'm cold," then we get a disconnection from the field. That is encapsulation in the feeling tone and leads very easily into the sense that something is making me cold: *"Why is this happening? There is some enemy-form that is doing something to me that I don't like."* All of that is the natural showing of the mind, complete and perfect from the very beginning.

Conflict, being seemingly divided, is one of the many ways in which the mind shows itself. We can look in the mirror and see some ugly reflection present there. Should we blame the mirror? Should we ask why the mirror why it is showing something ugly? This must be a bad mirror! Likewise my mind has got something in it that I don't like. I must have a bad mind. I need to change my mind. Something is wrong.

Here is the difference between paranoia and metanoia. When we are in paranoia, we start being very suspicious of what is going on, convinced that something bad is going to happen. Metanoia is the process of transformation and change. Something is wrong so do something different. Something seems wrong, and it's gone.

The problem is when we invest the 'gone-wrong' as if it were particularly significant. It doesn't mean that life's events don't touch us and don't move us. When tragedies happen, they have a particular flavour. We feel sad, we feel despair. This is normal; this is part of the human situation. Heartache happens to everyone. The fact that it happens to other people doesn't mean that it's not deep and significant when it happens, because its flavour is deep and significant.

Equalness doesn't mean homogenisation. It's not about ignoring what is happening. Rather, the issue is about identification, taking the current appearance, the formation which is happening at the moment, as being a true message about who I really am. We are always going on the middle way. If we say it is irrelevant, this is a kind of death. If we say it's the end of the world, and it's intolerable because this is all there is, this is a false perception. It is what it is. Sometimes the taste is bitter, sometimes the taste is sweet. Sweet and bitter don't taste the same. Then after some time, the taste transforms.

These are the key points of the meditation practice and of how we live in life – not taking life too seriously and not being over-defined by circumstances.

Don't pretend that circumstances are not happening. We have to work with our circumstances. As the texts say, eat when you need to eat, sleep when you need to sleep, cry when you need to cry, laugh when you need to laugh. If it's the time of crying, there's no need to pretend you are happy and laugh. Nor does it mean that you have to take on a tragic vision of your existence.

Drawing conclusions is a problem for us. To come to a final definition of a situation – *"things never work out right for me."* – is false perception. There is good and bad, happiness and sadness. We don't know when they're going to arrive; we don't know when they're going to leave. The mirror-like mind shows everything.

The less we interfere with the patterns, the more we realise that pattern is non-dual. That is to say, the world and myself are not two things. Being part of the world, we respond into the world. We don't have to protect ourselves against the world. Every flavour of life is what it is. It is its own taste, and it is empty of essence and substance. Our fragile ego-self says, *"I don't want the bad; I only want the good."* So it sets itself in conflict with the actuality of our existence. It fights how things are. This creates a lot of tension.

Of course we do need to participate – but with finesse, with grace, with attention to the potential of the current moment. We are neither the victim nor the controller. We're not in control, but we're also not out of control. We are part of the movement.

So, the purpose of doing the meditation and carrying that awareness into daily life is that by allowing the movement of forces, we may directly see that awareness is indestructible. This is what is meant by *dorje* [in Tibetan] or *vajra* [in Sanskrit].

My awareness is indestructible, but the formations which arise as the flow of experience are always changing. Awareness is stable but ungraspable, and appearance is ever-changing and is also ungraspable.

Ignorance, the root of all suffering according to buddhist teachings, is based on two things: we ignore what is stable, *nepa* in Tibetan, and we attend only to movement, *gyuwa* in Tibetan. We then try to make the moving stable. However the stable and the moving are inseparable. *Nepa* means stable, means empty awareness, and *gyuwa* means all the different movements of samsara and nirvana. These are inseparable, but they're not the same. To expect the moving to be stable will never succeed. We ourselves come into being through forces that we are not in control of.

It can be very helpful to look at politics, because we can see out there the dynamics of your own mind. Whether we inflate ourselves or hate ourselves, whatever position we take up, there's some country out there in the world doing exactly the same. We are all concerned about the conflicts and distress in the world. It's obvious that if the world is to get better, we have to collaborate but we can also see how difficult it is to collaborate.

This is what we try to do in our meditation, collaborate with ourselves, and sometimes that can be difficult but if we want to have peace, we have to learn to allow the conflicting parts of ourselves to have some rapprochement. That's what we're doing when we're sitting. We're allowing everything to be there without taking sides. When enemy countries meet to collaborate at first they find it quite difficult even to be in the same room.

Each of us can help the world by being more tolerant. When we're tolerant we realise that the bad dissolves, the good dissolves, and the solidity of our own definition of what is reasonable or what is unreasonable has no secure basis.

In this short time we've covered many things. If the ideas are helpful to you, massage them into yourself, reflect on them and see how this illuminates the actuality of your own situation.

We now come towards the end so let's just sit for a few minutes.

Sitting with our gaze open, we have more sense that we are in a building, that the building is in the street, that the street is in Berlin, in Germany, in Europe... Open to include all beings, so that whatever benefit there is from our study and practice together is not kept secluded in one small place but opens out to all.

Now we've come to the end.

Good luck to everyone. See what happens in life, maybe we meet again, maybe not – we never know – but it's a pleasure to be here with you now.

Teachings given in Berlin, Germany, 30-31 January 2016. Edited by Barbara Terris.

Finding your way home: an introduction to dzogchen

THE BASIC PRINCIPLES OF DZOGCHEN

The basic principles of dzogchen are important, because dzogchen, as a practice and as an understanding, is different from other paths in buddhism. In the dzogchen view the base, or the basis of awakening, is something that we already have, and therefore the path to awakening is not a path *going* somewhere else, and the result of awakening is not *being* somewhere else. Rather, it's to find a way of being fully present as oneself, which is revealed through opening up the possibility of exploring *'What does it mean to be oneself?'*

For this to occur we need to develop a capacity to observe ourselves across the range of our manifestation. Thoughts, feelings, sensations, movements of the body and so on form the constituents out of which we arise as ourselves. If we fully identify with these factors, they appear to be the definition of who we are.

One aspect of observation is the clarity whereby all these different factors are revealed just as they are. In fact we exist as the co-emergence or integration of the two factors: an openness which reveals *all* that is there and the *precise nature* of all that is there. This is not something mystical, it's not something symbolic; it doesn't belong to any particular system of interpretation. Dzogchen meditation resists the temptation to fall into interpretation.

From the time we were small our parents, school teachers and employers have been encouraging us to try to understand a bit more and to think a bit more and therefore to rest on thoughts as building blocks to establish understanding. Clearly, knowing about the world and how it functions brings a kind of clarity, but conditions change and our accumulated knowledge is quickly out of date.

In dzogchen we are aiming to awaken to a quality of awareness, a particular kind of knowing that is not dependent on circumstances. The most important aspect of this practice is trust in your ability to relax. Generally speaking when we read buddhist texts they explain that the basis of samsara is ignorance, leading to attachment. The word 'ignorance' can create the sense that there is some kind of cognitive disorder and that we need to learn more to get rid of ignorance. However from the point of view of dzogchen, the problem is more an ontological one about the nature of being. That is to say, in becoming alienated from ourselves and the ground of our being, there arises an anxiety, and this anxiety drives us into activity. For example, when there is an accident or something difficult in our lives we tend to think *"Oh what should I do?"* We become mobilised and ready to become very active.

Of course in that state of arousal and agitation our selective attention identifies many things that needs to be done and the more we do the more there is to do. Every religion is very generous in presenting thousands of things for us busy people to do! You can do prostrations every morning, then fill your water bowls, then clean your altar, and there are all these many mantras to say... So there is always something to do. In Tibetan buddhism there are thousands of different gods. First you praise the buddhas, then all the bodhisattvas, then all the gods, and then all the dharma protectors. That's a lot of praising to be done. Since you have said hello to them once, then the next time you go near them you have to call them by their name otherwise it's a bit rude... This kind of activity is good activity, but it *is* activity.

In dzogchen we are concerned to understand the nature of activity. That is to say, what is the movement of the body, what is the experience of speaking? What is sensation in the body? What is emotion? What is the experience of listening, eating, walking and so on?

[A phone rings in the room] These phones are invented to keep you busy. You can imagine the buddha sitting in Bodhgaya, under the bodhi tree ready to be enlightened and then a phone rings. It's his mother *'Are you alright, dear? I heard you were getting very thin...'*

SETTLING AND CALMING THE MIND

So now let us do some simple practice to arrive and settle in, allowing our attention to settle on a simple focus. Settle either on an external object such as a mark on the floor, or focus on the sensation of the breath going in and out of the nostrils. We sit with the spine straight, shoulders relaxed, chin slightly down, the tongue resting on the hard upper palate. The eyes are slightly closed and gazing down the line of the nose; the mouth is slightly open and we are not controlling our breath. Once you have decided on your focus, develop a clear intention that *'This is what I'm going to do'*. If you find your attention wanders off into something else, then as soon as you become aware of that, just gently bring your attention back onto the line of your focus.

The practice of tenderness and gentleness in meditation is very important. It's a way of healing some of the wounds which develop around the heart on the basis of the harsh messages which we have received from the outside and which we continue to give to ourselves, blaming, judging, and criticising and so on.

So just return to the focus and we stay with that. We will do this for about half an hour.

[Meditation]

The main goal of the practice we have just done is not to develop any particular insight but simply to calm the mind by cultivating a kind of disinterest. That is to say, the usual contents of the mind, which we normally find fascinating and which pull us into all kinds of developments, thoughts and associations, are now allowed to pass by without our paying any particular interest.

This kind of practice is something you may do from time to time to develop your capacity for focussed attention, but from the point of view of dzogchen it's not useful to have it as one's main meditation practice. The main goal of buddhist practice is to develop wisdom and compassion and if the mind is simply very calm and undisturbed then there is neither wisdom nor compassion. However, what this practice *can* do is start to give some kind of space, a kind of perspective, so that you begin to have a choice, 'Will I be involved or not?' When our mind is very distracted we get into a habit of reactivity to whatever comes whether it seems to be internal or external.

So in calming the mind we give ourselves the sense or the capacity to stop and look before we get involved. This helps us to start to see where is the main glue that binds us into what is going on. Is the glue in the object or is the glue in the subject? Sometimes we feel it is inevitable to be involved in something; the object seems so interesting or necessary that we have no choice. It is as if the object is pulling us towards it, causing us to fall into an involvement. *"What else could I do?"*

This is the basis of a lot of events in our existence. For example, if you go to any courtroom where the person has to explain to the judge why they did the bad thing they did, you will hear explanations which point to the inevitability of what occurred. *"Because I was poor"*... *"Because the person hadn't locked their car"*... There was some reason out there which made me do this. *"So you can't send me to jail; circumstances made this happen. I am a victim of circumstances."* We often think like that, as if the

294

outside is sucking and pulling us, or our thoughts, feelings and sensations are sucking us into something.

The advantage of calming the mind is that we can start to create a laboratory, a place of examination where we can see what is the nature of the forcefield of subject and object.

From a buddhist point of view we have been born many, many times before, and in all these lives we have developed likes and dislikes, habits, attitudes and so on. When we are born into this life we have particular vulnerabilities or susceptibilities. Some people, when they go to a party and hear the music, think *'I have to dance'* while other people at the same party, as soon as they see the bottles, think *'I have to get drunk'*. So in these ways we have a selective attention, that is to say, an attention that moves towards the world looking for things that are our particular individual patterning or a construction.

WHAT MAY FEEL NATURAL IS IN FACT QUITE ARTIFICIAL

This habitual involvement feels exactly normal for us so it's often difficult to see it because I am just doing what I do. How would I do anything else? This is me. But in fact in that moment our potential, our capacity to express ourselves in many different ways, is being caught by an old pattern and shaped in a very narrow form that is really limiting us.

So by calming the mind and being less immediately reactive or involved with the thoughts and feelings and so on which arise, we are able to start examining ourselves and the world around us and start to seeing how we actually function. An aspect of this is to start to see how other people function. It's always surprising to see what other people do. So for example, if you go to the supermarket and you come to the queue at the checkout, it's very interesting to look in other people's baskets. What are they buying? Why would they buy these things? What kind of person is that? How strange. Then we realise *'Oh they are not me.'* They have another life; they have another mind. Their mind is arising due to causes and circumstance due to their childhood, their education, their work or their not-work, and the same is true for me.

The function of looking in this way is to see that what I take in myself to be natural is actually something quite artificial. Because my mother was as she was, my father was as he was, my school was as it was, I have, through my integration with them, developed certain pathways inside myself, certain tilts of my gaze so that some things look shiny to me and other don't.

The real practice begins when we see that *'I am artificial; I am a construct; I am made out of habits, attitudes and tendencies, all of which have a historical basis, a contextual basis but no true foundation. There is nothing fundamentally reliable in them.'* If I keep following these habits and attitudes, I'm constantly winding myself into story time, into a narrative, into the myth of my existence. Inside of that many things are very important and many things don't bother me at all. So following the things I like and trying to get more of them, and avoiding the things I don't like and trying to have less of them, I spend my whole life going this way and that. I am always busy trying to maintain the sense of the continuity of this construct that has been created.

The view of dzogchen is a way of looking through the story to see if there is a different basis for our existence, one which is not simply our old individual patterning of the stream of experience, but something truly reliable which could be always there.

REFUGE IS LIKE AN UMBRELLA – YOU'LL GET WET IF YOU LET IT DOWN

In the general buddhist practice we begin by taking refuge in the Buddha, the teachings and the association of the people who practice. That is to say, we recognise that we are like a leaf in the autumn wind and we want to find something to hold onto.

Once you have a refuge you have to hold onto it. All kinds of refuge are like umbrellas; they will only keep the rain off if you hold them up. That is to say, without the effort of keeping up the umbrella you don't get any protection. As soon as your arm gets tired, your arm goes down and you get wet. So that's why it's very important to see the nature of religious practice. As long as we are trying to stop doing bad things and develop good things, we are engaged in activity. This activity may be a very good activity, but whenever you stop doing it, whatever you have constructed will start to crumble.

We can observe this again and again when you look in a garden; if the gardener is not working hard then many other things start growing. At one time, here in this nunnery [outside of Bilbao] there would have been many people living here, with many servants and everything would have been very perfect. Now there are just a few old nuns so things don't go so well.

The same principle operates in our mind, whenever you are creating something by your own effort, if your effort stops, that creation will become vulnerable. This is not a punishment; it's just how things are. You'll know this from any kind of possession, whether it's a motorcar or a house or an animal – you have to take care of it.

A NATURAL STATE OF PERFECTION

The central point of the practice of dzogchen is the clarity that from the very beginning in all beings – not just humans, but animals, insects, everything which has life – there is a natural state of perfection. The practice is designed to reveal this natural perfection. That is to say, we are not trying to construct ourselves in a better way; we are not trying to improve or develop ourselves since awakening is awakening to the perfection that is already there.

There are two aspects to this. There is what is sometimes called the nature of the mind itself, that is to say our own nature as we sit here together. This is openness, meaning that there is nothing closed or defined or conditioned about it. It's a naked quality, not covered with any habits or karmic accretions, and it's there automatically by itself. This is the state of awareness that illuminates everything in the same way that a mirror illuminates everything that is placed in front of it. Just as the mirror is not touched by any of the reflections that arise in it, so our awareness is not conditioned or distorted, or improved or contaminated by anything that arises in it. This state never moves and never changes.

Within this state everything moves, for nothing that appears is stable or reliable. The biggest problem in samsara is that people try to stabilise things which cannot be made stable. We try to make our own mental state stable; we try to make other people stable and reliable and what we find is that something is always happening, since, as the Buddha taught on many occasions, everything is impermanent.

When we are present in our experience rather than thinking about it, we can see that everything is dynamic and changing, unfolding moment-by-moment. We see that each of us is at the centre of this evolving world. The one who is at the centre of the moving world does not move. That is to say our awareness, which never changes, and this display which is ceaseless, are inseparable in non-duality. The infinite stillness of awareness and the ceaseless movement of the world, including ourselves, are not two different domains. What we call 'my body', 'my thoughts', 'my sensations' or 'my feelings' is the movement of energy; there is nothing stable about our existence. Breath is going in and out all the time; the blood is going round and round; electric impulses of the brain are ceaseless; the hormones and endocrine system are operating ceaselessly, bringing about communication inside the body. The body is not a *thing*, it's a great river of change, and the same is true for sensations and feelings and thoughts. Once we start to experience the ceaseless movement of experience we realise that within this movement there is nothing to hold on to. Yet we don't get lost, because the ground of this movement is completely still.

Our nature is always still and calm in the midst of the movement which is always happening. This is the basic vision in dzogchen. It's not about trying to become enlightened, where 'enlightenment' is some special state, which if we try really hard we can one day achieve, a place that will somehow be secure. When we look directly into the phenomenology of our existence we can see that thoughts come and go. Bad thoughts come and go, good thoughts come and go. All constructs are impermanent. And yet ungraspable, indestructible awareness is always right here.

Many things that people have thought to be very safe and secure are revealed by events to be not so secure. Year by year the Catholic Church is becoming less powerful in most countries and churches that were once full of people are fairly empty now. A hundred and fifty years ago this would have been unthinkable. When the Chinese came into Tibet and attacked the monasteries many of the Tibetan people could not understand how it would be possible to take a statue of the Buddha and break it up. They thought some big dharma protector would kill all the Chinese because they were doing something very, very bad. That did not happen. A statue is just metal; if you have faith it's more than metal, it's metal plus faith. Metal plus faith is very powerful. I myself have a lot of faith so I have lots of such pieces of metal in my home. However these things are very important because of our relationship with them; they let us see directly that *we* are making them shine. The energy of our mind is the radiance of the world.

BECOMING MORE AT HOME WITH ONESELF

The basic task is to become more at home with oneself by starting to observe what is reliably oneself. You can start with a general reflection on your own life. For example when you were young you had different interests from now. The dolls or the bike you played with as a child are no longer important to you but once they were really important. Then we can look at all the things that are in our life now and that seem very important to us, and ask what has real value? This doesn't mean rejecting everything and renouncing the world and going to live in a monastery but rather, we can start to see that value arises as the interplay as subject and object.

THE ILLUSION OF EXISTENCE

The Buddha explained many times that things are like an illusion, like a reflection of the moon on water, like a mirage, like an echo. Whether we are happy or sad it is just an illusion. An illusion does not mean that there is nothing there at all; it means that nothing is there that is inherently true, true from the inside out. For example, we might feel that meeting together like this is a useful thing to do; we might even enjoy being here, but then we look out the window and we see that there are many houses in this town and yet no one from this town has come here. So is it our duty to go out this evening and knock on peoples' doors and tell them, *'Friends, please come, enjoy'?* They will say *'Don't be stupid? Don't you know the World Cup is on television?'* It's like that. If *we* want to be here, it's *our* construction. This is an illusion too.

Everything is an illusion. Perhaps you have been out on a beautiful full-moon night by a lake and noticed the reflection of the moon on the water. It really seems that the moon is in the water, but it is not. In the summer if you are driving your car on the road you may have seen what looks like water, what has the appearance of water, but there is no true water there. It was a mirage. This is the nature of our experience here. There is nothing to grasp. That doesn't mean that there is nothing at all. There is **something,** but it is not a solid entity that you can build on or hold on to, and the same applies to ourselves.

Inside our body we feel the muscles tense and relax, we notice how our breathing changes, how our posture moves. That is to say, our body is something that appears for us, just as our bodies also appear for other people and this appearance is changing in time. Our skin looks different as the daylight changes, if the sun is shining, or if it's raining or there is artificial light. That is to say, ourselves and everything that we see is an experience which is arising. It is there as an experience but you can never get hold of it. This usually is hidden from us because we are caught up in our thoughts, being busy 'making sense' of the world. We have our ideas about how things are and on the basis of that we create a base of solid enduring entities. On the basis of that we start to build up a composite picture of outer things and inner things, and then we move these reliable entities around to create the world we want. But all the time it is really an illusion. I remember when I was in school we were always being encouraged to work hard to get through the exams. So every year in May and June I would be writing and writing for hours to do these school exams. Then a month later through the post I would get a letter telling me if I had passed or failed. Once I had opened the envelope and knew the result, well, life goes on. In English we talk about 'a storm in a tea cup'. This is what happens when we take things too seriously.

STORYTELLING

Sometimes I sit and eat with my colleagues at work. We talk about ourselves, where we have come from, what we have done at the weekend, what we plan to do in the summer... That is to say, we all tell a story about ourselves. But when we are relaxed and open, there is nothing to say. Most of our social interaction, even when we are interacting with ourselves on our own, is just a flow of stories. Stories about the past – what has happened, stories about the future – what we hope will or will not happen. While we are telling these stories there is the immediacy of our presence as ourselves, and this we can't talk about. We can't say what it is, yet it is the heart of our experience. Words describe things, events, manifestations – yet the mind itself is not a thing. It is beyond language, being the open field through which language moves. So the very ways in which we try to communicate with other people, which are the same ways in which we talk internally to ourselves, conceal the immediacy of ourselves in the very moment that they reveal the story about ourselves.

This is an important principle. It's not that story telling is wrong or bad, but it's to recognise the status and the function of the story. If I tell you something about my childhood, then I'm making little bridges from my world into your world, like some fast-growing creeper like Russian Vine or Virginia Creeper. When people are talking together little tendrils are growing out from their mouths and wrapping around each other. This creates the possibility of feeling connected and warm, and it also allows us to be helpful and to get a sense of the shape of the other person so that we can find a way to be close to them. That is to say, it is about compassion; it's not about wisdom. Wisdom is how things *actually* are, that is to say, staying relaxed open and present with the immediacy of our direct experience. Direct experience cannot be described because it is not a thing. Speaking can create the illusion of there being real entities.

The actual function of speaking is about connection and connection permits the movement of energy. For example in this room right now we are different types of people and we are moving together through time; we are *directly* the movement of time. Along this ceaseless gesture of time, we are all moving. It might help to imagine that this whole room is a big river with a strong current moving. This is what it is like being here; we are in the same river. This whole world is the same river, but each of us is a little movement.

However when we sit inside this bubble of ourselves then we protect our difference from other people because we want to be unique and special. Yet actually we are made out of the same stuff as everyone else. This does not mean that we are the same as other people. We are neither the same nor different; we are unique forms which are inseparable.

This illustrates the fact that wisdom and compassion are inseparable. In wisdom we are at home in the spaciousness that is the ground of all beings. In buddhist language it means the dharmakaya, or true nature, of all beings is exactly the same, but as we manifest we each have our own particular qualities. These qualities influence how we talk and how we walk and so on, and this influences the play of our compassion – how we can relate to other people. If we are cut off from our own experience of our spaciousness then instead of having this ungraspable and infinite openness at our centre, we find ourselves wrapped up inside stories. We talk ourselves into existence just like Scheherazade but these stories position us in particular ways that limit our capacity to respond to other people.

So the function of the practice is to integrate the openness with the expression, the stillness with the movement, so that our movement becomes an expression of the integrated movement of the situation as it presents itself moment-by-moment, rather than being the expression of 'who I am' in terms of my habitual story.

PRACTICE

We will do a little practice now. This is very, very simple, we just sit as we are and without doing anything artificial we just allow experience to flow. We are not trying to do anything special, we are not trying to develop something or create something in particular, simply to stay present with everything that is occurring. You can do this with your eyes closed if it's easier but normally we do this with our eyes open. If something moves outside, some sounds come in, just allow it to come. Don't block external experience, don't block internal experience.

If you find yourself spiralling into a particular pattern of thoughts, as soon as you recognise this just let go and let these thoughts vanish. As it often says in dzogchen, the mind is like the sky. The sky is open to whatever comes into it. Sometimes it's clouds, sometimes it's rainbows. Birds and planes fly through it, bombs go off in it but the sky stays open. So in the same way, just like the sky, remain relaxed and open... Whatever comes, you just let it be there. OK so we will sit like this for a while.

[Practice]

The basic instruction for dzogchen meditation is to not do anything at all. That does not mean that nothing will happen because, strangely enough, you are not the only one making things happen. The ego has a big fantasy about being in charge of mental activity, yet stuff is happening all the time – what Freudians might call the unconscious and Jungians might call the collective unconscious. Whatever it is, there is a lot of stuff going on that I don't know much about.

Since the instruction is not to do anything interfering or artificial, whenever a thought arises in your mind – and your next response is *'I like it'* or *'I don't like it'* – then following the instruction, just allow the thought to come and then just allow it to go.

The one who says *'I like'*, the one who says *'I don't like'* is just a thought. All that we think we are, is just thoughts. As long as we identify with these thoughts as being our true selves, our preoccupation with the transient arising moments gets in the way of just seeing ourselves in the moment of our openness. For example, if you are driving a car every time you look in the mirror you see something different. You are looking up in the mirror inside the car and you go *'Ah, that car is coming up behind me'*, *'Ah, that car is passing'*... Many things are appearing in the mirror for you. Then when you arrive at your destination you look in the mirror again and tidy your hair a little bit, maybe put on a little more lipstick. Now when you look in the mirror you see yourself. The mirror is full of you. Why? This is our attachment.

When you were driving, things were happening in the mirror; it was very dynamic but now when you look at your own reflection in the mirror it seems to be more real. This is because you invest it with a particular kind of significance. So when the meditation instruction is *'Don't do anything at all'*, it gives us the chance to see the process of investment of *me*. That is to say, one idea says to another idea *'I really like you'* and the next idea says *'I really like you too'* and in those way ideas chase ideas, chase ideas. This is what is called samsara. The freedom from samsara begins with seeing that an idea is only an idea. But when we live inside our habitual attachment we don't see a transient idea – we see another appearance. This is the illusion created by sitting inside an idea as if it were telling the truth.

OK so now we will break for today. You have to be in touch with your own condition since the heart of the practice is to make friends with yourself, to be so close with yourself that the internal division of subject and object is reintegrated, and that's when we can start to experience the state of non duality.

DZOGCHEN: EVERYTHING IS ALREADY PERFECT

Dzogchen means great perfection or great completion. That is to say whatever needs to be done is already being done, and therefore the idea that there is any fault or error is incorrect. The only fault or error is, in fact, to think that there is a fault or error! Clearly this makes it different from most religions. Most religions start with some kind of fall from grace, some variation on the stories of having to leave the Garden of Eden, some entry of ignorance... These myths involve two aspects: one is that the good place is lost, and the second is that the door to get back in is closed.

From the point of dzogchen, the natural state – or the open ground of our own existence and the existence of all beings – is not something that is lost. It can't be lost and it can't be gained. It can't be sold and it can't be purchased. It's always there, but one can *attend* to it or not. By taking it for granted we create a false notion of what it is we actually are dependent on. For example when you walk down the street, you are walking on your shoes, and our shoes are walking on the pavement, but both the shoes and the pavement are invisible to you as long as things are going well. But then if somebody has spilled oil on the pavement or if there is a banana skin or some dog shit, suddenly you become aware of the pavement and of your shoes. The very ease of our existence makes us not look very carefully at what is there. The practice of dzogchen is to avoid the extremes of either lazily taking things for granted or anxiously reacting to a crisis. Rather, we attend to what occurs without interpretation or bias.

In Tibet it was said that dzogchen was in Tibet before buddhism arrived. It was there before the bön religion too. That is to say, it is not an invented system, but is something that was, and is, always there and that people in all places, in all times, have access to. Very often, if you spend some time with small children you can have that sense that they are in this experience. Of course when children are small they do not make a commentary on what they are doing which means that their life, their experience, is open and immediate for them. It's wonderful to see people when they encounter a small baby and, generally speaking, something in the heart opens up and the face becomes light, and they are friendly and immediately connected with the baby. It's the very openness and undefendedness of the baby that invites the adult to enter that world. Of course a baby is rather helpless. Then as it grows up and learns how to take care of itself, it loses that openness. This is very sad yet it has happened to each of us. There was a time when we were just ourselves, and then we 'developed' ourselves, which is necessary for social adaption, but in the process we lost ourselves. We became turned into, or turned towards, the rhythm of the world, the necessary demands of existence. Moreover if our childhood is unhappy, then that process becomes even more complicated.

However from the point of view of dzogchen, openness is always there and the task in meditation is to integrate our capacity for complex 'being in the world with others' with the simplicity of the ground. The basis of the practice is to awaken to, to be fully open to, the state that is already here, a state that is hidden from us by nothing other than our own activity. This last point is very important since it means that all you need is already here with you; it is about how you pay attention to your existence.

If you are familiar with buddhism, this is not the usual presentation because usually it is described that a situation arises due to ignorance, that is to say, that we have lost touch with true knowledge and we have to find a way to this knowledge again. So, people will pray and make aspirations like *'May I become enlightened for all sentient beings'*, that is to say,

> *I recognise that my interests are small and I am mainly concerned with myself and I want to open this out so that my attention is with all beings equally. Through that I will escape this limitation, creating freedom for myself and so I will become more available for other people.*

To do that it is traditionally said that you need to have developed 'the two accumulations of merit and wisdom' which become the basis for achieving of enlightenment. This is often described in terms of removing all that has to be removed and gaining or developing all that has to be developed. The Tibetan word for 'Buddha', *sang-gye* comprises these two activities. *Sang* means to clear or to purify; *Gye* means to increase or develop. So the state of buddhahood is seen as one in which all faults, obscuration and limitations are cleared away and all good qualities necessary for the benefit of oneself and others are completely achieved, completely fulfilled. Buddhahood is seen as the result of a process. Should you enter a traditional pathway of training, as you get in the four schools of Tibetan buddhism, you are immediately concerned with these two activities of clearing away obstacles and developing whatever is useful. This activity is seen as taking many lifetimes. However the so-called 'higher tantras' teach how it can be achieved in one lifetime.

TANTRA: TRANSFORMS ORDINARY INTO PERFECT

The word 'tantra' means continuity and refers to the continuity of the states of limitation – called 'samsara', and the states of non-limitation – called 'nirvana'. The practice is to transform all that we take to be samsara – the world of separate objects, the world of truly existing phenomena – into the mandala of the deity. A mandala simply means a situation that has no limit. Essentially 'mandala' means that whatever aspect of existence you get fixated on and invest as being very important is not sealed inside an internal definition, but is actually a fractal of all the other things that are arising.

In that way we come to see that each thing, which in our ordinary perception we take to be something very strong and very real, is actually inseparable from the open field of actuality. In particular, our sense of 'I, me myself' which seems to differentiate us from all other people, is revealed as merely the play of empty signifiers which establish nothing. In the path of tantra we come to realise this through a transformation of our ordinary identity into the symbolic realm of the deity.

For example, we could visualise the yogini Machig Labdron in the clear blue sky in front of us, her body translucent so that you can see through it. She is there but she is an appearance without substance. Then by doing the meditation practice we link our energy with hers and out of her body rays of light come and dissolve into our body filling our body with light. So now her body is made of light and our body is made of light.

Her body now comes to the top of our head and dissolves into a ball of light and that ball of light comes down into our heart. Our body, which is light, dissolves into that ball so there is only one ball of light. That's all we are paying attention to, and this ball of light gets smaller and smaller and smaller until it is just one little dot, one point. The point now dissolves into emptiness and we rest in that open state. Then gradually thoughts, feelings, sensations arise and all of these are the forms of emptiness, the forms of the deity.

Gradually we become more aware of the world around us, tables, chairs, flowers, people and so on. Everything we see, we see as being inseparable from the body of the deity. For example we see flowers. Actually we don't see the flowers because 'flower' is the name we give to this. What we actually see is something quite strange, quite unbelievable – there is a little ball of something and gradually it opens up and wow! A flower. But as soon as we say *'It's a flower'*, life becomes easy, we feel safe. Now we 'know' what it is, but if we just look at it, it's just a pretty shape and colour.

The more we do the practice the more everything surprises us. Instead of being asleep in the dream of language, the fresh vitality of each moment can be revealed to us.

In order to enter into the path of tantra you have to get any necessary initiations and then do the practice every day, do the visualisations, recite the mantras. Then gradually you will get some experience. The danger with this method is that because it takes you a long time to do, and you know that if you don't make the effort you don't get the result, it becomes easy to draw the conclusion that 'I am making it happen'.

I might think that I am imagining this mandala, in the way a child imagines Batman or some other hero. That is to say, this activity comes out of me. That belief maintains the centrality of the ego – the very opposite of the intention of the practice. We have to imagine that we are entering the timeless world of the symbolic, of the sambhogakaya, in which all the aspects of the practice are unfolding by themselves. By merging with the deity we merge with our own true nature.

DZOGCHEN: KADAG AND LHUNDRUB

From the point of view of dzogchen, from the very beginning everything has been very perfect and the state of buddhahood is present in all beings. There are two basic principles in dzogchen.

The first is *kadag*, a Tibetan word, meaning 'primordially pure'. It means that your own mind, your own state, is pure from the very beginning. It has never been limited, or defiled or covered up by anything else. Whatever bad things you may have done in this life, none of this has conditioned or limited your own nature.

The purity of the mind is indestructible. This is a fundamental principle. Without this you cannot have any confidence. When you wear nice white clothes they look very attractive, especially if the sun is shining but you do have to be more careful when you drink your coffee because white cloth shows up every possible stain. Such relative purity is always a cause of anxiety but the purity described in dzogchen can never be stained or destroyed since its nature is empty. I will talk about the nature of emptiness a little later.

The second principle of dzogchen is called *lhundrub* in Tibetan: *lhun* means 'a heap' or 'a pile', and *drub* means 'to be made' or 'be accomplished'. Therefore *lhundrub* means 'made all at once', not bit my bit. This refers to the aspect of manifestation. Whatever we experience is immediately here, we don't need to construct it. The more we understand the openness and the purity of the mind, the more we see that the immediacy, the spontaneity of manifestation, is inseparable from that purity.

This might sound a little bit abstract but it is exactly our experience as we are sitting here. That is to say whatever thoughts, feelings, perceptions arise, they have an immediacy.

They show themselves. Who is this shown to? Me. Who is this one I call 'me'? It's a noetic capacity or a possibility of being aware. That is to say our ability to register experience is not done by *something*; it's not the product of a function, but it is a revelation. For example if I put my hand in front of a mirror, the reflection of my hand is immediately in the mirror.

Because the mirror has nothing inside it, because it has no fixed content, it can immediately show what is there. Because our **mind** is naturally empty, it also has no fixed content and therefore it immediately reveals whatever is arising.

Yesterday, when I came here with Marta, we looked a little at the room to see how we could fit the seating, Marta had already been here some days before and moved some of the chairs. That is to say, the room was already occupied or filled in a particular way, and we had to work with what was here in the room. This is the way our ordinary consciousness works. We already have furniture in our head and when you come into a new situation you can only manage these new experiences according to the amount of remaining space you have. A very normal way we have of dealing with this problem is to say this new experience is very like this old experience.

By comparing and contrasting events, two functions arise. The first is that I have a kind of confidence that I know how to make sense of the world, and the second is that I am protected against the shocking freshness of each new experience. Because if you really look at the flowers they are very very strange, even if you look at just a plastic cup, it's very, very strange. When I was a child things like this didn't exist. Suddenly someone developed the capacity to make this, something that is so cheap you just throw it away. When I was a child you always had to clean everything and keep it very safe. Maybe we could say that this plastic cup is part of the Buddha's teaching because this is a something that is already nothing, but this kind of nothing is simply capitalist consumerist nothing! It's very strange, very strange and we tend not to see the strangeness.

In that way we tend to exchange the unsettling immediacy of freshness for the power of knowing. If you're with children – especially boys about seven, eight or nine – it's sad to see how they become very obsessed with knowing things. It starts with knowing the names of all the different kinds of dinosaurs, then the names of all the motorcars, and then all the football teams and so on. If you don't know all these things people say you are stupid. Of course from a developmental point of view this is the accumulation of knowledge, but it is an empty kind of knowledge, knowledge as a defence against the anxiety of not knowing who you are. Now that we have the internet and knowledge banks like Wikipedia the problem is much worse. This is because there are a lot of things in the world that you can know; you can spend hours and hours on a computer getting more and more information, and all the time you are looking at the information you are not looking at yourself. So the existential question of 'Who am I?' becomes hidden within the search for information about other things.

EMPTINESS IS LINKED WITH THE QUESTION OF TIME

OK, now I am going to say a little bit about emptiness and then start to look at different kinds of meditation in relation to understanding our own nature and relaxing our body speech and mind. Then we will have plenty of time for questions you may have especially about how to apply this in your ordinary life.

Emptiness is very strongly linked to the question of time. Generally speaking we move in what is called the three times, the past, the present and the future. When we talk about the present, we usually mean *'Here I am in this room with you. I know I am here and it's already 11 o'clock because we have already had breakfast and lunch is still to come'*. That is to say what we can generally consider to be the present is something which stands at a crossroads between the past and the future. It's not the radical present of being fully awake to what is here, with a great freshness, rather it's the point where the past turns into the future.

The past moves into the future on the basis of there being the continuity of truly existing entities. So, here is my watch, my watch shows the time because it continues in time. If it turned into an apple it would not be very useful. When I put it on my arm in the morning I put on a watch. If after two hours when I looked at my wrist, it was a fried egg I would be very surprised! That is to say I expect some*thing* to remain some*thing*.

It's the same watch I had yesterday, which makes sense. But from a buddhist point of view this is not correct, because when I look at this and I say *'It's a watch'*, then 'watch' is itself an interpretation. It's an abstract concept and what I have in my hand seems to be an example of that abstract concept. For example, maybe you're out shopping and you stop for a moment outside a jeweller's shop, you'll see they have a hundred different kinds of watches. All of these are watches but they don't all look the same. So the watch-*ness* of the watch exists outside the particularity of this watch. When you were small you had to learn to tell the time. There's a big hand and a small hand. The big hand shows the minutes and the small hand shows the hours. You have to look again and again and eventually you get able to tell the time.

Now, when you are a child it is presented to you that everyone knows how to tell the time and if you want to be a normal person you also have to learn to tell the time. You are given to understand that time is in the watch and if you know how to read the watch you will get the time! The *watch* however doesn't tell you anything. In fact *you* tell the watch that it is the watch that is telling you the time. That is what is happening. You are deceiving yourself in the name of giving knowledge.

You develop a mental capacity which you project into the movement of the hands of the watch and with that you revolve within the cultural construction of the frame of time. The sense of time is different in this nunnery where we are now for clock time is not the most important time. The most important time is the time of the bell which brings you to the different church services through the day. This goes right back to the 6th century when the religious day was divided up into its six periods of devotion. It was the same in Tibet; the day was divided into six periods. It starts with the middle of the night, and then cockcrow and so on.

So, watch time is a cultural construct, and when you live inside that construct it appears to be just how it is. Its artificial nature, its conditioned nature, is hidden by the fact that we all take it for granted that it is two minutes past eleven. In buddhism when they talk of the root of suffering being attachment, this operates on different levels.

On the outer level I am attached to this watch; this is *my* watch, I have had it for some years and so I have grown accustomed to this particular watch, but if I lose this watch I can always buy another watch. For a while I'll still remember 'Oh, how much nicer my old watch was!'... but then I'll forget about it and become used to the new watch and then it will just become *my* watch.

Much more dangerous is attachment to the idea of watch-*ness* of the watch. So that every time I see something like this I think *'Oh it's a watch'*. Between the arising of the object and the arising of the thought in my mind there is no gap, which means that instead of being able to really look and see what this is, I look at it through the lens or the filter of my knowledge or assumption of what it is. In the western tradition of phenomenology Merleau-Ponty, Husserl and others struggle with, as they say, the epoché, the bracketing off, of assumptions that we put onto the object. They attempted to put the assumption into parenthesis but thoughts come so quickly and are so plausible that it is very difficult not to be taken in, in the moment they arise. And analysing and using the thought patterns after they have occurred does not take us very far.

For example when I was growing up and was around eighteen or nineteen it was still possible as a man to say that women are like this or like that; but in my thirties I came back from India and the new feminism had occurred during my absence and so now it felt very dangerous for any man to voice any assumption about how women were. Women said if you want to know who I am, you can ask me. I will show you, but you can't know me before you see me.

This is very important, because it is a beginning of a kind of freedom. So long as men can define women according to an old patriarchal structure, that knowledge of the woman precedes her own individual existence. So, you could say that buddhism is applying a similar level of consciousness-raising, but is applying it to everything in the universe.

That is to say, if you want to know what things are, you have to look. You can't just assume, especially since your assumptions are full of old limited patterns. Although it seems very clear to *you* how to see things, this is the pseudo-clarity, the false clarity, of the intensity of your own opinions! Therefore, instead of telling the world what it is, we need to receive the world and let the world tell *us* what it is.

This is why, as I was saying yesterday evening, there is a paradox in the main function of the practice, which is not to do anything at all. The less you do, the more you will receive, because there is so much – in terms of the colours of the tiles of the roof, the shade of the trees, the way different people walk and talk – there is so much richness in the world and it will show itself if we just let it be absorbed into us.

THE UNGRASPABILITY OF SELF

The buddhist notion of emptiness can be made very, very complicated, but it's not complicated. It means essentially the absence of inherent self-nature. Which means there is no essence inside the object for you to grasp, and its

315

ungraspability means that the move of the ego to gain power over the world by knowledge is exposed as something ridiculous.

In the same way, in the first wave of feminism in Britain, from the 1890's to about 1910, the suffragettes had the explicit aim of getting the vote for women. Then in the second wave in the 1960's and 1970's women were saying that women can define themselves, that they were not a puppet of the male gaze or the male definition. Nowadays we have what some people refer to as the 'third wave feminism', where women do many, many different things. Last year was an anniversary for many of the founding writers of 'second wave feminism' and it was very interesting because many of these women had been very passionate about establishing rights for women and there had been a sense of solidarity, of women being sisters, and of going in the same direction. But when I went to conferences about this, I heard these women saying *'Now it is much more difficult. These young women nowadays do things that we would never, never do. They think it's a sign of freedom to wear a skirt so short that it shows their knickers'.* The older feminists think *'How can this be? How can it have come to this?'* and the younger ones respond, *'If I want to look like a tart, I will look like a tart. That is part of my freedom.'*

That's very, very interesting, because the more that you have freedom, the less you can grasp anything, what can you say? As long as you have an enemy and you're fighting for something, you can define yourself. *'I am against this; this must change.'* But once you have some degree of freedom, life can go in all sorts of directions. If you take that change in the feminist movements as a metaphor, you can see that something similar happens with our relation with our own mind. When you stop struggling to gain enlightenment by overcoming your obstacles, you find yourself participating in a realm of infinite possibilities. Of course this brings a lot of freedom but also its own particular difficulty, because we still have the question

'How shall I live?' If you follow the theravada path, and think, 'Inside me I have many impulses and if I indulge these impulses I will get into trouble. Therefore maybe I should become a monk or a nun and then I will have many rules to follow and these rules will show me what to avoid and what to do.' then you can always check the rulebook on how to proceed.

In mahayana buddhism what is developed instead is the intention, *'I want to help all sentient beings'*. So this gives a sense if direction. That is to say that in any situation I try to think what would be beneficial for the other. So you have something to refer to, which is the vow, the bodhisattva vow or intention.

If you practice according to tantra you have the commitment to see the whole world as the mandala of the deity and to see everyone you meet as a god or a goddess. So, again, you always know what to do.

But in dzogchen there is no rule. *'What should I do?'* Nobody can tell you; you have to be an adult and that's not so easy. Life is easier if you are a child. Somehow you can find a mamma or a papa and they will tell you what to do. Sometimes mamma and papa are mad. In the last century we had many mad mammas and papas, Stalin, Hitler and Franco and so on… somebody who always knows what is right. This is a big problem.

The view of dzogchen indicates that you have to be fully present so that you are as connected as possible to everything that is there in the undivided uninterrupted phenomenological field, which includes yourself. From the state of relaxation your spontaneous movement will be connected with the situation. Then activity is effortless and intrinsically ethical. Dzogchen texts describe this as 'the path of non-meditation', for whether we are sitting or whether we are moving around and being with other people, we don't have any imported object of meditation.

The object of meditation is always simply that which is arising. Sometimes it feels inside, sometimes it feels outside. Without editing, without trying to improve or change, without falling into a fusion with the object or seemingly protecting yourself by trying to maintain a distance, stay completely close to whatever is arising, letting it come and letting it go. This is illustrated by the traditional image of the mirror. The reflection seems to be in the mirror, and yet when the mirror moves, that reflection vanishes; it doesn't leave a trace. The more you open and you experience the indestructible emptiness of your mind, the more you lose the fear that experience is going to mark or condition your openness. Your mind can remain fresh and clear. This is not a position of macho indifference, like the attitude of a matador, because if somebody says something that upsets you, you can cry. The one who is crying is the patterning of energy. The content of the mind and the nature of the mind are not the same. Nor are they two different things. If you cry you have not shown yourself to be a weak pathetic person. Everything is possible. When you are happy you can be happy, when you are sad you can be sad. The difference is, who is the one who is happy, and who is the one who is sad?

The sadness is me, as an experience which is manifesting. The one who is experiencing or revealing this manifestation is the unchanging awareness. These two aspects are present simultaneously. If we were *only* this absolute clarity, nothing would touch us; we would not be human. But if you are only passionately involved in your life, you don't have any clarity. Awakening to the integration of these two is the basis of dzogchen.

[Break]

RELAXING OUR BODY, SPEECH AND MIND

Our body speech and mind are aspects of our existence which are not separate from each other but rather are mutually influencing. They indicate our having a kind of dignity, of welcoming yourself into existence. Think of a cat. When cats look at you it is as if they are telling you *'I'm here too'*; that's a quality of their vitality. Body, speech and mind refers to not leaking out into the world... to neither pouring out all your energy, nor hiding inside yourself, but really being alive in your own skin, with the sense organs fully alive. This quality of just being in one's skin, not too far out and not too far in, is the basis for abandoning neither other people nor oneself. Usually we tend to tilt in one way or the other.

In terms of relaxing the body, make friends with your skeleton, particularly the spine. When the weight of the head is properly balanced through the vertebrae, the muscles in the neck can become very soft, allowing all the muscles in the body to relax. We tense up when there is something to be done but now, when there is nothing to be done, if you are *still* tense, then there is a double message. The mind may be telling you to relax, but the tension in the body is saying *'Oh what next?'* Western medicine describes the autonomic nervous system as having two regulatory systems: the sympathetic and the parasympathetic nervous systems. For most of us our parasympathetic nervous system is not very healthy, that is to say we are over-aroused a lot of the time and we are used to feeling relief by even more arousal! For example you might watch television in order to relax, but television is a stimulant; you might smoke a cigarette in order to relax but tobacco contains many stimulants. In these ways we become habituated to a state of alertness that is not necessary to the actual environment we live in.

Maybe we had bad or frightening situations in our childhood, which have left an impact on our capacity to self-soothe, so it's very important to allow the body to come to rest. There are many western techniques for doing this. A common system is autogenic training which involves consciously working through the whole body, tensing and then releasing the muscles. Such systems are often easier to learn than yoga.

Yoga is very useful but it can be difficult to integrate into ordinary life. Patanjali, who taught the yoga sutras in India about two thousand years ago, laid the basis for the development of eight paths of liberation, with each of the eight paths having its own particular kind of logic. Sometimes people may do a little bit of yoga just to keep their body flexible and that's ok though perhaps not something you can do in the office. Say you're at work and your boss gives you a hard time you might be feeling angry and humiliated which is immediately presented in tensing of the muscles, changing of posture, of breathing, of capacity for eye contact and so on. At such times it's very important to breathe freely and openly from the diaphragm and to release the tension in the muscles. Although you have been attacked, and have felt attacked, you are no longer being attacked so you can release the arousal and tension in your body. As human beings we often have to cover things over, to hold ourselves together in public. This is much less helpful than immediately releasing as soon as the causal situation has passed.

BEING FLEXIBLE

Although it may be good to learn Indian or Tibetan systems of yoga, the essential thing is to start to know your own body. For example, when you are sitting at your computer you can check for yourself if some of the muscles in your body, maybe in your neck, are tense. We adjust our posture to our mental image of what is right for us, so very often people think that they are sitting straight up when they are not, because they have developed a habitual sense of their posture that feels right, but is actually off-centre. Ballet studios have a wall of mirrors because the line of balance you feel inside yourself is not always the true line. There are modern methods like the Alexander technique and the Feldenkrais method which will help you identify when and where you are going off-centre. You can pursue the enquiry: what are the factors that tense me up, what are the factors that help me release? Our body, as the vehicle of our movement into the world, needs to be flexible because we do not know what is going to happen.

You have the most freedom to move when your body is in a non-committed position. By 'committed' I mean that when you have an intention to move your body in a particular way, you have less freedom. You can see how important this is for goalkeepers, for example. The goal area is quite big and the goalkeeper can't show the striker which way he is going to dive, so he has to be like a master of martial arts, able to move from zero to a hundred very quickly. As soon as he leans in any one direction, that makes the other possibilities less likely. So, it comes back to finding the central position, to resting in the middle way.

Do we operate from our own intention or do we operate from a central point that is outside ourselves in the co-emergence of self and other? For example, some people can dance but they can't really dance with other people. That is to say, they dance doing whatever they do, and in their own world they are expressing themselves, but they are sealed within their own relation to the music – there is no room for anyone else. To dance with another person, their movement and your movement have to work together. In many dances, like waltzes or tango, this problem is solved by one person leading and the other person following.

However the goal in dzogchen is not to have a dominance and submission movement but to have a co-emergence, that is to say, that the subtle interchange of messages between the two people allows something to arise between them whereby for each, their response to the other provides them with a holiday from themselves. I am sure we have all had this experience, parents especially. When the parent relates to the child, the child leads them into doing things that the parent wouldn't do for themselves. The parent might have to go into school and confront the teacher about the way their child is being spoken to. The parent might be able to do that but then find that they cannot bring their faulty goods back to the shop and ask for their money back. The mother or father might lack the confidence to be strong for themselves, but for their child they can transcend their own limit.

NOT FEELING STRETCHED LIKE AN ELASTIC BAND

When dzogchen talks of non-duality it refers to the lack of a real separation between subject and object. So, if we stay connected with the world and with other people we are always being called into conversation and into ways of being which are not our familiar territory. As long as you have a home territory, a familiar position, and as long as you feel that in order to make contact with other people you have to go out of that territory, then this can be like stretching an elastic band. At a certain point you feel you have gone far enough and you need to come back to being yourself. At the end of the day you might think *'Oh, thank God that's over. I've had enough for one day. I don't want to talk to anyone; I don't want to see anyone… Where is my wine?'* Maybe all day you were quite happy to be with these people, but then if a friend calls you in the evening you go *'These bloody people, they are on my case all day long…'*

This is important, because this is where compassion and wisdom have become separated. That is to say my generosity towards the other person, which I gave freely, which I enjoyed giving, is still linked to a tight definition of myself. So when I'm giving it, it may be feely given, but inside there is a meter, like a taxi meter, and at a certain point I think *'Oh, that was too much.'* Many people who work with other people get what is called burnout because of that.

This is why deeply relaxing is important and opening up every fixed position we have, so that we are not resting anywhere and so that our movement is always from this place to that place, with no home place to come back to. That is to say, where we live is where we are.

How do we apply this in our meditation? You can be sitting doing your meditation and you go off on some sequence of thoughts, then suddenly you realise – '*Oh oh, I am way over there...*', and then you come back to doing the meditation. This is what we do when we are meditating focusing on the breath; we come back to the breath.

However in the practice of dzogchen since the object of meditation is whatever is arising, you cannot get lost. If you are present, then wherever you go, there you are. You are simply presence. There is no rulebook that says this is where you should go, or this is how you should be, or this is how your mind should be. Sometimes when we do meditation we may find ourselves crying – suddenly we are full of a lot of grief and sadness and maybe we don't even know why. You don't have to push that away or change it; just stay present with it and then, after some time, it will change into something else. The danger in thinking '*I don't want to be like this. I shouldn't be like that*', is that you then try to find a 'right' way to be. Don't do that. Whatever state you find yourself in – angry, proud, bored, whatever – just be with it.

OUR BREATH IS OUR FRIEND

To go back to the body, sit in a comfortable way, with the spine holding your weight. You can be aware of particular tensions that turn up, and if you feel you want to stretch your limbs, then just do that. In some systems of meditation everyone has to sit in a particular posture and try not to move. Here it's fine to move, but to move with awareness so that the movement of the body is moving *through* the awareness and you remain aware. The movement of the body shouldn't disrupt the meditation because while the body is moving, that is the object of meditation.

Relaxation of the body follows from having free easy movement of the diaphragm. Yoga has many methods for holding the breath, for extending the period that you can remain without the flow of breath and the associated flow of thought. However, in daily life deep slow breath, using the diaphragm is the most important.

Many of us breathe in a very unhelpful way. When we get a bit anxious, or excited or frightened, we shift into upper chest breathing whereby we have rapid short breaths, with slightly longer in-breaths than out-breaths. This increases the amount of oxygen going into the bloodstream, which prepares mobilisation for fight or flight. When we have habitual shallow breaths what we are doing is saying to the body there is danger. Often people slouch on the sofa at home watching television, maybe leaning forward and with their shoulders collapsed so that they can hardly breathe. They may be trying to relax but actually there is a biochemical wind-up or tension.

When you breathe in, imagine it's like pouring a bottle of water into a jug; the jug fills up from the bottom. So as you breathe in, your belly comes out a bit as the diaphragm comes down and there is space for the lungs. When you breathe out, breathe out first from the bottom, slow and steady. So, we will just sit and consciously do this for a little while.

To develop the useful habit of breathing deeply and slowly you need to consciously practice it several times a day. For example, once you become used to sitting with your spine straight, it becomes easier to recognise when you are slumping and so you can straighten your spine as required. The more you maintain this slow deep steady rhythm, the more you can monitor when you move away from it. Then you can start to notice what are the external situations and the internal thoughts and feelings that are bringing about any change in your breathing pattern.

For example, a tightening of the breath may be grounded in the sense of not wanting to be somewhere. When we notice this it is helpful for the shift in our breathing has alerted us to how we have gone into a narrow vision of our potential. Some situation or some thought pattern is arising which seems to be controlling me or defining me, or putting me in a place where I don't want to be. The expression *'it's getting to me'* is quite helpful in this context because it indicates that I have become a thing which something else can get. Gradually we start to recognise this pattern of thinking and feeling and see that it's just a temporary construct, and on a deeper level, that there is none to be caught.

In that way the body and the breath – which is linked to the voice – and the mind all collaborate together. If you get stuck in one aspect, you don't have to work on that area in order to free yourself. For example, if you get caught up in habitual negative thoughts, rather than trying to think about the thoughts and think your way out of thinking..., if you shift into focusing on your breath and relax the breath and have it free and deep, then the lock into the thought will go. You could achieve the same by standing up and shaking your body because when we lock into a thought very often we lock into a posture; if you change your posture you break the lock.

LOOSENING UP WHEN YOU GET LOCKED IN

I used to regularly have dinner with a couple of psychotherapist friends. Sometimes we would be joined by a colleague of theirs whom I did not know well. We would be sitting having dinner, having some wine and talking and predictably, inevitably, I would get into some sort of an argument with their colleague. We would get completely locked into something. Then one of the others would clap his hands and say *"Everyone stand up and move around the table!"* Then we would get up, move around and sit down in different places and the conversation would become very sweet again.

It's very interesting how you just lock into a particular place and then more and more, like an accelerator or an amplifier, you get locked in. This can be useful in the sort of meditation that says sit still and focus your mind in order to decrease the likelihood of distraction. But if you get locked into something unhelpful, then clearly it makes sense to do the opposite, that is to say, to move about, to distract yourself from whatever you are trapped in. Most of us will have seen this working with small babies. They start to cry but if you bounce them up and down, do something with your fingers or maybe sing a song then once you catch their attention, they stop crying. It's the same principle with ourselves.

Being aware of tightening and loosening, its pulsation and triggers, is very helpful for regaining a sense of balance. Yet it is predicated on us having a sense of who we are, on the primary identification that we make with certain constructions as if they were our true self. In dzogchen our practice is to rest in the state of openness free of constructs, our self-balancing natural freedom.

THOUGHTS ARE MOVING *THROUGH* ME

We have already looked a little bit at impermanence. When we become aware of the flow or stream of our experience, we see that the same sort of feelings and patterns arise again and again. If we focus on the semantic content of them then there seems to be a reaffirmation of the sense of the continuity of our existence established by them. But if you pay attention to the energetic *movement* of the thought then you start to see that although I am frequently like this or I am frequently full of this kind of thought, these thoughts are moving **through** me. As such I cannot hold a thought nor repeat it. The second occurrence of the 'same' thought seems identical with the first occurrence only because I am focused on the semantic content. Actually the context within which the thought arises, is changing. The outer field of what other people do is changing. The inner field of my own emotions and sensations is changing and the thought itself is different. It is different because along the line of time it is actually a *new* thought.

Thus we might ask, *'Do you want another cup of coffee?'* This could mean, *"You have had one cup of coffee. Do you want another which is the same?"* It would be the same because it's just another cup of coffee, but it's *another* cup of coffee. It's not the same cup of coffee because the first one is already gone. It's a *new* cup of coffee; it's really new, and it's really a different cup of coffee. But it's also 'another cup of coffee'. Does that make sense? These two things are happening at the same time; it's both fresh and familiar.

If you focus on the familiar it seems to be almost solid; you know where you are. If you focus on the freshness it's something new, and this brings us back to ourselves.

—Oh what is this that is happening for me?

—What is this thing in a cup?

—Oh, what an amazing smell!

—You call this coffee?

Each moment is new. The fact that we bring some knowledge to it, which helps us to manage it, doesn't need to make it old and stale so that we fall asleep inside it.

OK, now we will do a little sitting meditation and bring together these elements. The breath flowing easily, deeply through the diaphragm: the skeleton holding our weight so that the muscles can relax: the awareness open so that whatever is coming is not interfered with. Now our consciousness – that is to say our conscious sense of self, our conscious sense of what is happening to us – is always busy with what is going on, but we can also be aware of this movement of our consciousness. As we looked earlier, we are these two aspects. We are this open awareness, and as a quality of its display or radiance, we are also the movements of the engaged consciousness.

In the meditation we want to gently tilt the focus of our attention towards the experience of spacious awareness and not be so interested in the movement, in the movement of the particular thoughts and feelings that are arising. The practice is very easy to do but it's also easy to slip out of, so for that reason we start by doing it for short periods of time. If you get a bit tired or a bit spacey then you focus more on the breath, slow and deep breaths that will bring you back into a more grounded state. When you have done that for some time, release the focus of your attention. Be aware of whatever is occurring. Often our attention is like a torch on a dark night, creating a circle of light outside of which everything else is a bit dark and recedes into the background. However in this meditation we want to have a more panoramic vision. We are sitting with our eyes open, not staring at anything in particular but incorporating our peripheral vision. Have a sense too of the space behind you so that all the potential of awareness through the senses is open to whatever is occurring. This takes a little while to get used to. You're not trying to do anything in particular, but simply to offer the widest possible welcome to what is occurring.

THE IMMEDIACY OF PERCEPTION IS SELF-ORGANISING: NOTHING MORE NEED BE DONE

The key focus is not going after past thoughts, not expectantly waiting for future thoughts, but staying present exactly with the moment of time as it unfolds, because time is a quality of our own existence. Very often we can feel trapped by time; there are so many things to do in the course of a day and we have to fit into time.

From the point of view of dzogchen this is a very alienated vision, because the immediacy of being present here now is itself inseparable from time and when we integrate openness and movement we escape from the prison of sequentious time. We also escape from the building up of patterns, so that we can truly experience what is occurring without being caught by it. We don't fall in to thoughts like 'what if...', 'if only...' and 'maybe...' that starts streams of speculation.

Now at first when we are just with the immediacy of the moment, it can seem that everything becomes fragmented, because our habitual pattern of organising what appears to us in terms of narratives or stories falls away. But if we just stay open we find that we don't need to make sense of it; the value is immediately transmitted and doesn't leave any trace.

If you are drawing with a child who is about four years old, very often they draw circle shapes with little things coming off them. While they are doing it they are concentrating very hard and when you ask them what it is, they will tell you *'This is a house...'*, *'This is my mamma...'*, *'This is a car...'* It doesn't look anything like that but in the moment the child is doing it, it *feels* like that to them. That is to say, in the experience of making the mark there is the affirmation *'Yes, that's it.'* It doesn't have to leave a logical trace that has to be followed or justified and explained. It just *is* and the child has a full belief when he tells you *'This is a motor car'* which gives some indication of their sense that it just is. The immediacy is self-organising; it does not have to be tided up into some familiar category. This takes us more and more close to the immediacy of perception.

GARAB DORJE'S FIRST POINT: AWAKEN ON YOUR REAL NATURE

Awareness of the natural state of being was transmitted directly to Garab Dorje by the primordial buddha, Kuntu Zangpo. Garab Dorje then brought these teachings into the world in his famous *Three Statements*. According to the tradition, he rose up into the sky and from a mass of rainbow clouds he pronounced these three simple statements. The first of these statements is to awaken on, or in, your real nature. The second is to keep finding yourself in that nature. And the third is to never leave that nature.

This raises an interesting question. If it's our real nature, how is it that we are not in touch with it and we need someone else to teach us about it? To answer this we need to look at the nature of mind itself. The mind has three aspects. The first is natural openness, which is to say that our capacity to know is not a construct; it is not a thing resting on other things. This is not a materialistic view. It may well be that our consciousness – our interactive sense of who we are – is linked through the brain and the body and the five senses into the world around us. However awareness itself is not created out of anything. It is the state which reveals all that is created.

This has many implications for who we are. All that we take ourselves to be is an illusion, momentary identifications that cannot, and do not, remain. We are not what we think we are. And the very thing that we don't recognise about ourselves, well, that is our actual nature. This is what Garab Dorje is pointing out.

The transmission of these teachings requires no formal initiation, but in order to awaken to ourselves, it helps if our nature is pointed out both through words and through the co-emergence of joint practice. Our nature is pure from the very beginning. From this morning from when you first got up, you have had many, many experiences, such as walking in the garden and seeing the trees blowing in the wind, having a chat with people whilst you were drinking coffee, sitting in here and thinking about these various issues. There are different kinds of experiences; when they are there, they are there, and then they are gone and another experience arises. There is a simplicity to this. Yet when we are inattentive or split our attention we can create jumbled, hazy confusing experience. For example last night at the meal I had some water to drink and then I thought I would have some wine. Not paying attention, I put the wine in the glass which was half-full of water. The wine did not taste strong and mixed with water, it did not taste of anything, neither water nor wine. It's like that. If everything gets mixed up you never know what's what.

Our mind offers us the same choice, clarity or non-clarity. We have two aspects. One is our open awareness which, like the mirror, allows experience to come and come and never gets filled up. The other is our consciousness, which is the aspect of our mind whereby we engage with and make sense of the world. This has a limited capacity. We all know the experience of being filled up until we have had enough. We can only absorb so much and then we need some fresh air.

Knowing about these two aspects, in the meditation practice we can recognise when we need to shift our focus if we are getting trapped in involved consciousness. It's not that consciousness is bad and awareness is good. Fundamentally they are not two different things, but they have different qualities, different functions. It's like a bicycle which has gears on it. Some gears are very good for going on flat ground, and some are good for going up a hill. If you have a bike without gears you really know the difference. It makes sense to change gears and get this support when you are going uphill or over a difficult surface.

The Tibetan word for awareness is *yeshe: ye* means from the beginning or primordial and *she pa* means to know. The word for consciousness is *namshe. Nam* means 'shapes or forms' and *she pa* means 'to know'. These two words have the same root in 'knowing'. Awareness indicates just knowing, like the shiny surface of the mirror, it shows what is there. While consciousness attends to knowing this and that, knowing how things are, knowing what to do. If you were just in a state of open awareness all the time you could not do anything.

Chogyam Trungpa, one of the first lamas to come and teach in the west used to say that if the mind was only open and shining then you would need to have a special hospital ward for buddhas! So it's very important to have both capacities: to be in the world with all the detail but not get caught in it – to be relaxed and open but not to hide in it. When consciousness is integrated in awareness it is deconstructed, freed of its enmeshment with reification. Then it is revealed as being the energy of awareness, its modality of participation.

ALL THAT WE SEE IS LIKE AN ILLUSION BUT ILLUSIONS HAVE THEIR OWN LOGIC

Garab Dorje describes how from the naked open state that is not artificial, not covered up or conditioned in any way, an illumination arises, which is the natural clarity of this open state which reveals everything that is here. It reveals dreams in the night-time and all the experiences in the daytime. All that we see is like an illusion. Here in this place where we are now, we can see a train running along the tracks across the valley. You might think that the train can't be an illusion since if you stand in front of it and it hits you, you will die. This idea would indicate that we do not understand the buddhist meaning of illusion.

Illusions have their own logic. Each form in the world has its functions and structures, yet it exists in a dimension which makes it inseparable from everything else that is manifesting. Thus the train is on the train tracks; it has to be *somewhere*. When you wake up in the morning you don't find a railway track parked outside in the street beside you. When you come home from work and you open the door into the kitchen, you don't find a train. Everything is somewhere, that is to say everything is connected with other phenomena. All phenomena arise together. If I look out of this window I can see sheep on the hill, but I also remember seeing one of Bunuel's early films where there were a lot of sheep inside a rich person's house. Do you remember this film?

Group: Yes, *The Exterminating Angel.*

It's very shocking to see sheep in the house because we expect everything to be where it should be, and generally that's the case. Everything is coming in its own particular place. This is the quality of clarity that does not have to sort things out but just shows, '*Oh everything is where it is*'.

Our particular manifestation is arising from and within this clarity, and changing moment-by-moment. That is to say, every day we are doing something; all day long something is happening to our voice, to our thoughts, to our bodies. What I call myself is an unfolding. Now, if the flower has the right conditions it will unfold as the flower we know it can be, but we do not know how *we* are going to unfold. We may be happy in the morning and sad in the evening or vice versa. It depends on what happens. That is to say, between myself and the world, there is not a wall. This is the great freedom and creativity of the human situation.

THE CENTRE OF MY EXISTENCE IS ALWAYS OUTSIDE MYSELF

My existence is revealed to me through my participation in the world. I can't find my existence by looking inside me. It's not an essence like the bulb of a flower, closed in and of itself, and which will reveal itself if the conditions are right. Rather we have many many different potentials and how these arise in not dependent primarily on our intention but on the possibilities that arise in the interaction we have with the world.

In the course of my working day at the hospital I see many patients and each person has a different kind of conversation with me. The way the conversation develops is influenced by how they are when they come into the room. I may have decided beforehand that it's time we talked about some particular thing but if they come in and say *'Oh, I have just found out that my child is ill…'*, then my idea about what is important to talk about is suddenly not so important. That is to say how I found myself coming into the situation is defined by the quality of the space. It's not all up to me; it's not all up to the other. So it means the centre of my existence is always outside myself since it is at the point where self and other are interacting. Both self and other are potentialities, not entities.

I think this is actually how it is for us, but it is not the usual way we think about it. Normally we have the idea that you have to be in charge of your own life. The powerful and pragmatic view is that we need to form a practical engagement with the world, in order to get what you need and ensure that the things you want, happen. It's a view of dominance and control: I assert my own individual existence by living life on my own terms.

From the buddhist point of view this is madness, since it means that each little person sets out to be the world dictator. The main mood is competitive but competition is not all that helpful for various reasons. It alienates us from each other, it reduces empathy, and it gives us the sense that *my success can be established through your failure*'. But if of course ***my existence*** is tied to my lived interactive environment, then I don't have my existence with me as a personal possession like something in my pocket. Rather my existence is co-emergent with the field of experience. So, if I then become competitive with you, I am really becoming competitive with myself, because I need your existence in order to develop mine.

Now if we are friendly together, and do things together then the quality of me being me is quite nice, quite happy, quite relaxed. But if I think that in order for me to be happy I need to squeeze you so that you work harder for me to give me the things I need even if you are not happy, then at the end of the day I sit in my room on my own counting all my money. Outside I hear you crying, I imagine your tears. *'Don't disturb me. I am victorious.'* What kind of a life is that? From this point of view, ethics in dzogchen isn't a rulebook about how you should behave; rather it is based on the principle that if we stay connected with each other an ethical connection arises automatically within the field of our experience.

It's not something you can know in advance. Just as you can't know how you are going to be in advance, you don't know how you ***should*** be in advance. This is what is meant by *'being time'*: that you are exactly in the moment of your arising in existence. It is not an abstract concept but rather a reminder that activity arises in the field of awareness and so we don't have to struggle to work out what to do. Unborn openness, and the ceaseless display of clarity, and the precision of our gestures moment-by-moment are the three inseparable aspects of our experiences and we can start to trust that, and it will be fine.

PRACTICES FOR OPENING UP: PHAT!

We can use the sound of Phat! to help us get a sense of our open dimension. Phat! is a sound which represents cutting and is used to cut away the thoughts and feelings that wrap themselves around you. First relax into the meditation practice and then whenever you find you are getting distracted into some thought pattern or feeling or bodily sensation, simply release this sound. It comes right up from inside you and you imagine it coming out of the top of your head.

In the commentary by Patrul Rinpoche he said we should be shocked open. *Hedewa* is the Tibetan word used to describe this state. It means very open, without any thought in your head, but not spaced out. Here, but nothing. There are two aspects to this: the first is cutting off the immersion in thoughts and the second is being completely balanced, present and open. We are not attacking ourselves but we are freeing ourselves to see what is there without obscuration.

Try to have the sound of Phat! coming from deep within you. You don't want to shout it out from your mouth or throat for that will hurt. As the force is coming up, try not to be trapped in anything but you just stay open. Have the feeling of the force coming up and through, cleaving everything away.

[Practice shouting Phat!]

Your throat may feel a bit blocked and you may have some tension around shouting. As children we are often told to be quiet, to not make a noise or disturb other people. This can lead to retroflection whereby we push things back into ourselves out of fear and anxiety.

Phat! is an uninhibited sound. For example in India there are many dogs wandering around in the roads and sometimes these dogs carry diseases with them, especially rabies. So if an unknown dog comes towards a villager, they shout out Phat! Phat! Poor villagers cannot afford any treatment for rabies so a dog biting them is something important. Something is at stake.

It's the same here with us. These thoughts, which on an ordinary level are like your best friends, are so friendly that they might be stopping you from getting your one big chance. Imagine you've saved up all your money and now you're going on a pilgrimage to India. Five of your friends come to the airport to say goodbye to you. They say *'Let's drink some champagne before you go'*. So there you are, drinking and laughing and joking and kissing and saying goodbye. Then you look at your watch and… the plane has gone!

This life is going by. Our friends, our little thoughts, our feelings inside ourselves, are always giving us something to think about. There is no end to the conversations inside our head. You're sitting there trying to focus on your breath going in and out and a thought pops up, *'That was quite interesting, what we were talking about yesterday…'* and off you go on another little journey. It is important to see how something very important is at stake here. Now we have a chance to drop this immersion in the thoughts and feelings. Don't worry, they won't vanish forever!

All we are going to do is open a space in which we see this unborn ground or spaciousness, which we actually are. Then the thoughts arise again as an expression of this state, connecting ourselves with everything else that arises. The thoughts – which act as a kind of blanket or duvet around us – need to be dropped in order to reveal the fact that they are the energy of emptiness. We have to stop them spiralling around this illusory solid self, like candyfloss winding around a stick. Phat! cuts the thought and the thinker simultaneously, revealing natural effortless clarity.

In this practice we need simplicity and total commitment. If we feel inhibited, a little shy, a bit embarrassed, thinking that we are going to make a funny noise or we won't do it right, we have to recognise that these thoughts themselves are the limit of our existence. If we believe such thoughts, they will continue to define how we can manifest but if we see each thought for what it is, as an illusory phenomenon whose only power is the fact that we believe in it, then by saying Phat!, we break free. We break the investment that we have put in the thought that is our own prison guard.

PHAT! IS THE SOUND OF WISDOM AND COMPASSION

No matter what kind of thoughts are inside us, happy thoughts, sad thoughts, proud thoughts, frightened little thoughts... whatever kinds they are, we want to taste what is hidden behind them. So instead of being frightened by our own reflection, which is all that our thoughts are, allow this sound to come though. In the commentaries it says this is the sound of wisdom and compassion together. It's the sound of wisdom because it cuts through attachment, and it's a sound of compassion because, in freeing us from this self-centred view, we are immediately part of the world with others.

OK so now we will try it. We don't want to make it too serious because that's another kind of heaviness. We are just loosening ourselves up. So we sit and relax and go into the practice. First we just relax, breathing in and out, sitting quietly. Then whenever you find yourself wrapped in thoughts, release the sound.

[Practice]

This is a good practice to do on your own. There is more detail about it in Chapter 11 of SIMPLY BEING.

When you read in books about the empty nature of the mind it's not like going into an empty room and finding nothing there. The familiar furniture may not be there but *the empty room* is there. Sometimes we think there is going to be nothing at all, but if you think of the mirror, the mirror always has reflections inside it. The fact that the reflection is in the mirror doesn't diminish the capacity for the mirror to show reflections and in fact it is the presence of the reflection that shows the emptiness of the mirror.

Compare a mirror with a picture like this one here. It's not a mirror although the glass surface is a bit shiny. It is a particular picture and although it can look slightly different according to the changes of light in the room, generally speaking we can say it's the same picture in the morning as in the evening. Nothing else is going to arise inside this picture. Whereas with a mirror it shows what is there, *because* it doesn't show itself. So the picture shows itself, and by being full of itself, it can't show anything else. The mirror never shows itself but it always shows reflections and through showing reflections, it shows its emptiness. Is that clear? That's very important. If you get a sense of that then you get a sense of what buddhist 'emptiness' means. Emptiness refers to both the empty ground of the mirror and the empty experience of the reflection. Both are devoid of inherent self-nature; they have no intrinsic defining essence that can be established as something truly existing.

For example, if you decide to have a party you might move out some of the furniture. The first people who arrive may think your house looks a bit empty but then more people come and the place fills up, the music gets going and people are dancing. The emptiness of the flat was the basis of your hospitality. If you run around saying *'This is a new white carpet. Be careful with the red wine'*, it's not going to be much of a party because hospitality means letting things happen. It means that the flow of experience, the coming together, the moving, is more important than trying to keep everything in its proper shape.

It's the same when we do meditation. The emptiness of our mind is revealed through the flow of image and sensation. If you do the Phat! or some other practice intensively then for a very brief moment of time, it's as if there's nothing at all. But it's the very nature of the mind to display thoughts, feelings, sensations, colours and so on. Their presence in our mind is not the problem. The problem is if we lose our openness to what is occurring and become over-identified with whatever is arising, then it becomes strongly real in our experience. Then, whatever occurs seems to be inherently important and so the seemingly real object and the seemingly real subject seem to resume their familiar interaction. Identifying ourselves as our specific, personal consciousness we try to push away bad thoughts and try to hold on to good thoughts. And the endless activity of samsara keeps rolling on.

Relaxed openness is non-defensive presence with whatever is happening. Part of what is happening is the familiar sense of 'I, me, myself'. But because we are not strongly identified inside ourselves the hospitality includes *everything* which is arising including ourselves. Through this we awaken to the primordial integration of the three aspects of existence. These are, firstly the empty open hospitable ground, the source and sphere of everything. Secondly there is the infinite field of spontaneous expression, the richness of the potentiality of the ground – the immediacy of non-duality. Thirdly there is the unique specificity of each moment of the movement of the field – the exquisite, ungraspable 'thusness' of our being alive as participants in the shared field. Although these aspects can be described separately, they are not 'things', and they are inseparable.

In the meditation we are not trying to go from one place to another place. Sometimes when we see pictures of Buddhas, they look very bright and shiny and we might have an idea that if I recognise my own nature I will see rainbows in the sky. I will feel completely different inside; no one will ever be rude to me again, and so on…. This is a nice fantasy, but actually the experience of existence continues; now we are present in it as movement in time.

Rather than moving our life around like pieces on a chessboard, trying to get to a better safer place, it is more like movements of water *within* a river. Movements or currents or little rivulets running inside the general flow of the water. Experience never stops; it continues but now we can be more light, more playful, more an integrated part of it.

If bad times come we won't feel so determined by them or downcast. If happy times come, we can enjoy them but without imagining that they are going to last forever. Then our life becomes more simple, more direct. We find that we are not afraid of death.

PRACTICES FOR OPENING UP: GURU YOGA

Now we will look at another method for opening ourselves to the natural state. In our ordinary existence we are caught up in a duality of subject and object. We become very concerned with the difference between ourselves and other people. The differences are manifest but that doesn't mean that there is a true *essential* difference between ourselves and others. This is to say, we have different ways of existing but the nature or structure of our existence is the same. We see, we hear, we taste; sensations arise and pass and so on. So if somebody tells us about their life and we listen with an open heart, generally what they say makes sense to us. But our belief in the duality of self and other can operate as a limiting threshold. Dzogchen is concerned with non-duality.

Non-duality is not the same as homogenisation. We don't put everything into one pot and stir it around. Rather, non-duality, in some ways, is the same as co-emergence. It means everything is arising at the same time, within the same dimension, with mutual influence. In order to get a sense of this we have to be aware that we are always in relationship.

There is a kind of elliptical movement in the development of beings and cultures, that is to say, we tend to go towards one extreme and we get so far and then we have to come back. You could say that from the time of the European enlightenment we have been moving in the direction of individualism. Exemplified by the French Revolution, we have the collapse of the royal hierarchy and also of the religious hierarchy. People start to think that just because my father was a peasant farmer it does not mean that *I* have to spend all my life following a cow. I can look inside myself and find out how I am and then try to bring this potential into the world.

As this idea developed more and more people left the land and went to the city where, with the opportunities and the anonymity, they could forget who they were according to their class or family occupation, and become somebody new. We start to develop the idea that my life belongs to me and it's up to me how I use it. I want to be independent and autonomous, I don't want other people to define who I am. But of course when that goes to a radical extreme we end up being disconnected from other people. In the city of London now, people are so alienated now that they find it very difficult to talk to other people. When children throw rubbish on the pavement, adults don't feel able to say *'Hey what are you doing?'* If someone is attacked on the street, other people often look away, because there is no sense of relation.

From the point of view of buddhism the loss of the direct experience of our own ground is definitely leading us in the direction of individualistic alienation. There are two aspects that go together: awakening to the non-duality of our manifest form and this open, aware ground of our being, and awakening to the non-duality of self and other; these are inseparable.

In order to relax our fixation on duality and open to the givenness of non-duality, we can make use of our connection with another. Traditionally this is done with what is known as guru yoga. 'Yoga' can be interpreted in many ways. One aspect is linked to its root which means 'yoke', the wooden beam that is used for joining two cows together when they are pulling a cart. The Tibetan translation of 'yoga' is *naljor*; *nal* means relaxed and *jor* means to join or to be in the state of. Thus the heart of yoga is relaxation. In guru yoga we relax into the inseparability of our mind and the buddha's mind.

'GURU' INCLUDES ALL THE PEOPLE YOU HAVE LEARNED FROM

All our teachers are linked to the path of awakening for they have opened doors to a wider world. 'Teacher' 'guru' thus includes our parents and our schoolteachers, because without their help we would not have been able to enter the door of dharma.

You can read these accounts of children who have been abandoned in the forest when they were very small. Sometimes they were raised by wolves. When they are found again years later they find human contact very difficult and cannot easily develop the capacity to speak. What's very nice is if our parents spoke to us, even if sometimes we did not like very much what they said to us.

Reflecting on what others have done for us we can start to have a sense of gratitude and to see that right from the very beginning as a baby our life was connected with other people. Of course for nine months we were growing inside our mother's body. The distillation of her food, the strength of her body was going into ours. The first music we heard was the rhythm of her heart, then we drank her milk. In these ways, our body develops through relationship. Through all the different ways people have talked to us and listened to us we develop the sense of the extension or contraction of ourselves.

We imagine all the people who have ever helped us, including meditation teachers and so on in the sky in front of us. We imagine then in space because *everything* has the nature of space, they are the radiant appearance of space manifesting in space.

We imagine them all contained in the form of a white letter Aa. You can think of it in the Tibetan form or as a capital A. Aa represents emptiness, emptiness in the form of a 'plenum void', a full void, a void which fills itself up. It's a void, it is empty, but it is full of everything. It's not empty, empty, nothing, nothing, but it's empty and full at the same time.

The sound Aa represents nothing at all, yet as the root vowel it is our first sound. From Aa you have mama, papa, then all its variations as the words and sounds of the world. In that sense Aa is stillness and movement. It's the first sound that arrives from silence and it contains within it all the potential of the other sounds. So with Aa you can go into nothing at all, and out into everything.

When we imagine the letter Aa, it is surrounded by a ball of light, like the sort of shimmering bubble ball that children blow from washing up liquid. We have the sense that this is in front of us. We say Aa slowly three times. As we say Aa we release the tensions in our body, our voice and our mind and open into integration with the presence of the qualities of all the teachers.

The space of our heart – the openness of our heart – and the openness represented by Aa are inseparable. After we have said Aa three times, the letter Aa dissolves and we sit in space. Now our awareness is open and empty, inseparable from the mind of the Buddha and we stay relaxed in this state and allow whatever comes to come.

[Meditation]

THE GROUND OF EXPERIENCE IS EMPTY

As we looked before, in terms of ordinary consciousness the ground of our experience is the movement of the thoughts, sensations and feelings that we seem to be resting on moment-by-moment. But awareness itself is not resting on anything. That is to say, it doesn't have a base; it doesn't have a ground. The ground of experience is empty, just as a rainbow appears in the sky though there is nothing supporting the rainbow. Everything we see, and hear and touch has the same nature.

On one level this sounds completely mad because you can think *'Well my feet are on the ground; there is something there supporting me'*, but that sequence 'something there supporting me' is a mental sequence. I am the one that says that this is the floor. I am the one who say that this is me. One idea follows another idea, and together these two ideas create some image, or some expectation that something is truly the case. But as we started to look earlier, each thing is related to other things. The seemingly solid floor beneath our feet has a space underneath it. Then we can go right down to the foundations of the house. One piece of earth is resting on another piece of earth; we go down and down and down, and the earth becomes very hot, it becomes magma. One atom of magma is resting on another atom of magma, then another and another. Eventually you come to Australia! So in fact we are resting on Australia! In that way ideas sit on ideas and we create this structure of our interpretation, this structure of our meaning, and for as long as it makes sense, we think that it must be true.

From the buddhist point of view, there is no solidity in any of these aspects. If we look at the walls of this building we can see that it's made of big blocks of stone. If you have the right tools you can cut into any so-called earth substance. So the stonewalls may feel very solid to me but eventually someone will decide that they are going to knock the building down and they'll bring a big machine and within two days everything is knocked flat.

What holds this building in shape is not the strength of the stones but the fact that the church has enough money to fund the continuation of the building for now. When they can no longer pay for it, it will be sold. Maybe some business will buy it or will knock it down and build some houses. So what we take to be a very solid structure which seems to have some integrity of its own is held in place by the contingent fact that people like us come here and rent this space, by the fact that the local council probably does not charge too much to the church for rates, water and so on, by the fact that people like to have their weddings here... It's like that. There are factors of maintenance or continuation that keep this place going.

Again and again we have to inspect what are the seemingly solid self-existing phenomena that seem to create a limit to our mind leading us to say *'This is mental. This is physical'*.

EXPERIENCE IS ALL WE HAVE: DIFFERENT WAYS OF LOOKING AT THE WORLD

I use the word experience many times because actually all we have is experience. Part of our experience is our capacity to use abstract concepts. So we can say that the table is quite solid and that is a fact because the things resting on the table don't fall through it. But, with the idea that the table is solid, we tend to link the assumption that the table is therefore truly existing. Because in the west our main polarity is reality and fantasy. We can say that the table has a reality; you can touch it, you can lick it, you could run your hands up and down it; it shows that it is there. To imagine the white letter Aa and rays of light spreading out would normally be described as a fantasy, like watching Bambi in the cinema. Better to stay with reality. Get a good job, work hard, and don't waste your time on all this funny buddhist stuff. Think of your future. This is the sort of thing that anxious parents say. *'What are you going to do when you get older?'* These two categories are very powerful: the solid, the tangible, the facts of what really exists and the rest, which is just some kind of fantasy.

It's very important for us to explore this because it is one of the organising systems which we were educated to believe in. Here in the west we take the material as something reliable and the imagination as something deceptive. The material is reliable and the immaterial is unreliable. For people who were raised as children in Tibetan buddhism it's very different; they are taught that everything is illusion. Either you grasp at the illusion and try to make it real or you accept that it is an illusion. Grasping at the illusion and trying to make it real will make you stupid, whereas trying to directly understand illusion and live within that free movement, will set you free. So you can see, how that is a completely different way of looking at the world.

It is still the tradition in India to see the world in terms of the five elements. According to this view there is space, and the most subtle movement of space is the wind. Space you can't touch or feel in any way, it's just the arena in which you are moving. The wind you can't catch, but you can feel it when it blows on you. You can see it by the effect it has on a tree; we see the tree moving and impute the action of the wind. Then, with more shape, we have fire. Fire exists in relation to fuel. The fuel can be like the wind element, gas for example; it can be liquid like the water element, petrol for example; it can be like the earth element, wood or coal for example. You can see fire but it's difficult to catch. If you have a fire burning outside the flames are moving all the time. Water has more shape than fire. Water flows easily and adapts to where it finds itself. If you put your hands into the sink, the water rises to give them space. Earth is the most solid and tangible of the elements. It holds a shape but that shape can be altered by other elements acting on it.

It is generally believed in buddhism that everything is created out of the interaction of these five elements, and from the point of view of tantra and dzogchen, the basic nature of all these elements is light. The energy of the universe, the energy of existence, manifests light and sound. The light takes on many different shapes and this is what appears to us in the universe.

Light and sound are vibration. If vibration becomes dense and 'heavy' it can take on the form of earth. So something like this metal object [*James is holding a metal bell*] is quite heavy and hard; you can say that this really is the earth element. It is created out of metals which are created out of the earth yet it is *revealed* to us through our senses. Because I am holding it now, I can feel the weight of it but primarily it is revealed through our being able to *see* it. As with all we encounter, the quality of light which is displayed from them, shows our relation with them in this unrepeatable moment. If you look at the flowers and then you look at this brass bell, their ways of showing themselves are very different. The qualities of the 'object' are relational, not intrinsic; they are both attributed to the object and uniquely revealed in each moment of experience of them.

My experience of myself emerges at the same time as my experience of the world

All experience is moment-by-moment revelation. It's not that *I* am seeing things outside *myself* – that I am real and they are also real – but rather my experience of myself emerges at the same time as my experience of the world. The experience of both is always changing. What appears to be solid and real and reliable is only concept.

It is a paradox that the things which seem most reliable, are the most abstract. We are now in Spain; this is a fact. Spain is a concept; it's a concept people are willing to die for, to die for the dignity of Spain. 'Spain' is a word, and it's an idea. As with everything you can see in the world, what seems solid and real and reliable is actuality an idea, while experience itself is tumbling and changing. It is immediate, it is phenomenological; it's what you get, except you can't get it because it's already gone. Names, words, concepts seem to

347

endure – yet they have no substance. And what they seem to refer to is only available to us as fleeting experience. The actual world is ungraspable. The usual world we inhabit is a mental world made of the rapid flow of mesmerising concepts.

For example in the worst practice of psychiatry, some person, often a young man of eighteen or nineteen, starts to hear voices and see strange visions. The parents or friends get worried and eventually he goes to his doctor who refers him to a psychiatrist. After asking a range of questions for half an hour to an hour, the conclusion is that the person has a psychotic illness and that they need medication. *"If you take this you will feel better."* So the psychiatrist opens up a file and writes in it 'Psychosis'. Now the person *has* something. When they went into the room they had voices and strange visions, now they have psychosis as well! This is called adding value! Now that we know what is wrong with the person we don't need to listen or try to understand. There is nothing more to be found; it's just that the person has psychosis. Because now we 'know' what the problem is. This is, of course, not very helpful, but we ourselves are doing something similar all the time when we rely on our *concepts* and don't attend to what is there.

QUESTIONS TO ASK ABOUT OUR MIND: IT'S SHAPE, SIZE, COLOUR...

It is important to explore how our mind is. We can do this now in a very simple way. We will again do the three Aa practice and then, when you have been sitting relaxed for a while, I invite you to take up the questions: What shape is my mind? Is my mind inside my body? Is my body inside my mind? Does my mind stop here, or does it go way back? Is this building in my mind? How far does my mind extend? If I think of Madrid, is it in my mind? Does Madrid exist somewhere in itself? If I go to Madrid will I experience Madrid itself, or my mind experiencing Madrid?

Hold the question very gently: Are there any walls at the end of your mind? Is there anything you can find that is outside your mind? As you think about the thing that is outside your mind, while you think about it, the thought about it is inside your mind. While you are thinking about something that appears to be *outside* your mind, you are thinking about it with thoughts that are *inside* your mind. So is there something outside your mind that is different from the thoughts that you are having about the thing that is inside your mind? This is a chance to put into question the assumptions you have about the world you live in.

Question: When we talk about the ground, is it one ground for one and everything or has each person has an individual ground?

James: According to tradition everyone has their own ground, but it's all the same ground.

Question: So they are individual but everyone has the same, identical?

James: We each have our own unique experiences yet their nature is identical because the ground of experience is itself emptiness and emptiness tastes the same in all directions. By looking we can see that our existence is arising moment-by-moment out of this emptiness – not arising out of it like a fish jumping out the sea, but more in the way that reflections seems to come out of a mirror but remains in the mirror. Then we can experience, *"Oh, there is no solid basis for 'me'. I am movement. The base of my existence is empty because I can't find anything there, and yet it's always full, because there is always something happening."*

Each person who looks to find who they are, how they are, will find exactly the same thing. This is the case because as far as I myself can tell, and according to the lineage, it's not a cultural construct. It's not created out of concepts, although in order to talk about it we make use of concepts. Therefore it's not conditioned by your age, your gender, the culture you grew up in, the colour of your skin and so on.

However of course, on the level of personality, our experience is exactly individual. It's not direct in the manner of awareness, but is mediated through our history, our language and so on. So when we examine ourselves, if the limit of our enquiry is our individual history, our personality traits and so on – the kind of enquiry you have in psychotherapy for example – then each individual looks completely unique. They have their own special personal package.

If the enquiry is based on the nature of your personality, and your own personal history is the limit of the definition of yourself, then you will find the particular details of your life determine who you are. These details are not shared by anyone else. And so, from *that* level of analysis we are completely unique, sealed inside our own private world. However, dharma enquiry is seeking to go through concepts, not to push them to one side, but to see how they function, and to reveal that they themselves have no solid basis. That enquiry shows an openness, which I think is shared by everyone.

QUESTIONS ABOUT MINDFULNESS AND AWARENESS

Question: What does 'mindful' mean?

James: 'Mindfulness' is nowadays often linked with cognitive behavioural therapy as a method for disrupting neurotic patterns. Traditionally in buddhism 'mindfulness' means remembrance. The word for it in Tibetan it is *drenpa* which means memory or recollection.

I lived for quite a long time in India and I developed a habit of remembrance of my money. So now many, many years later, when I'm walking down the street, I check that my money is still there. In India I got very used to knowing where my bag was and not just being in a daydream and giving someone the chance to take it away from me. Thus mindfulness means being careful. It is a focused intentional use of attention. That is the traditional sense of it.

You can be mindful of the body, of the breath, of the emotions. You can be mindful of the passage of time, of death and so on. In that sense mindfulness is narrow and focused; it's a method; it's not a state to arrive in. It is an artificial method of increasing your receptivity to a particular area. However because it's a focused attention, whilst you are focussing on that one thing, something else is happening and you are not attending to that.

Also, generally speaking, mindfulness is self-referential. That is to say, *I* know *I* am being mindful because I am the one who decided to be mindful. So although it frees me from being distracted into this and that, it has within it a subtle reinforcement of my sense that *'I am the agent', 'I am the actor', 'I am the one who is doing this'*. This can increase the sense of *'I really exist'*. Mindfulness is a technical intervention.

In dzogchen open awareness is sometimes compared to the sun. The sun gives out rays of light and illuminates everything. The sun doesn't decide what to illuminate and what not to illuminate; it just illuminates. It is active but it is not intentional. Sometimes awareness is also compared to a mirror. The mirror doesn't have to do anything to show an image; its capacity to show the reflection is more like the way the moon receives the light of the sun, and thus, without any effort, it seems to give out light all by itself. It's a more passive way of showing what it's got, which is the light of the sun.

Likewise, in the state of awareness everything is registered, without any particular choice. Out of this state of awareness, energy arises. What's called *rigpa'i tsal,* the manifesting energy of awareness itself which illuminates particular situations. This is compared to the heat or the light of the sun, because it can make something happen. This does not have any intention either, so from the point of view of dzogchen, activity is not concerned with doing anything. Benefit will happen automatically if there is the unimpeded flow of the energy of manifestation non-dual with the ground. This is different from the quality of conscious intention, which is connected with mindfulness.

When a child is learning to ride a bicycle, at first they can't find their balance; then they find their balance but they can't yet steer very well. We can see children in the local parks learning to ride their bikes and their little legs are going round and round and they are very excited and talking to each other and the bicycles are going all over the place. We want to say *'Hey, be careful! There are people walking. Look, there's a dog. Be careful!'* That is to say, don't forget where you are and enjoy the space with others. However once somebody is used to riding a bicycle they get to a place where it just flows through them. Then although they are relaxed, their peripheral vision will pick up any difficulties so that they move smoothly and easily dealing with every problem, without having to be especially attentive.

People in that state could either become more aware or become more complacent. They could close down their attention and lose a little bit of their competence or they could open their attention to the wider field and enjoy being on the bicycle while being completely relaxed and present.

The key thing is we are never aware. We can be conscious, we can be mindful, because these are activities of the individual organising their energy of manifestation. But awareness or presence is a state we relax *into* it's not something we *do*. So I can't 'make myself aware'. It is not that 'I' am aware, but that I find myself in the state of presence or rigpa.

For example, if you are walking in the summer and you are very, very hot and you might come to a place where the river is tumbling down the mountainside and there is a waterfall. All you have to do is to walk into the waterfall. The waterfall will cool you. You can't cool yourself. You could say you are cooling yourself using the water which would affirm your ego agency, but actually you are letting the water cool you – no effort or agency is required.

Similarly the state of openness or presence is always there, and according to the tradition we are never more than one hair's breadth away from it. But that hair's breadth makes a big difference. Our natural freedom is always here saying, *"Here I am. Here I am"* but we reply *"Shh, I'm busy getting enlightened. Go away and leave me alone. When I get enlightened I will have time for freedom. But first I have to do this and it is very important."* From the point of view of dzogchen, trust freedom. Doing less could be enough. But this is the big sacrifice; this is what is hard because the ego feels as if it is being made redundant. The ego has been the centre of our existence for as long as we can remember. Usually after some years have gone by our heart has a few scars on it. We are a little less trustful and that brings with it a certain heavy feeling, *"Oh, better be careful. It's all up to me."* Because we remember when we were still young and more fresh and open and spontaneous – we got burnt. So in terms of the practice we have to confront these anxieties and the desire to go back into an isolated sense of ourselves and protect ourselves, because it is our attitude of self-protection that is causing our limitation. When life is hard it is difficult to trust that awakening is easy.

HOW DO WE LEARN?

Now we can explore what it means to make progress with this practice. The main traditions of spiritual learning are very hierarchal and so they tend to privilege the teachers, but the teachers already know something, so that's not very exciting. Much more interesting is the learner, because the learner is the site of potential. How then do we learn? If you want to learn, the most important thing is not to know. Not-knowing can be both exciting and anxiety-provoking. We might feel that we should know, we might become very hungry to know, we might try to be knowledgeable by accumulating bits of information. But I think learning actually involves a kind of self-forgetfulness, a leaving of the places that are familiar to us and a moving out, with trust, hope and confidence. Learning is about enquiring, about putting what occurs – including ourselves – into question.

This is a work only you can do. If I eat a very nice dinner when I'm back in London, even if I am thinking of *you*, your stomach won't get full. You yourself have to put the food in your own mouth, and you yourself have to chew it.

So there is a particular way one has to find one's own style of learning. For example in the dzogchen tradition, there is the notion of the teacher 'showing the nature of the mind'. You could say to the teacher *'Please show me the nature of my mind'*. Then somehow you imagine it's like being in the barber's; you sit in the chair and in front of you is the mirror. The hairdresser does something to your hair and then they come behind you and they hold up another mirror, and the reflection of the back of your head goes from that mirror behind you into the mirror in front of you. In that way they show you what you cannot see yourself. Without the barber you would never see that aspect of yourself although it is always there with you. Yet when you leave the barber's shop you are likely to forget it.

METAPHOR OF A TENT AND TENT POLE

In teaching we can create some kind of mood, use words that operate as metaphors to open up a kind of space. But each of us has to explore that space and find our way of being at home in it. It is a bit like if you have a big round tent; you stretch out all the pieces on the ground and you put in the pegs and then you put the pole in the middle and up it all goes.

The teaching is like the pole. For a moment you understand a little bit more, but then the teacher has to go and takes the pole with them and you find the tent has collapsed all around you. You have a tent but it's not much use, in fact you can't even walk now. So the main thing is to find your own pole. The pole needs to be straight, like your spine; it's about your dignity. By putting yourself in that place gradually you understand more.

This relates to the second point of Garab Dorje, 'Not remaining in doubt'. That is to say when you become full of different ideas, don't follow after the **content** of the idea but observe what is the nature of the thought that is arising. Because if you follow after the thoughts they will lead you astray. They may start to create fantasies of your being stupid, of not understanding, or of it being too difficult. This is the problem of not knowing what thoughts are.

Yesterday we looked at how thoughts themselves are like Janus, they have two faces each looking in a different direction. In terms of the semantics, in terms of the content, the thought is looking towards the construction of meaning but the same thought, simultaneously, is looking at its own ground which is this open dimension of presence. So once one has a sense of openness and relaxation, the central point is to observe how every experience which arises is inseparable from its own ground. That ground is empty – we won't get to a secure or solid place. Yet because that basis or ground is not a **thing**, it gives the freedom to manifest in every possible way, which is why the instruction is, 'Don't interfere with your mind'. If you become sad then be sad. If you feel hopeless you can feel hopeless. If you feel jealous you can feel jealous.

This is where this path is very different from many other paths. Some paths would say, *'Don't become sad. Put on a cheerful face and think of good things'*.

But this practice supports equal opportunities for *all* kinds of mental events. For too long happiness has been made too important, but we dzogchen practitioners are members of the Buddhist Sadness Party! We defend the right to cry, since everything that arises in the mind is illusory and impermanent. If we take it as strongly real – if we say, *'this is bad'* or *'I really don't like this and therefore I have to change it'* – then the site of our operation, the place we are entering into experience from, is our narrow, historically developed ego consciousness. But we are not the masters of the world. Dharma is not a path to narcissistic inflation. We are participants in the flow of existence, neither in charge nor a slave to it, but finding our way, taking our place.

The more we can offer hospitality to whatever is arising and find ways of being with that, then the more we become flexible; we start to be able to allow our energy to flow according to the situation. Because we are not holding onto a self-referential identity we become more useful to other people. Actually, the flow of existence is **always** being interrupted. Interruption *is* existence. You do one thing and then something happens, then something else happens. Openness means available and that means welcoming, or at least accepting, interruption.

THE MORE WE TRY TO BE IN CONTROL, THE MORE DANGEROUS THE OTHER SEEMS

This is one reason for being a little bit careful with meditation. You can get into the idea that if you do a retreat then life would be better – that you could then have space and uninterrupted time to practice. Yes, that is useful for developing wisdom, but a key aspect of wisdom is knowing that you can't control your mind.

Why would you want to be a dictator of yourself: *'I am the boss. I know exactly what to do. I am in charge. Now I will tell myself exactly what to do.'* The myth of control, the fantasy of control is very poisonous.

When I was about seven years old, I once got stung by a wasp when I was out playing. I became very angry with all wasps, and so every time I saw a wasp I'd try to hit it with my stick and kill it. My mother asked me what I was trying to do? She did not like killing things at all. I said that these wasps were very dangerous and you've got to kill them. Then she very nicely explained that there are many wasps in the world and that I was one little boy with one stick and that life would be better if I found a way to live with the wasps. It's like that.

The more we try to be in control, the more dangerous the other thing seems. Eventually dictators become paranoid, always imagining that they are going to be betrayed, initially by outside enemies, and then towards the end, they are always looking at the people around them wondering which one is going to betray them.

If you apply this fantasy of control to your own mind, if you try to control all your thoughts and only have very good thoughts, then any bad thought that suddenly arises can destroy all you have created. I remember when I was first studying buddhism reading in Santideva's *Bodhisattvacharyavatara* that a thousand aeons of practicing virtue will all be destroyed by a single flash of anger. This can mean either of two things: first, you must try harder, or second, why bother being virtuous since clearly it's very vulnerable to events.

Virtue has to be done for other people, not for gaining anything for yourself. It is a fantasy that I can somehow create an ideal self. As the Buddha explained, everything that is created will come to an end, everything with a beginning moves inexorably towards death, towards its extinction. In dzogchen, we are working with the nature of the mind, which is *not* born, and is *not* a thing.

In practice we have a chance to observe the precise point at which the construction of samsara occurs. One thought is flowing along, then another thought lands beside it and something seems to be created. My mind is resting on this idea; it is the basis of my activity. Whatever we find in the moment seems to be an adequate support for my identity. The ego can rest on anything, identifying with anything. The thought that appears to be me, and the thought which appears to be the site of the mind, are both moving.

For example, if you go out on a boat and the wind is blowing a bit, you can see the waves moving. Then along comes a seagull, and it lands on the sea. It *was* flying and now it's sitting on the water. It's having a little rest, but what it's sitting on is moving. It's like that. The thought is moving in your mind like the waves on the sea. Another thoughts arises, and *'Ah'*, you think, *'I can stay here.'* In the very moment that you think, *'Ah, this is where I belong'*, you are being moved along. All manifestation is dynamic, which is why we have to look again, and again, and again, so we really *see* the essential difference between stillness and movement. Movement is never still; you cannot make it still. The only thing that is still is presence, and it *never* moves.

So when you look for the shape of the mind, or where the mind rests, or where the mind is coming from, or where the mind is going to – in all of these cases the temptation is to choose something familiar, which *seems* to us to be right, but which is actually an aspect of movement. We look at something that is moving, and try to imagine that it is still. As we explored in some detail yesterday, the dynamic nature of experience is hidden by the projection of assumptions regarding fixed stable entities.

For example, some of us have been in this building before. That seems quite a reasonable thing to say. We were here last year; we're back in the same place now. But is it the same place? We can say *some things* are in the same place, and we know that because what we see fits the map that we have created. So I am using the memory, or the map in my head, as the proof that these phenomena as the same as they were last year. But of course when we do that we are not looking very carefully, because many, many things will have changed.

For example, I can see from the way the sun is shining that there are many marks on the windows. They are dirty this year in a way that they were not dirty last year. Does this matter? Well, it's what is there; it's what is actual. If we say, *'It's a window with a bit of dirt on it. What does the dirt matter?'* this is a concept. Whether we are interested in the windows being clean or dirty does not matter; the fact *is* that the window as a window is there *with* the dirt on it. So once we start to look really carefully, we see that everything is changing.

This is a very simple thing to do but if you bring it into your life you will be able to see that everything is an illusion. For example, when I go to work in the hospital, I go on the underground. There is an announcement which says when the next stop is London Bridge. The doors open and I get out onto the platform along with some other people from my compartment. I always get off at London Bridge because that's where my work is, but as I come on to the platform and go up the escalator, it's not the same people every day. We don't have the Half-Past-Seven London Bridge Club where we agree to meet. So each time I get off, London Bridge is very different. It's called London Bridge Station, but my experience of it is always very different. Different commuters, different underground staff, the lighting a bit different, and so on.

So we have these two worlds that exist simultaneously: the world of immediate experience – what is here – and the world of concepts, of maps, of interpretations. When the buddhist teachings say that everything is an illusion this means that the construction which is created in the world of concepts is not truly existing. If you attend to what is actually there, it's there but ungraspable. You can't catch it, you can't keep it, and you can't build on it. This is true for everyone, however your life is. If you have to take children to school, every day is different. One day they are very slow in eating their breakfast; the next day they can't find their shoes; the following morning they are worried because they have forgotten to do all their homework. This is how life is. So, when you say you are taking your children to school, this is a concept. What is revealed in the moment of participation in our existence, you cannot know in advance.

This is the meaning of illusion. It doesn't mean that there is nothing there at all but it's like a dance – a dance is revealed as you dance it. If you are trained in the Laban notation of choreography you can denote the movements of the body, but that's abstract. It's when the music starts and the body is moving that dance is revealed, as when a fish suddenly breaks the surface and you see its shining silvery body and then it's gone. If you're not there you don't see the fish. There's nothing to get, but you get it.

Translator: But you get it? If you are there?

James: Yes, if you are there!

GARAB DORJE'S SECOND POINT: STAY TRUE TO THE EXPERIENCE OF OPENING

Thus the second point from Garab Dorje is to stay true to the experience of opening. Probably it's not what you thought it would be. You see all these pictures of buddhas sitting very peacefully, but our life is not like that. We have many, many things to do. So it's very tempting for us to focus our attention onto activity and onto the sense of making things happen. Of course if you are doing an activity like driving a car, you have got to make it happen, you have got to control the steering wheel and so on. But of course you drive your car according to the road, according to the other cars. So again you could say *'I'm driving my car'* or *'I am participating in the traffic'*. When you're participating in the traffic you find that the car is moving according to other cars, according to the curve of the road, whether it's raining or not, whether you are in a hurry or not, whether you are happy or sad… All of these influence in some way how you are driving.

By opening and welcoming life as it is and seeing the impermanence of thoughts, feelings, sensations and experiences we come to see that the only place to be alive is now. The dreams which tempt us – which send us spiralling into a place which is both in time and outside time – these become less interesting.

Translator/Question: In time and out of time too?

James: Yes. So for example, you're sitting here and your mind goes off and you think *'Tomorrow is Monday so now what do I have to do?'* Your body is here, the clock is going round, you are in that flow of time but simultaneously you are somewhere else. There is not really another place you have gone to. You're not quite here, but you're not quite somewhere else either. Phenomenologically it can be very interesting to examine what it is like to be caught in a thought. It's a kind of limbo, a kind of dream. Although that state may feel familiar and reassuring to you, the experience is often generated by anxiety. *'If only I think more, if only I prepare more, my life will go better.'* Sometimes that's true, but a lot of the time it's not true at all.

If life is about participation, the most important quality is availability. What is it that stops our availability? All neurosis, all psychosis, and everything else! Any kind of preoccupation is a foreclosure; it closes things down before they have had a chance to open up. Expectations, hopes, fears, all of these create a slight tilt, or a slight turn, which cuts us off from the free open availability of the widest aspect of ourselves.

WE ARISE IN RELATION TO OTHER PEOPLE

So in the practice we come back again and again to being present in the moment, but not just present *in* the moment but present *as* the moment. Our nature is itself the space within which everything occurs. This includes time; we are ourselves time. Everything flows through us. Each person is the centre of the world. It's not that there are some big people and everyone has to turn round them.

There is room for everyone to be the centre. It's quite unique, **your** way of emerging into the world. Imagine a hundred people go to the seaside, then they are all swimming under the sea and suddenly they all pop their heads out of the water! They are all in the centre of the sea! Each one has the sea all around them. It feels like *my* sea, but the sea is big enough for everyone to be at the centre.

It means that when we meet other people we share the similarity of being the energy of the ground and therefore by attending to the particularity of ourselves as we arise in relation to this person – because each person has their own way of embodiment – that embodiment will bring a resonance or a response in other people. That is the actuality. That is what is there. So if we are present in ourselves we also receive the particularity of each person and then we allow ourselves to arise in that situation. So, we say different things to different people…, which makes life interesting. It's dynamic; it's fresh into the situation.

GARAB DORJE'S THIRD POINT: SIMPLY TO CONTINUE IN THIS WAY

Garab Dorje third point is simply to continue in this way, which is to say, to continue integrating every experience into the natural open spaciousness of your presence. In order to do that we are continually deconstructing our habit of reifying personal pronouns.

For example, we might say 'to integrate everything into my presence'. For each person it is 'my presence' but 'my presence' and 'my watch' is not the same kind of thing. We have a long habit of appropriation of things that are the part of the world, including our body, which is a part of the world. So when we say 'my presence' it is mine because of the unique vital experience of being there, but it's not something we can possess or own because the one who says 'my presence', is itself the energy which arises as a quality of the presence.

For example, if a child says 'my mother' and a mother says 'my child', these are very different statements. The mother can pick up the child but unless the child is called Superman, he can't pick up the mother. So the mother's ownership of the child is to know what food to give them, what things they like, what stories to tell them at bedtime and so on. This is a particular kind of possession. For the child, 'mother' is just mother... Mum! Mum!

When we speak to other people, we are of necessity swimming in the sea of language, and this is a sea formed out of the movement of individual egos trying to define and adjust and relate. So when we speak, it's very tempting – it's a strong pull – to identify with our individualised sense of self as if *it* was the centre, and then from that state to experience the moments of presence as some nice things that I have, like having my holiday.

Garab Dorje is describing something very different – relaxed open presence, which continuously integrates everything, including the voice of the individualised person, saying 'my presence'.

PRACTICE: RELAXING INTO THE OUT-BREATH

OK, so now we will do a little bit more practice. This time we will start in a very simple way, relaxing into a long deep out-breath and staying present with whatever happens. Now there are advantages and disadvantages of this way of doing things. If you do a lot of chanting first and some mudras and so on you can create the sense of a sacred space and therefore you create a sense of something different which can help you to maintain a particular quality of attention. Of course you then have the problem of how to integrate the kind of experience you have in the sacred space, into daily life which is not at all sacred. But here we just relax into the out-breath it's not very far from where we have just been. Life is going on as before; the same sort of thoughts in your head; the room looks the same... So there are many hooks to getting distracted and being caught in familiar patterns. This is where we just very gently apply the basic instruction: don't go after past thoughts; don't wait expectantly for future thoughts; just here and now in this moment, open to whatever comes letting them go as they go.

Let it come, let it go. OK.

THE FUNCTIONS OF RITUALS

In our time together, because it's not so long and also because it is in harmony with this style of practice, we haven't done any rituals. That's not to say there is something wrong with rituals and of course many of you have your own rituals from other traditions you are practicing. Learning new rituals is not necessarily better. The key thing is to discover the function of the ritual. So if we take refuge and develop bodhicitta, this operates on different levels. On the outer level we say, *'Here I am wandering in samsara, a dangerous place, and I get lost very easily.'*

Translator: When we take refuge, do we say that?

James: Well we *feel* that. Then we think that we want something which is more reliable and that we can hold onto. So we can rely on the Buddha, on the teachings and on the sangha. Similarly, we can think, *'I'm rather self-obsessed, rather selfish in my approach to life, but I recognise that I have a connection with all beings'*, so I develop a bodhisattva aspiration or intention, that in this and in all my future lives may I help all beings.

Essentially these are ways of shifting our energy. We take refuge because we are very reactive to many things that are happening, and we make an intention to have some kind of path, some kind of line to follow. When we take the bodhisattva vow, we want to step outside of the enclosure of ourselves, to find ourselves as part of the world.

From the point of view of dzogchen, we are not trying to go anywhere else. We don't *need* to have a path; rather we need to be present. If we are present then *where* we are is revealed to us in terms of what it actually is rather than the fantasies we have about it. When we relax and open, our experience arises as the undivided field of self and other. We see that what I call 'myself' and what I call 'other people' are not two different things. Because immediately, directly I am aware that if I look down, I see my leg and I see the floor. The long black shape I say is 'my leg'; the flat light brown shape I say is 'the floor'. These are names that my own mind is putting. If I don't attend to these names, what there is, is colour and shapes. There is no real separation between the two. All the shapes and colours of the world are organised by my mind according to what's inside.

In terms of relating to the details of the world this can be quite useful, but in relating to the actual nature of ourselves, it's not helpful. This is because it creates the sense that the function of naming and dividing is somehow the central point of our existence when in fact, this capacity to put names, to distinguish, to separate things out, is just a function of energy. Energy that arises and passes as movements out of the natural clarity.

All sadhanas are activities. In Tibetan they are often referred to as *'trinlé'*, which means 'activity'. An activity is a mobilisation of energy in a particular direction towards a task. When we start to see that, everything we do is a participation in the field of movement and the ground of this movement is not 'I, me, myself' because actually, most of the time we are conscious *after* the fact of our activity. In English we say, *'I found myself doing...'*. That is to say, my activity was preceding my consciousness. The situation *called* me into a kind of response, a gesture, which is not something I planned. Not something arising out of a pot inside me, but what I call 'myself' has somehow being flowing out in this particular shape.

This we can observe all day long: that we are essentially a flow within a flow. Some of the flows you can call 'religious' and some you can say are 'not religious'. Some are called 'helpful', some are called 'not helpful'. If you have a bottle of wine for breakfast and spend the day just falling about, that's one way to spend time. If you cook some food, and give some to your sick neighbour, that's another way of passing the day. We say that the second way is better than the first way. But that's from a relative, conventional point of view. Both are activities. The person who is helping the neighbour could be quite proud and so their mental state would be undoing the virtue of what their body was performing.

Generally speaking in buddhism there is the idea that the value of an action lies in its intention, not in its outcome. Particularly, in dzogchen we say that the nature of the action lies in its ground, because all activity is the energy of this open dimension. So integrating your activity into the ground is – at least while you are learning the path – more important than trying to do good things. This is a very big world and many situations arise; sometimes our behaviour needs to be quite radical, and if you develop a strong notion of what is 'good behaviour' or 'proper behaviour' you might not be able to help people very much. For example, trainee therapists are generally very good nice people. So when they sit in a room with a patient who is quite tricksy they can sit, week after week, and the patient is just dancing on their head. Eventually they have to learn how to say to the patient, in a very nice way, *'Don't mess with me'* because if they can't say that, then there is no therapy. At first they think this is very rude, *'I just have to give some space to this lost person, and then they will find themselves'.* Why would they want to find themselves, when they are playing with you, the way a cat plays with a mouse?

So in that way, every kind of behaviour can be useful according to particular circumstances. Very often formal, ethical maps don't help us sort this out. In order to help people, we have to be willing to let our activity flow into the situation and that involves taking a risk.

Rituals are useful as a way of observing yourself when you do something quite artificial. When we do this namaste gesture and we bow this creates a particular kind of feeling. If you do a full-length prostration on the ground, this creates a different kind of feeling. Then when we learn to chant you have a different kind of feeling. The function is to observe what happens to yourself. It's not so much about saying these holy words but about seeing how the situation acts as a stimulus, calling you forth to allow you to express your energy.

So in whatever situation you are – if you are working with friendly supportive people or working with difficult people, if you are caring for sick relatives or if you yourself become sick – *whatever* happens, just observe yourself. Don't stand apart from the situation thinking *'I like this. I don't like that'*. It is **your** life and since you are in this situation, don't protect yourself from your own experience. Just open to it and see what it is. See what it does to your breathing, your posture, what feelings arise, what thoughts arise... Then something changes and you will find yourself manifesting in a different way. And **you** become different, open, free, spacious. This is very important. Then you will discover that no situation ever catches you. Even if something is horrible, it's there for a moment and then it's gone.

The moment leaves no trace if the one who experiences it is integrated in space. But if you turn the event into the beginning of a story – *'Why did they say that? I hate this person...'* – then you start to get scratches all over you and next thing is that you're bleeding. So who has harmed us in that situation? Is it the other person? Or is it our own mental activity? The *Dhammapada* records the Buddha as saying,

> *Not father, not mother,*
>
> *not brother, not sister,*
>
> *not friend, not enemy,*
>
> *no one can harm me more than myself.*

and it continues,

> *'Not father, not mother,*
>
> *not brother, not sister,*
>
> *not friend, not enemy,*
>
> *no one can help me more than myself'.*

This is why our main practice is to observe ourselves. What am I up to? And in particular *how* am I up to it, how do I do myself? What is the process of becoming myself? What is the pattern I habitually bend myself into? What are the expectations and beliefs behind the movement into that pattern? And particularly from the view of dzogchen, what is the **ground** of myself and why am I drifting away from it?

Our expectations and beliefs are the pseudo-ground. As long as we are caught up in them they seem like the true basis of our existence. So we might say *'I am angry'*, *'I don't like people who behave in this way.' 'I don't like that'. 'This is just how I am'. 'This is what I believe, enough!' 'Don't talk to me anymore'. 'I don't want to change my mind. This is me.'* But actually it is an illusion; it is just a habit. And what we bring from the practice of meditation is the capacity to just observe this place which seems so definite so secure. Observing again and again that it is here and then it is gone.

OK so now is the time to do some final practice together. Just sitting in a nice relaxed way. Relax into the out-breath and remain just open. *[Practice]*

So our short time together comes to an end. It has been very nice for me to come here and be amongst such warm and friendly people.

Meeting and parting is part of our lives. Nothing lasts for long, but everything reveals itself when you are most free and present with it. So if we bring the quality of attention and openness and presence that we have here – if we bring this out into every aspect of our lives – then I believe we will all have more and more richness and depth. So it's been a pleasure, thank you.

Teachings given in Amorebieta, Spain, 18-20 June, 2010. Edited by James Low and Barbara Terris.

APPENDIX

1. Buddhism and personal identity. *Public talk given in Frankfurt, Germany on 14th October 2015.*

2. Anxiety, awareness and ease. *Teachings based on a talk given to psychotherapy trainees in Milan, Italy on 14th November 2013.*

3. Finding freedom when you feel trapped. *Teachings given for the people in prisons, June 2015.*

4. Being at ease with yourself. *Public talk given in Devon, UK on 28th November 2014.*

5. Seeing identity and buddha-nature. *Public talk given in Berlin on 25th October 2017.*

6. The glue of duality. *Teachings based on a Zoom discussion, 21st November 2021.*

7. Why emptiness is liberating. *Public talk given at Shang Shung Institute, London on 25th February 2016.*

8. Mindfulness, contact and healing in psychotherapy. *An article written by James Low in May 2019.*

9. Depth and light. *Teachings given in Berlin, Germany, 30-31 January 2016.*

10. Finding your way home: an introduction to dzogchen. *Teachings given in Amorebieta, Spain, 18-20 June, 2010.*

Other books by James Low

1. Love Your Mother

(Published by Simply Being, UK, 2023. ISBN: 978-1739938185)

2. The Open Door of Emptiness: a collection of public talks and teachings

(Published by Simply Being, UK, 2023. ISBN:978-1739938178)

3. Buddha Shows the Way: a collection of public talks and teachings

(Published by Simply Being, UK, 2022. ISBN:979-8825841762)

4. Proud Little Cloud: letting in the light

(Published by Simply Being, UK, 2022. ISBN: 978-0956923998)

5. Me First!: an account of the rise of the Wrathful Buddhas

(Published by Simply Being, UK, 2022. ISBN: 978-0956923981)

6. Sweet Simplicity: Mahamudra doha songs

(Published by Simply Being, UK, 2022. ISBN: 978-1739938154)

It has been translated into German, Spanish, Italian and Hungarian.

7. Lotus Source: becoming Lotus Born

(Published by Simply Being, UK, 2021. ISBN: 978-1739938123)

8. The Mirror of Clear Meaning: A Commentary on the Dzogchen Treasure Text of Nuden Dorje

(Published by Simply Being, UK, 2021. ISBN: 978-1739938130)

9. Longing for Limitless Light: Letting in the light of Buddha Amitabha's love

(Published by Simply Being, UK, 2021. ISBN: 978-1739938109)

10. This is it: revealing the great completion

(Published by Simply Being, UK, 2021. ISBN: 978-0956923974)

11. Chöd Khandro Gadgyang by Jigme Lingpa (Sound of Dakini Laughter: The Method for Cutting the Ego)

(Published by Wandel Verlag, Berlin, 2020. ISBN: 978-3942380294)

This has been translated into German.

12. Finding Freedom: texts from the Theravadin, Mahayana and Dzogchen Buddhist traditions

(Published by Wandel Verlag, Berlin, 2019. ISBN: 978-3942380270)

The book has been translated into German and Polish.

13. Sparks

(Published by Simply Being, UK, 2017. ISBN: 978-0956923943)

The book has been translated into German, Italian, Polish, Spanish and Turkish.

14. Collected Works of C. R. Lama

(Published by Simply Being, UK, 2017. ISBN: 978-0956923929)

The book has been translated into French, German, Polish, Spanish and Portuguese.

15. Radiant Aspiration: The Butterlamp Prayer Lamp of Aspiration

(Published by Simply Being, UK, 2011. ISBN: 978-0956923905)

It has been translated into German, Polish and Spanish.

16. Simply Being: Texts in the Dzogchen Tradition

(Published by Antony Rowe Publishing, UK, 2010. ISBN: 978-1907571015)

This has been translated into French, German, Italian, Polish and Spanish.

17. The Seven Chapters of Prayer: as taught by Padma Sambhava of Urgyen, known in Tibetan as Le'u bDun Ma

(Published by Wandel Verlag, Berlin, 2010. ISBN: 978-3942380027)

The book has been translated into French and German.

18. Being Guru Rinpoche: A Commentary on Nuden Dorje's Terma Vidyadhara Guru Sadhana

(Published by Trafford Publishing, 2006. ISBN: 978-1412084079)

This has been translated into French, German, Polish and Spanish.

19. Being Right Here: A Dzogchen Treasure Text of Nuden Dorje Entitled the Mirror of Clear Meaning

(Published by Snow Lion, 2004. ISBN: 978-1559392082)

The book has been translated into French, German, Italian, polish and portuguese.

20. The Yogins of Ladakh: A Pilgrimage Among The Hermits of The Buddhist Himalayas

(Published by Motilal Banarsidass, 1997. ISBN: 978-8120814622)

The book has been translated into Italian.